The Timeline of Presidential Elections

Chicago Studies in American Politics
A series edited by Benjamin I. Page, Susan Herbst,
Lawrence R. Jacobs, and James Druckman

Also in the series:

ELECTING JUDGES: THE SURPRISING EFFECTS
OF CAMPAIGNING ON JUDICIAL LEGITIMACY
by James L. Gibson

FOLLOW THE LEADER?: HOW VOTERS
RESPOND TO POLITICIANS' POLICIES
AND PERFORMANCE *by Gabriel S. Lenz*

THE SUBMERGED STATE: HOW
INVISIBLE GOVERNMENT POLICIES
UNDERMINE AMERICAN DEMOCRACY
by Suzanne Mettler

DISCIPLINING THE POOR: NEOLIBERAL
PATERNALISM AND THE PERSISTENT POWER
OF RACE *by Joe Soss, Richard C. Fording,
and Sanford F. Schram*

WHY PARTIES? A SECOND LOOK
by John H. Aldrich

NEWS THAT MATTERS: TELEVISION AND
AMERICAN OPINION, UPDATED EDITION
by Shanto Iyengar and Donald R. Kinder

SELLING FEAR: COUNTERTERRORISM, THE
MEDIA, AND PUBLIC OPINION
*by Brigitte L. Nacos, Yaeli Bloch-Elkon,
and Robert Y. Shapiro*

OBAMA'S RACE: THE 2008 ELECTION AND
THE DREAM OF A POST-RACIAL AMERICA
by Michael Tesler and David O. Sears

FILIBUSTERING: A POLITICAL HISTORY OF
OBSTRUCTION IN THE HOUSE AND SENATE
by Gregory Koger

IN TIME OF WAR: UNDERSTANDING
AMERICAN PUBLIC OPINION FROM WORLD
WAR II TO IRAQ *by Adam J. Berinsky*

US AGAINST THEM: ETHNOCENTRIC
FOUNDATIONS OF AMERICAN OPINION
by Donald R. Kinder and Cindy D. Kam

THE PARTISAN SORT: HOW LIBERALS BECAME
DEMOCRATS AND CONSERVATIVES BECAME
REPUBLICANS *by Matthew Levendusky*

Additional series titles follow index

The Timeline of Presidential Elections

How Campaigns Do (and Do Not) Matter

ROBERT S. ERIKSON AND
CHRISTOPHER WLEZIEN

The University of Chicago Press
Chicago and London

Robert S. Erikson is professor of political science at Columbia University and the author or coauthor of several books, including *The Macro Polity*. Christopher Wlezien is professor of political science at Temple University and coauthor, most recently, of *Degrees of Democracy*.

The University of Chicago Press, Chicago 60637
The University of Chicago Press, Ltd., London
© 2012 by The University of Chicago
All rights reserved. Published 2012.
Printed in the United States of America

21 20 19 18 17 16 15 14 13 12   1 2 3 4 5

ISBN-13: 978-0-226-92214-0 (cloth)
ISBN-13: 978-0-226-92215-7 (paper)
ISBN-13: 978-0-226-92216-4 (e-book)
ISBN-10: 0-226-92214-6 (cloth)
ISBN-10: 0-226-92215-4 (paper)
ISBN-10: 0-226-92216-2 (e-book)

Library of Congress Cataloging-in-Publication Data

Erickson, Robert S.
    The timeline of presidential elections : how campaigns do (and do not) matter / Robert S. Erikson and Christopher Wlezien.
        pages. cm.—(Chicago studies in American politics)
    ISBN-13: 978-0-226-92214-0 (cloth : alkaline paper)
    ISBN-10: 0-226-92214-6 (cloth : alkaline paper)
    ISBN-13: 978-0-226-92215-7 (paperback : alkaline paper)
    ISBN-10: 0-226-92215-4 (paperback : alkaline paper)
    [etc.]
    1. Presidents—United States—Election. 2. Political campaigns—United States—History. 3. United States—Politics and government. I. Wlezien, Christopher. II. Title.
    JK524.E84 2012
    324.973—dc23

                                                                2012002385

♾ This paper meets the requirements of ANSI/NISO Z39.48–1992 (Permanence of Paper).

CONTENTS

Acknowledgments / vii

ONE / Election Campaigns and Voter Preferences / 1

TWO / Uncovering Vote Intentions using Trial-Heat Polls / 17

THREE / Thinking about Campaign Dynamics / 41

FOUR / Vote Intentions over the Campaign Timeline / 59

FIVE / From the Campaign to Election Day / 83

SIX / Sources of Change over the Campaign Timeline / 109

SEVEN / Campaign Dynamics and the Individual Voter / 139

EIGHT / The Evolution of Electoral Choice
over the Campaign Timeline / 165

Appendix / Vote Intention Data / 179
Notes / 181
References / 195
Index / 203

ACKNOWLEDGEMENTS

The book has been long in coming. The origins can be traced to our initial collaboration twenty years back. Before the 1992 presidential election, we considered what explanatory models of past presidential elections could tell us about the then upcoming election between George H. W. Bush and Bill Clinton. As it turned out, our forecast was accurate, but it was designed to work near the end of the campaign. Then, starting with the 1996 election, we considered how the effects of the economy come into focus at particular stages in advance of the election. After this, we turned to trial-heat polls of voter preferences between the candidates for the White House, and then began to crystallize our thinking about the campaign "timeline." The result of that work is an article in the 2002 *Journal of Politics*, which introduced our initial thoughts on the subject. In later election years, we began to explore how polls came to reflect the economic fundamentals over time and what they added to our understanding of the outcome. Our book builds on all of this previous work, and develops and extends it in significant ways.

The research would not have been possible without two separate grants from the National Science Foundation. The first enabled us to amass all of the macrolevel poll data, the second to pull together the various microlevel data. We received additional support from Columbia University's Institute for Social and Economic Research. For assistance in collecting and organizing the data, we thank Joseph Bafumi, Christopher Carman, Bruce Carroll, Albert Fang, Yair Ghitza, Joe Howard, Kathy Javian, John Kastellec, Jason Kelly, Krystyna Litton, Jeff May, Quinn Mulroy, Sharif Nesheiwat, Eldon Porter, Kelly Rader, Amy Ware, and Alexander Wu. For generously sharing other critical data, we thank Michael D. McDonald, James A. Stimson, and John Zaller.

We have many people to thank for helpful input over the years. There were participants in seminars at Columbia University; the University of Essex; Gallup Organization; Leiden University; the University of Manchester; University of Mannheim; Massachusetts Institute of Technology; University of Minnesota; University of North Carolina; Oxford University; University of Surrey; Texas A&M University; University of Texas, Dallas; Trinity College, Dublin; and Washington University. There were participants in panels at professional meetings in Cardiff, Chicago, Houston, Montreal, San Antonio, Savannah, and Washington, D.C.

A large number of people have made significant comments. Jane Green read every chapter and in great detail and helped us see more clearly at numerous points. Others made important marks, including Cristina Adams, Joseph Bafumi, James Campbell, Tereza Capelos, Harold Clarke, George Edwards, Harry Enten, Geoff Evans, Steve Fisher, Rob Ford, Andrew Gelman, Thomas Gschwend, Michael Hagen, Sunshine Hillygus, Tom Holbrook, Bill Jacoby, Will Jennings, Richard Johnston, Brad Jones, Andrew Karch, Paul Kellstedt, Kathleen Knight, Yph Lelkes, Joseph McLaughlin, Brendan Nyhan, Costas Panagopoulos, Josh Pasek, Colin Provost, Robert Shapiro, Daron Shaw, Michael Sobel, Stuart Soroka, Evan Parker Stephen, Marianne Stewart, Laura Stoker, and Dan Wood. We surely have missed the names of others who contributed in important ways over the long life of the project—we have tried our best to remember and apologize for not doing better. We also thank the two anonymous reviewers of this book, especially for helping us focus more on the forest and less on the trees.

We also thank people at the University of Chicago Press. Of special note is the contribution of the editors. Jamie Druckman read the book from beginning to end and had an important impact on its parts and their sum. We can't thank him enough. John Tryneski provided critical input and guidance in framing the book's contribution. We are grateful for this and for his patience throughout the editorial process. Rodney Powell helped us negotiate final revisions and begin production.

Finally, we owe special thanks to our families for letting us take the time and energy needed to finish the book, something we weren't able to do prior to the 2004 and 2008 elections.

ONE

Election Campaigns and Voter Preferences

Imagine the timeline of a presidential election campaign. We begin the timeline at some early point before the election, perhaps as soon as polls ask voters whom they will support. The timeline ends on Election Day. At the beginning, the polls reveal the electorate's preliminary vote intentions. On Election Day, at the end of the campaign, the electorate reaches a final verdict. In this book we trace the national vote division as it evolves over the campaign timeline.

We ask: How much does the vote change over the timeline? Is the shift a smooth trajectory, or does the aggregate vote lurch over the timeline in a series of bumps and wiggles? What are the forces that influence the vote and when do they occur? When new events affect the vote decision, how long do the effects last? To what extent are their effects temporary and to what extent do they persist to affect the outcome on Election Day? These are some of the questions we address in this book. Their answers inform us about the importance of the election campaigns—often beginning before the national party conventions—on the outcome of the presidential election.

How much do campaigns matter? Here, some division can be seen between the views of political practitioners and journalists on the one hand, and academic scholars on the other. Especially in the heat of the campaign, practitioners and journalists emphasize elections as a battle of rival campaigns, with the winning team determined by campaign quality plus the random shocks from unexpected campaign events. In the extreme, elections are decided by which side is better at the public relations art of persuading voters.

Of course, all observers recognize that campaign outcomes involve more than a combination of salesmanship and luck. When political scientists study elections, they tend to emphasize the political environment—often referred to as the "fundamentals" of the campaign. Many concede that campaigns may matter, but that they do so mostly to channel the vote toward a verdict that can largely be seen in advance from the fundamentals. Always prominent in discussions of campaign fundamentals is the economy's performance. But the fundamentals can also include the electorate's net evaluation of the competence and perceived ideological positioning of the major political parties and candidates (Lewis-Beck and Rice 1992; Gelman and King 1993; Holbrook 1996; Campbell 2008a; also see Popkin 1991). In the extreme, the fundamentals of the election are in place before the campaign begins, and the campaign is a mere conduit to drive the voters' decision to its deterministic decision.

Election outcomes are not simply the residue of campaign quality plus a dose of chance. Neither are they the automatic result of deterministic forces that can be foreseen in advance of the campaign. Voters are influenced by a variety of factors, some stemming from the candidates' campaigns and some beyond the candidates' control. The general puzzles that motivate many discussions of elections remain: how much do campaigns affect elections, and how much do the fundamentals shape the campaign and its effect on the voters? (See, e.g., Holbrook 1996, 2010; Campbell 2008a; Stimson 2004; Bartels 2006; Ansolabehere 2006; and Vavreck 2009.)

In this book, we translate general arguments about the effects of campaign events into a set of formal expectations. We then analyze all available national polls from the fifteen presidential elections from 1952 through 2008. We have three main goals. The first is to identify the dynamics of the electorate's vote intentions over the campaign timeline. The second is to assess the extent to which changes in voter preferences over the campaign timeline persist to impact the Election Day vote. The third is to model the sources of electoral change over the campaign timeline. To complement the analysis of aggregate poll results, we also examine individual-level poll responses. This allows us to observe the crystallization of voter preferences over the campaign timeline.

At the beginning of an election year, trial-heat polls reveal little about the eventual Election Day verdict By April, however, the electorate forms impressions of the candidates that bear some resemblance to the final verdict. As the campaign progresses, the electorate's vote division typically resembles the outcome that analysts predict from the fundamentals, though not perfectly and sometimes not much at all. The vote division rarely ends where it starts early in the election year, but, except (occasionally) in the aftermath of the party conventions, change is usually gradual. As we will see, the relative stability of the electorate's preferences is often masked by sampling error in polls. And the real movement in the electorate's preferences often is nothing more than short-term change that fades quickly. Elections are decided by the slow evolution of campaign events that leave an impact that lasts until Election Day.

This book analyzes all available national vote intention polls for the fifteen presidential elections from 1952 through 2008. The sheer volume of polls—nearly 2,000 of them—allows us to assess the dynamics of aggregate electoral preferences in considerable detail. We can determine whether and how preferences change over the course of the election year; indeed, we can quantify and date the change. We also can determine whether and the extent to which the change in preferences we observe actually lasts to affect the outcome. Finally, we can assess the causes of aggregate preference change.

To complete the story, we analyze individual vote preferences at different points of the campaign. This makes more understandable those patterns we see at the aggregate level. We are thus able to offer a comprehensive accounting of preference evolution. What we glean from our analysis provides answers to important questions about electoral preferences: how do they change over time, why do they change, and with what effect on the final outcome?

In some ways, the timeline of a presidential campaign is like a season of major league baseball. In the spring, each team and its fans believe they have a chance at getting to the playoffs and winning the World Series. It may seem that, with a few good breaks, any team can go all the way. In the end, however, the teams with the highest caliber of talent at the start of the season usually get to the playoffs. The list of postseason entries still can include occasional surprises, which makes the long season interesting.

The electoral parallel is obvious. In the spring of election year, parties and candidates, plus their supporters, see a pathway to victory. Political journalists and pundits speculate that the outcome will depend on who runs the smartest campaign and how the outcome may turn on chance events. But the outcome can typically be foreseen from the fundamentals of the campaign; the candidate favored by the economy and presidential performance usually wins. Surprises are possible, however. Just as in baseball, the season must be played out to determine who wins.

We show how, over the timeline of presidential campaigns, the electorate's collective vote choice undergoes a slow evolution. Most of our analysis concentrates on what polls show within 200 days of the election. The

200th day before the election (ED-200) occurs in mid-April. At that time, the likely major-party candidates are identified and matched up in the pollsters' trial-heat questions in each of our 15 election years. Those polls, however, are an uncertain guide to the final outcome. After the fact, we know that polls at ED-200 can explain slightly less than half the variance in the final vote division. (We also show that polls from the beginning of the election year have virtually no predictive power, which means that preferences start to come into focus as the nomination process unfolds.) The polls from April also provide a useful guide to the Election Day winner, as the polls are "right" more often than not. Polls as of ED-200 "erred" only in 1980, 1988, and 1992, while showing a plurality for the final winner in eleven other instances.[1] (In 2004, the ED-200 polls showed a virtual tie.) In short, the early polls are fairly useful for identifying the winner. Where they "err," we do not blame the early polls but rather attribute it to the flow of subsequent events. In other words, the campaign seems to matter.

As everyone who closely follows election polls knows, the numbers bounce around a lot from day to day, and can vary from poll to poll within the same reporting period. Much of this is noise from sampling error. Our book attempts to extract the signal of the ever-moving division of voter preferences over the campaign. This electoral movement is slow—far less than one might think from comparing two polls from nearby dates. With a series of graphs and statistics, we track this slow evolution of voter preferences.

We also identify some of the sources of this slow evolution. Early polls typically start with one candidate ahead by a more one-sided margin than the final vote. Seemingly, if surprise snap elections were called in April, voters would give lopsided verdicts often quite different from their Election Day verdict. We see three periods in the campaign timeline during which aggregate preferences get reshuffled more than usual. The first is during the early stages of the primary season, when voters often are first learning about some of the nominees. The second is during and after the period when the political parties hold their national conventions. The third is the final run-up to the election during the final campaign week, a time when many voters decide. In each instance, the electoral verdict tightens, moving closer to 50–50.

Of course it is important to know what drives electoral change over the campaign. We show that even by April, trial-heat polls incorporate considerations that no longer matter by Election Day. Yet April polls also contain information that persists to become part of the final electoral verdict. Between April and November, something happens. In some fashion, the campaign delivers the economic and political fundamentals to the voters. It also delivers less tangible information that analysts cannot readily identify.

1.1 Electoral Campaigns and the Presidential Vote

It is well known that presidential election outcomes are predictable, at least up to a point. Despite all the media attention paid to the many events and drama during campaigns, there are certain things that powerfully structure the vote on Election Day. At the individual level, party identification is of great importance. Other factors also matter at the individual level, including class, other social cleavages, and policy preferences, to name but a few of the many things that structure individuals' votes. The point is that voters tend to line up in fairly expected ways on Election Day (see Gelman and King 1993; Campbell 2008a; Andersen, Tilley, and Heath 2005).

To point out the obvious, the electoral verdict changes from election to election. It is not that everyone changes or even that most do, as the bulk of partisans vote for their parties or candidates of their parties year in and year out. The ones that change tend to be those who are least attached to particular parties. These "floating voters" are more likely to reflect short-term considerations, such as the state of the economy or the more general performance of the incumbent president (Zaller 2004).[2] There is more to election outcomes than the recent degree of peace and prosperity, but incumbent presidential performance in these domains tells much of the story (see, e.g., Fair 1978; Hibbs 1987; Erikson 1989; Lewis-Beck 2005; Holbrook 2010). Political factors, including the candidates' policy positions, are also important (Erikson, MacKuen, and Stimson 2002; Vavreck 2009).

1.1.1 The Fundamentals

A common view is that the campaign delivers the fundamentals (e.g., Gelman and King 1993; Campbell 2008a). The fundamentals are typically described as a set of economic and political circumstances known long before the election, so that the results are knowable in advance, perhaps before the eventual outcome is evident in the polls. The campaign effectively brings home the fundamentals to voters. If the final result departs from what the fundamentals predict, then the campaign must have failed to fully enlighten voters by Election Day.[3]

Our view is different. We conceive of the fundamentals not by their content but by their persistence. The fundamentals are those things that cause a long-term shift in voter preferences—long-term, that is, for the length of the campaign. Some campaign effects come and go. The fundamentals have effects that last. Some of these are anticipated early on in the campaign; others evolve over the course of the campaign. We would like to observe all the forces that affect the fundamentals directly. Although we can identify some of the major culprits—such as the economy, candidates' positions on issues relative to voters, and aggregate party identification—many sources go unmeasured. However, the distinction between underlying (and somewhat movable) fundamentals and short-term fluctuations frames our analysis. In subsequent chapters, we describe vote intentions over the campaign timeline as a combination of long-term fundamentals—the accumulation of permanent influences on the campaign—and short-term influences with little consequence (unless they occur close to Election Day).[4]

1.1.2 Fundamentals: External and Internal

As we have discussed, the notion of the fundamentals of a campaign can incorporate many things. They include the electorate's partisan identity and its evaluation of the sitting president's performance. Voters also respond to their social and economic self-interests and policy preferences, among other personal motivations. The fundamentals also include the policy positions of the major presidential candidates. In one sense, the fundamentals represent the vote that occurs when the electorate focuses on the task and becomes "enlightened." (We elaborate on this process later.) Of course, reasonable people disagree about what it means to be enlightened. What are voters' interests? To what extent do the candidates represent these interests? Is it enlightened to judge the sitting president on the basis of late-arriving economic growth? We are agnostic on these issues. To us, fundamentals include anything that has a lasting impact on voter preferences. We can identify some of the factors that do matter on Election Day but not all.

It is useful to distinguish between "internal" and "external" fundamentals. As we have seen, some of the factors are internal to voters and apply personally. Voters are members of different groups. Although group characteristics are stable over the course of the campaign, their electoral effects may grow, emerging as the election becomes salient. When a person's group characteristics or group interests affects his or her vote, we can include that among the fundamentals. Voters also have partisan (and ideological) predispositions that form a basis of vote choice. As voters rely on these dispositions for their vote choice, that too can be included as part of the fundamentals.

Other fundamentals are external to voters in that they arise from the political environment and the candidates themselves. The economy is the usual suspect. Economic prosperity benefits the party of the sitting president; recession favors the out-party. Political factors are important as well, such as candidates' position-taking and the popularity of the sitting president. Economic and political circumstances are powerful influences on each election. These external fundamentals together with the internal fundamentals largely determine what happens on Election Day.

1.1.3 The Fundamentals and the Campaign

How can a discussion of fundamentals help to frame our understanding of election campaigns? One's first thought might be that the influence of fundamental variables tells us that campaigns do not matter. From this perspective, campaign effects are the difference between the result and the prediction from the fundamentals. To the extent the outcomes are predictable, therefore, campaigns have "minimal effects" (see, e.g., Finkel 1993). This view resonates in certain parts of the literature (Lewis-Beck and Rice 1992). After all, candidates who are likely losers will not embrace the fundamentals (e.g., the economy) but rather seek another tack. (On this point, see Vavreck 2009.)

There's another view, which James Campbell (2008a) refers to as the "predictable campaign." Here, predictability does not mean that campaigns do not matter, just that the effects of the competing Democratic and Republican campaigns cancel out (also see Fiorina and Peterson 2002). Strategists for both presidential campaigns do the best they can with the cards they are dealt. All we observe is the net effect of the fundamentals. If both candidates do well, the logic goes, we should expect partisanship to structure partisans' votes. We also should expect that things that are important to voters, such as the economy, will swing their votes and the final result. When campaigns do what they are supposed to, the result turns out as we expect.

This latter interpretation may appeal. It fits the facts and explicitly incorporates the effects of campaigns, at least conceptually. After all, while the contrast with the minimal effects view is clear, the empirical regularity is precisely the same. What differentiates the two views are their assumptions: one presumes that predictability implies minimal effects, whereas the other presumes that it means there are substantial campaign effects but that they cancel out.

1.1.4 Enlightenment (Learning)

The conventional political science wisdom is a bit different from the general caricatures we have just described. Here, Election Day predictability implies that election campaigns "enlighten" voters about their interests and things that are important to them, for example, government performance (Gelman and King 1993; also see Andersen, Tilley, and Heath 2005). From this view, campaigns deliver the fundamentals by providing information to voters. In the course of taking positions, emphasizing issues, and challenging each other, campaigns help people sort themselves by party and take stock of performance (also see Arceneaux 2005). This view overlaps some with the "predictable campaign" perspective. It also appeals for much the same reasons: it fits the facts and includes a role for the presidential candidates' campaigns to help shape the election outcome.

There is other support for the enlightenment thesis. Cross-national research shows that fundamental variables matter more the longer the campaign (Stevenson and Vavreck 2000). Voters are more likely to "learn" the more time they have. Research on US presidential elections shows that big campaign events, such as the parties' nominating conventions, effectively "correct" preferences, bringing them in line with the fundamentals (Holbrook 1996). Campaigns evidently help voters focus on and learn (or relearn) the positions of the parties, the candidates, and government performance. Moreover, as the campaign unfolds, voters increase their political attention. They seek out further information, reflecting their "need to decide" as Election Day approaches.[5]

There are further complexities, of course. To begin with, consider that election outcomes do not always play out as the fundamentals would have it. The 2000 presidential election is a classic example. The prosperous economy under the eight years of the Clinton presidency made the 2000 election Al Gore's to lose. And he lost it. Why didn't voters learn that the economy was booming in 2000? Or did they learn it but not transfer any credit to Gore? If so, why not? Why did they give appropriate credit in the other election years, which created the expectation that the economy would propel Gore to the White House in 2000?

1.1.5 Priming

One way campaigns can influence voters is by affecting the salience that voters attach to different considerations. In other words, campaign content shapes what voters think about. This is commonly referred to as "priming" (see Krosnick and Kinder 1990; Bartels 2006; Iyengar and Kinder [1987] 2010; also see Miller and Krosnick 1996). There is a long history of research on priming effects in election campaigns, which traditionally has emphasized the activation of voters' partisan predispositions (Berelson, Lazarsfeld, and McPhee 1954). Other research examines priming based on racial cues (Mendelberg 2001) and gender (Kahn and Goldenberg 1991). See Hillygus (2010) for a useful summary.[6]

Lynn Vavreck (2009) addresses priming and its effect on election outcomes. To Vavreck, the issues that candidates choose to emphasize help to dictate the outcome. The economy is the main contextual feature of the election. Although it is important to voters to begin with, the economy does not matter magically on Election Day. The economy matters because candidates prime it. Those candidates who are advantaged by the economy need to explicitly run on the issue of the economy to capitalize on their advantage. Candidates who are not advantaged by economic circumstances need to get voters to focus on other issues, ones on which they can effectively take a position that the opponent cannot and with which the public agrees. This provides the opportunity for success when facing economic conditions that do not favor the opposition.

This priming model is an appealing model of campaign effects. It is highly intuitive and comports with most of the existing literature—indeed, it is not fundamentally different from the other perspectives we have discussed. What differentiates it is that it can account for both the influence of certain fundamental variables, like the economy, on Election Day as well the departures from what the fundamentals would predict. This is not what we would expect from the predictable campaign. Consider also that, while the activities of candidates surely may influence which issues matter on Election Day, priming may impact learning itself. That is, the attention candidates pay to issues may improve the information voters acquire. This can happen either directly through the give-and-take of the campaign (Geer 2006) or indirectly, as voters seek out other information and/or others provide it. The two "types" of campaign effects thus may be (closely) related.[7]

1.1.6 Persuasion

Although much attention is paid to learning and priming, the holy grail of campaign effects is persuasion. What matters most, after all, is changing voters' electoral preferences. Scholars often distinguish persuasion from learning and priming, but we know that voters' preferences can change because of learning and priming, as voters acquire information and candidates emphasize issues—indeed, they actually may account for most of the change in voter preferences we observe

Campaigns can persuade voters in several ways. They can teach voters which candidates are more likely to move policy in their preferred direction; they can also affect change by convincing voters to change their own policy preferences. And they can certainly influence voters' assessments of candidate competence. Accumulating evidence shows that campaigns can actually change voters' preferences (see, e.g., Bartels 2006; Hillygus and Shields 2008; also see Hillygus's 2010 review). Much of the work emphasizes the influence of advertising (Shaw1999a; Johnston, Hagen, and Jamieson 2004; Huber and Arceneaux 2007; Gerber et al. 2011).

1.1.7 Voter Dynamics

The preceding discussion may make it seem as though voters are highly malleable in their vote choice. Voters are buffeted by all sorts of information during presidential campaigns, and one might think that each plausible argument individuals are exposed to might cause them to change their mind. One can picture the typical voter as constantly pivoting from one candidate to the other based on the latest information received.

Such a view would be wrong. As the earliest voting researchers (e.g., Berelson, Lazarsfeld, and McPhee 1954) discovered, voters tend to hold stable candidate preferences over the course of presidential campaigns. In large part, these preferences are the result of people's stable partisan predispositions. For many American voters, identifying as a Republican or a Democrat (or perhaps a conservative or a liberal) anchors their beliefs so that their candidate choice becomes a long-standing decision that is difficult to disturb. Those without firm political preferences naturally tend to be those with the least interest in politics. Thus, the least politically involved are the ones most likely to be swayed by campaign information (Converse 1962; Zaller 1992).

How then do we study the dynamics of change? As we stated, not all voters hold partisan leanings to keep them persistent, and some do not have preexisting political views at all. Importantly, some may be temporarily aroused by campaign information to go against their initial leanings, only to return home again. These short-term changes are of little relevance to the vote choice and the election outcome, unless they are close enough to the election to have an impact.[8]

A related way of looking at the long-run versus short-run distinction is to distinguish between decision-making that researchers call "online processing" and that which is "memory based" (Lodge, Steenbergen, and Brau 1995). When answering a survey question, online processors recall their answer from their past. If they are asked whether they favor a particular policy, they respond automatically from long-term memory. They know what their position is, so they reveal it to the survey researcher. Memory-based processors would answer the question differently. They consult their recent memory for considerations that might lead them to favor or oppose the policy. The content of their short-term memory—what they have been thinking recently—governs their responses.

Of course it is an oversimplification to say that people can be divided specifically into two types—online processors and memory-based respond-ers. Realistically, for most people most of the time, both processes are at work.[9] People tend to hold long-term predispositions that can be tempo-rarily derailed by short-term considerations that do not last long. At times many voters are influenced to shift uniformly in one partisan direction by the events of the moment. In these cases, the national vote division will shift but return to normal when the event is forgotten.

1.1.8 Elections and Campaigns: A Summary

The literature on elections and campaigns reveals a lot about presidential elections. The following summary encapsulates much of what we know. Although voters generally hold stable partisan choices over the course of the campaign, the rival campaigns and the accompanying discussions do sway some voters' choices. Yet, to an important degree, the final Election Day outcome reflects certain known fundamentals. Campaigns wield their greatest influence on those voters with the least interest in politics. In do-ing so, campaigns arguably enlighten their electoral choice.

This literature on election and campaigns is the backdrop for our cur-rent study. We pursue questions such as, What is the origin of voter prefer-ences at the outset of the campaign? How much do aggregate preferences shift over the campaign timeline, and why? When events cause voters to shift their candidate preferences, to what extent do these changes persist to Election Day? We turn next to a discussion of campaign events.

1.2 The Events Perspective on Campaign Effects

Electoral analysts—academics, journalists, and political professionals alike—typically focus on particular events as the source of change during presidential campaigns. These key events are structured focal points, such as nominating conventions and general election debates (see Geer 1988; Campbell, Cherry, and Wink 1992; Holbrook 1996; Shaw1999b; Johnston, Hagen, and Jamieson 2004). This attention is understandable for a number of reasons. First, conventions and debates are prominent events, which a large number of people watch on television and/or acquire information about them in other ways. Second, we can anticipate these events, so our interpretations of their effects are not subject to the post hoc, ergo propter hoc reduction that characterizes interpretation of the seeming effects of other campaign events. Third, there already is evidence that party conventions and, to a much lesser extent, presidential debates affect voters more than other events.

We know that the full list of campaign events includes many political "shocks," of which the highly visible conventions and debates are a tiny fraction. There are campaign visits, speeches, advertising campaigns, and mobilization efforts, to name but some of the inputs to voter evaluations during election campaigns. It is fair to wonder about the effects of these more common events; indeed, it may be that, taken together, they matter more for their influence on voters than do conventions and debates. The difficulty is in identifying their effects. Survey error is the culprit.

It is very difficult to estimate the effects on the vote of some seemingly big events, such as presidential debates. We can measure voter preferences in trial-heat polls before a debate and compare it to those reported in polls a few days after. As elaborated in chapter 2, however, much "change" we observe in surveys is simply the natural result of sampling error. And we know that ordinary campaign events such as major speeches, embarrassing gaffes, clever TV ads, and the like rarely have major long-term impact. As we will see in subsequent chapters, the response in terms of change in the aggregate vote is not only hard to measure; true change (as opposed to change in the reported polls) tends to be slight and often of temporary duration. Rarely can we point to a campaign event and say that it made a difference of a size and duration that can be identified in the polls (see Zaller 2002).

An exception to this rule is provided by two major events—the Democratic and Republican National Conventions in the summer of every presidential election year. The electorate cannot help but pay attention (and respond) to the shows the two major parties put on at their national conventions. And, as we will see, the convention effects are strong enough to be discernible in polls. They also have consequences for the Election Day result.

1.3 The Campaign Timeline and Electoral Preferences

Consider again the timeline of election campaigns. Campaign events occur over the timeline. For now, consider campaign events very broadly to include the full range of campaign behavior—from highly visible party conventions and political debates to the more routine day-to-day activities and everything in between—as well as the net result of voter discussion and evaluation. Do these "events" matter?

Let us assume that we have trial-heat polls at regular intervals over the course of the campaign. For this mental exercise, let us further assume that we have perfect polls, that is, no bias, sampling error, and so forth. Now, if campaign events do have effects, we would observe poll movement over the course of the campaign. Events would change voters' true preferences. This expectation reflects the standard characterization of campaign effects, as is clear from existing literature that focuses on the effects of particular types of events discussed earlier.

The existence of campaign effects is only half the story, however. Campaign effects are important to the extent their impact survives until Election Day. Effects either are permanent or else decay with the progress of time. It may be that effects decay. Here there is relatively short memory. Preferences tend toward the equilibrium in a particular election year, which represents the fundamentals of the campaign. Note that the equilibrium does not represent the final outcome, which would equal the fundamentals *plus* late campaign effects that have not fully dissipated by the time voters go to the polls. This expectation is consistent with some forecasting models of elections, namely, those that hold that the election campaign has little ultimate effect on the outcome (Lewis-Beck and Rice 1992).

Campaign effects might cumulate rather than decay. Here, there is no forgetting. Everything matters, as each effect makes a permanent contribution to the time series. Effects on different days may cancel out. Or they may compound. There is no equilibrium, and preferences shift up or down over time. The election outcome would be the sum of all of the campaign effects that occur over the timeline.

It may be that both processes are at work. Some events may have effects that decay and others ones that last. Yet other events may cause preferences to shift and then bounce back, but to a level different from before. In this model of the world there is an equilibrium, but it isn't static. That is, it moves up and down over time with events. The election outcome then is the sum of all lasting effects that happened over the campaign *and* any other late effects that have not fully decayed. The important point is that some campaign effects persist and the rest decay. This model is consistent with studies of selected campaign events and also accords with Gelman and King's (1993) evidence of enlightenment.

These different "models" of campaign effects are not musings. As we have noted, they summarize general arguments in the literature about the role of campaigns on electoral preferences. They also capture what we ultimately want to know—whether the campaign has real effects on electoral preferences and whether these effects matter on Election Day. They also can be explicitly tested and form the guiding force behind our analysis. Our analysis focuses first on aggregate preferences. Of course, we also are interested in individual voters. An understanding of macrolevel change, while important, does not tell the whole story. And an understanding of the microlevel makes more understandable patterns we observe at the aggregate level.

1.4 The Plan of this Book

As a study of presidential campaigns, this book has a decided focus. Contrary to much of the literature on campaign effects, this book has little discussion of specific campaign events, such as who said what in debates, or whether certain candidates were helped or hurt by a specific campaign controversy. We take a broader view and focus on more general patterns. This emphasis partly reflects what much of the literature itself has shown— that there are limits to studying the effects of events. With the exception of party conventions, it is difficult to find the effects of particular events, even the general election debates, as we also will see.

What we offer is an assessment of more than a half century of trial-heat polls. Our approach focuses not so much on the time series of polls in each election year. There are too many gaps in polling for that. Instead, our attention is to repeated cross-sections of the trial-heat polls at different time points in the campaign from ED-200 to Election Day. For the different points on this timeline, we assess underlying voter preferences for each of the fifteen elections, and the pace and direction of the movement. With these data we assess how the polls change from time point to time point across the fifteen elections. We also assess how the polls from different points in time relate to the Election Day vote across the election years. We can then assess what factors drive the change in polls over time. Finally, we turn from poll results to explore the vote motivations of individual respondents who make up the surveys, all with the goal of understanding how the vote intentions of voters evolve over the campaign timeline.

In this book, we show that voters' preferences change over the course of the campaign. Much of the change does not last to impact the outcome but some of it does. Early on in the election year, polls inform about the Election Day vote only modestly. During the year, preferences come into focus slowly. There are periods of real churning to be sure—the early nomination season, the conventions, and the very end of the campaign. Much of what matters on Election Day, however, comes into focus in between these periods, and this evolution is gradual, almost glacial.

The changes we observe aren't random. To a large extent, the campaign brings the fundamentals of the election to the voters. The external fundamentals emanating from the campaign inform voters of the issues; the internal fundamentals from voters' predispositions activate as the campaign progresses. Of course we don't know all the variables that, substantively, constitute the fundamentals of the election. Importantly, some of those we can identify and measure are not fixed—they change over time to influence voters' preferences and sometimes even determine which candidate wins. The fundamentals represent only the effects of the campaign that are long-lasting and persist until Election Day. Some events influence vote intentions in the short term but with no permanent trace. These short-term effects are of consequence only if they occur at the end of the campaign.

The book proceeds as follows.

Chapter 2 introduces the national polls that we use in our investigation and presents an initial depiction of the evolving voter preferences over the campaign timeline. Critical to the analysis is the separation of the signal from the (sampling) error in trial-heat polls. Much of the seeming change from survey to survey is the noise of survey error. The chapter also shows how vote margins tend to tighten over the campaign, which is a puzzle to be explained.

Chapter 3 theorizes about campaign dynamics, for individual voters and the national aggregate. Here we set out the different possibilities and explicitly model them using basic time-series technology. The modeling discussion suggests how poll results can tighten even as the campaign serves to polarize voters. On the one hand, we model the long-term accumulation of campaign effects as a "random walk" that should veer the outcome off center. On the other hand, voters can become increasingly attracted by their partisan roots, which makes the final verdict closer.

We begin to assess dynamics in chapter 4, focusing on voter preferences over different periods of the campaign timeline, as aggregate vote intentions change (usually slowly) from one week to the next. Aggregate vote intentions are most volatile during the convention season. They are most stable during the final weeks, ironically the period when the campaign heats up the most. The chapter presents evidence that campaign dynamics typically consist of both short-term effects of events and the more important long-term effects depicted as a slow-moving random walk.

Chapter 5 examines how well the polls at different points in the cycle predict the Election Day vote. Following the polls from day to day over the campaign timeline, we see their predictability zoom from virtually zero in January to reasonable accuracy on election eve. The periods of greatest growth in predictability—when preferences reshape and harden—are the early primary season and the convention season. A further period of preference reshuffling (relatively speaking) occurs at the last minute—the time between the final polls and the election.

Chapter 6 introduces the content of the economic and political fundamentals, and considers how they influence vote intentions over the campaign timeline. This chapter links directly to the literature that predicts presidential election outcomes from tangible aspects of the political environment during the campaign. At the outset of the campaign, voter preferences virtually ignore the economy. As the campaign progresses, the economy is an increasingly salient factor. The chapter also shows how partisanship and the candidates' ideological stances relative to the voters affect the election.

Chapter 7 changes the focus from aggregates to individuals. The object is to assess crystallization of vote choices and clarify linkages to the aggregate-level patterns established in previous chapters. The chapter follows individual voters from Gallup surveys at key points during the fifteen campaigns and also follows vote choice over the final two weeks among panel respondents surveyed by the American National Election Studies in the fifteen elections. We show that over time, voters' candidate choices evolve toward their internal fundamentals (partisan and demographic predispositions). At the same time, vote choices are highly stable as remarkably few voters change their minds over the course of the campaign.

The concluding chapter 8 reviews our findings and considers what they tell us about the predictability of presidential elections in general and for each of the fifteen elections in particular.

TWO

Uncovering Vote Intentions
using Trial-Heat Polls

Pollsters have been seeking Americans' opinions about their presidential choice for over two-thirds of a century. The practice has now intensified to the point where hardly a day passes during an election year without encountering results of new presidential polls, often from multiple organizations. In these so-called trial-heat polls, citizens typically are asked how they would vote "if the election were held today," with some differences in question wording, although in some early polls respondents were asked who they "would like to see win."

The first scientific polls to ask presidential preferences were conducted in 1936; their architects were the now-famous trio of Crossley, Roper, and Gallup.[1] By 1944, Gallup was conducting trial-heat polls on a regular basis. In that election year alone, Gallup asked twenty-eight different national samples of voting-age adults about their preference for the major-party presidential candidates—Franklin D. Roosevelt and Thomas E. Dewey. Since then, Gallup has conducted polls on a monthly or more frequent basis in every presidential election year.

By 1980, each of the leading broadcast networks (ABC, NBC, and CBS) were conducting surveys. Some newspaper organizations were too. The number grew through the 1980s. Independent organizations joined the ranks, and the proliferation of cable news networks added still more. In 1992, no less than 22 organizations conducted at least one poll. In 2000, more than 36 different organizations did. Over 19 fielded at least five polls. Five conducted tracking polls during the last month of the campaign, putting them in the field every day. The PollingReport.com website showed results from some 524 national polls of presidential election preferences during the 2000 election year. By 2008 there were more than 800 national polls.

Improved polling technology—especially the switch to telephone—accounts for much of the growth in presidential polling. Until well into the 1980s, most polls were conducted in person, as interviewers met with respondents in their homes. Given the logistics of interviewing a representative national sample in person, in-home polls typically were conducted over many days, over a window as wide as two weeks. By the mid-1970s, some pollsters were turning to telephone interviewing, which allowed quicker results at much less cost. By the mid-1990s, the transition to telephone was almost complete. One result is the greater density of polling we see today. During recent presidential election years, hardly a day passes without new presidential polls, often from multiple organizations.

The twenty-first century has seen still further technological innovations that have allowed quicker and cheaper polling. We refer to the rise of Internet polls—in which respondents are recruited for web-based interviews—and interactive voice response (IVR) polls—in which people are interviewed over the telephone but by recorded voices rather than live interviewers. For this book, we ignore polls conducted with the use of these new technologies.[2] The reason is not that they are certifiably wrong or inferior to live-interviewer polls, because that is not the case. Internet and IVR polls sometimes give results that differ from those of live-interviewer polls, however. When comparing polls historically, we conclude that it is safer to only include the live-interviewer polls from recent presidential races. The density of polling using this approach in recent elections is more than sufficient for our analysis.

Concern about comparability across time also compels a further restriction of our analysis. We start our analysis in 1952 and ignore earlier presidential polls from 1936 to 1948. Before 1952, pollsters often employed the flawed "quota-sampling" method, which allowed interviewers the freedom of whom to interview as long as they were within designated demographic quotas. It was the bias from quota sampling that misled some pollsters to predict Dewey would defeat Truman in 1948. Since 1952, the samples for national presidential polls have been drawn using some variant of random assignment, typically "multistage random samples."[3] The theory of random assignment is that it allows every voter (or citizen) an equal chance of inclusion in the survey.

To summarize, our focus is on polls conducted by survey organizations using live interviewers and beginning with the 1952 presidential election, when quota sampling had been displaced by variants of random sampling.

2.1 The Polls, 1952–2008

Employing a cutoff of 300 days before the election, roughly the beginning of the election year, we consider all live-interviewer polls involving the eventual major-party candidates. Using these criteria, we have located what we believe to be all of the available national polls of the presidential vote division that included the actual Democratic and Republican nominees for the fifteen elections between 1952 and 2008. In analyzing these polls, we ignore differences in question wording. Lau (1994) shows that variation in question wording has little bearing on trial-heat results.[4] Until 1992, the data are mostly from the vast Roper Center's iPOLL database, the standard archive for such data. We also supplemented using the *Gallup Report*, the now-defunct *Public Opinion*, and the more recently defunct magazine *Public Perspective*. In 1996, the data were drawn primarily from the also defunct *PoliticsNow* website, supplemented by data from the *Public Perspective* and the iPOLL database (see Erikson and Wlezien 1999). Beginning with the 2000 election, the data are from PollingReport.com and the iPOLL database. The amassing of data is only the first step. Decisions are required regarding how the data set is put together. We identify three concerns and our solutions.

First, although our interest is in the support for the two major-party candidates, we have to deal with surveys that include minor-party candidates among their choices. When a survey organization asks its trial-heat question two ways—with and without minor-party candidates on their ballots—we use the results without the minor-party candidates. Where the organization only offers respondents a choice among three or more candidates, we include the poll but only count the major-party choices.

Second, in recent years—especially since 1992—survey organizations report multiple results for the same polling dates, reflecting different sampling universes. For example, early in the election year, Gallup may report results for samples of adults on the one hand and registered voters on the other. Later in the election year, they may report results for samples of registered and "likely" voters, where the later focuses only on those considered likely to vote.[5] Clearly we don't want to count the same data twice, so we use only the data for the universe that seemingly best approximates the actual voting electorate. Where a survey house reports poll results for both an adult sample and a registered voter sample, we use data from the latter. Where a survey house reports poll results for both registered voters and a sample of likely voters, we use data from the latter.[6]

Third, especially in recent years, survey organizations often report results for overlapping polling periods. This is understandable and is as we
would expect where a survey house operates a tracking poll and reports
three-day moving averages. Respondents interviewed today would be included in poll results reported tomorrow and the day after, and the day
after that. Clearly, we do not want to count the same respondents on multiple days, and it is very easy to avoid. For the hypothetical survey house
operating a tracking poll and reporting three-day moving averages, we only
use poll results for every third day.

Applying these three basic rules has dramatic effects. Consider the 2000
election year. Recall from above that the PollingReport.com website con-
tained results for some 524 national polls of the Bush-Gore (-Nader) division reported by different survey organizations. Eliminating results for multiple universes and the overlap in polling periods leaves only 295 separate
national polls. For the period 1952–2008 we identify 1,971 different polls.
The polls are not evenly distributed across elections and cluster in more
recent years. Table 2.1 summarizes the data. Here we see that more than
90 percent of the polls were conducted in the eight elections since 1980.
From 1980 through 2008, the number of polls averaged 225 per election.
For the period before 1980, we have only 25 polls per election on average.
Thus, the data offer much more frequent readings of electoral sentiment
for the last six elections. Even in these recent years, the polls tend to cluster
late in the electoral seasons, especially after Labor Day, when the general
election campaign begins in earnest.

Most polls are conducted over multiple days. The median number of
days in the field is 3 and the mean 3.75, though there is a lot of variance
here—the standard deviation is 2.83 days. We "date" each poll by the middle day of the period the survey is in the field. If a poll is conducted during
the three days between June 12 and June 14, we date the poll June 13. For
surveys in the field with an even number of days, the fractional midpoint is
rounded up to the following day.

For days when more than one poll result is recorded, we pool the respondents into one *poll of polls*. With the use of this method, the 1,971
polls allow readings (often multiple) for 1,158 separate days from 1952 to
2008 (see table 2.1). Since 1980, we have readings for 125 days per election on average, more than one-third of which is concentrated in the period after Labor Day. Indeed, we have a virtual day-to-day monitoring of
preferences during the general election campaign for these years, especially
for 1992–2008.

It is important to note that polls on successive days are not truly inde-

Table 2.1   Summary of presidential polls within 300 days of the election

Election year	Number of polls	Number of dates with polls[a]
1952	17	17
1956	24	16
1960	27	17
1964	22	21
1968	22	22
1972	38	26
1976	31	29
1980	118	63
1984	159	108
1988	153	97
1992	247	129
1996	222	118
2000	297	168
2004	273	152
2008	351	175
Total	1,971	1,158

[a] The variable indicates the number of days for which poll readings are available, based on an aggregation of polls by the mid-date of the reported polling period. Counts represent only live-interview polls involving the two major-party candidates.

pendent. Although they do not share respondents, they do share overlapping *polling periods*. That is, the polls on each particular day combine results of polls in the field on days before and after. Readings on neighboring days thus will capture a lot of the same things, by definition. This is of consequence for an analysis of dynamics, as we will see.

Figure 2.1 and 2.2 present the daily poll-of-polls for the final 300 days of fifteen presidential campaigns. For the quick overview, figure 2.1 displays all the polls over fifteen years on the same page for ready comparison. Figure 2.2 displays the data in larger scale over several pages. In each instance, the graphs depict the Democratic share of the *two-party* vote intention, ignoring all other candidates (such as Nader in 2000), aggregated by the mid-date of the reported polling period. To be absolutely clear, the number on a particular day is the Democratic share of all *respondents* reporting a Democratic or Republican preference in polls centered on that day, that is, we do not simply average across polls.[7] Where possible, respondents who were undecided but leaned toward one of the candidates were included in the tallies.

To enhance comparability across years, in figure 2.1 we subtract out the actual Democratic share of the two-party vote; thus, the numbers in the

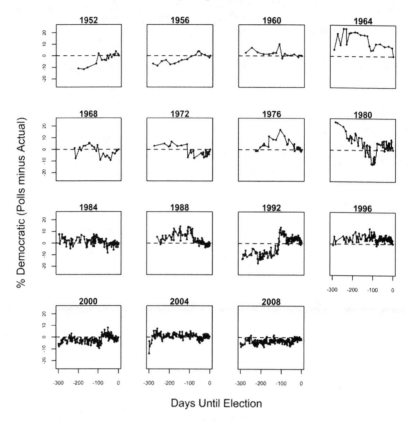

Figure 2.1. Trial-heat preferences for the final 300 days of the campaign, 1952–2008: A global view.

figure reflect the degree to which poll results differ from the final vote. A positive value indicates Democratic support that is above what we observe on Election Day, while a negative value reveals support that is below the Democratic candidate's ultimate vote share. Ignoring the scattering of trial heats conducted in the year prior to the election, we concentrate solely on polls over the final 300 days of the campaign.

For the larger set of fifteen graphs in figure 2.2, the scaling is the percentage of Democratic rather than the deviation of the Democratic vote from the outcome. We group the fifteen elections into five graphs, with each showing the time series of the polls for three consecutive elections, starting with 1952, 1956, and 1960. The graphs show the final vote divisions as solid dots at 0 days before the election.

As can readily be seen from a perusal of figures 2.1 and 2.2, the daily poll-of-polls numbers exhibit considerably more within-year variance in

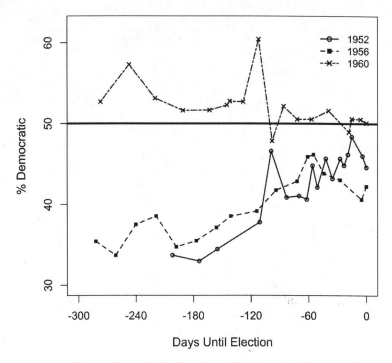

Figure 2.2A. Trial-heat preferences for final 300 days of the campaign, 1952–60. Observations represent daily polls of polls. The Election Day results are on the far right.

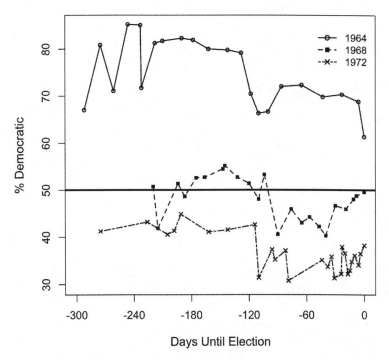

Figure 2.2B. Trial-heat preferences for final 300 days of the campaign, 1964–72. Observations represent daily polls of polls. The Election Day results are on the far right.

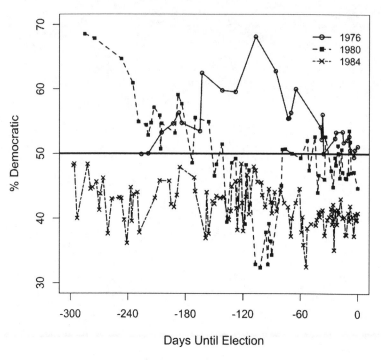

Figure 2.2C. Trial-heat preferences for final 300 days of the campaign, 1976–84. Observations represent daily polls of polls. The Election Day results are on the far right.

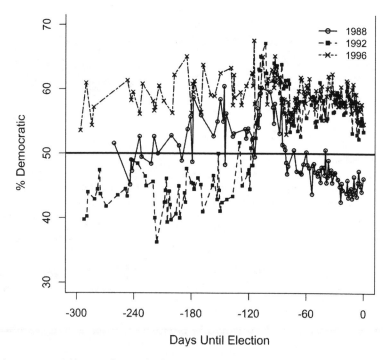

Figure 2.2D. Trial-heat preferences for final 300 days of the campaign, 1988–96. Observations represent daily polls of polls. The Election Day results are on the far right.

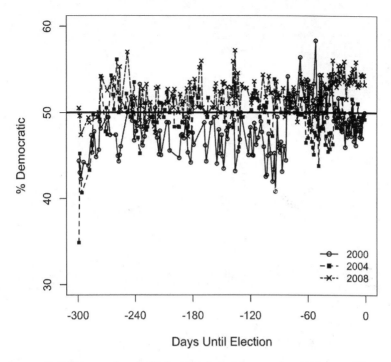

Figure 2.2E. Trial-heat preferences for final 300 days of the campaign, 2000–2008. Observations represent daily polls of polls. The Election Day results are on the far right.

some years than in others. Consider first some instances in which change was clearly evident. In 1992, the polls began somewhat favorable to President George H. W. Bush but then surged dramatically toward Democrat Bill Clinton after the Democratic National Convention, which was followed by tightening at the end of the race. The polls for 1980 show a similar degree of movement, with President Carter's vote declining, then spiking upward, and fading at the end as he lost to Reagan. Interestingly, these were both elections in which the incumbent president sought and lost reelection. The other extreme is depicted by the polls of 1996 and 2004, when the incumbent presidents (Clinton and G. W. Bush) sought reelection and emerged victorious. In each instance, the polls were nearly constant, as shifts in voter sentiment were limited to a very narrow range. The 2000 G. W. Bush–Gore election and the 2008 McCain–Obama election are somewhere in between those two extremes. Real differences clearly exist across election years in terms of the volatility of voter preferences.

Just as the within-year variances of the poll time series differ from elec-

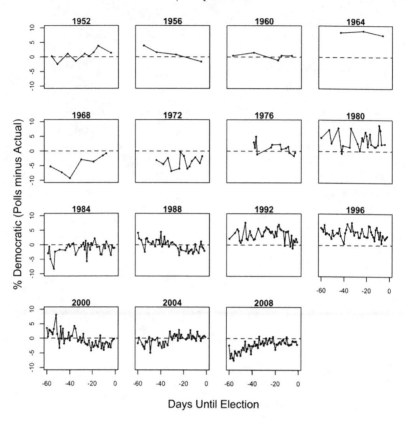

Figure 2.3. Trial-heat preferences for final 60 days of the campaign, 1952–2008.

tion to election, the within-year variances of polls also differ from one time period to another over the campaign cycle. The time serial variance in the polls drops noticeably as the election cycle unfolds. This compression of variance is particularly pronounced after Labor Day, the unofficial beginning of the fall campaign. Figure 2.3 zooms in on this period and displays the daily poll-of-polls for the final 60 days of the campaign. (With the magnification, the range of the y-axis is now half of that shown in figs. 2.1 and 2.2.) On average, the variance of vote intentions as measured by polling in the fall is only about one-third of the variance for observations over the campaign's previous 60 days. As we will see, much of the volatility of the polls is concentrated in the run-up to the fall campaign (including the period of the party conventions), not the fall campaign itself. We return to this point shortly.[8]

2.2 True Variance in Preferences versus Sampling Error

In discussing trial-heat polls, we distinguish between *the polls*, which we observe directly from survey samples, and the underlying unobserved *electoral preferences* among the universe of potential voters. The observed divisions in trial-heat polls represent a combination of true preferences and survey error. By "true" preferences we mean the average response to the poll question among the *universe* of potential voters—the outcome of a hypothetical election conducted on that day. Of course our surveys do not perfectly reflect true preferences, because surveys are based on samples. Even if the electorate's net true preferences remain unchanged over the course of a campaign, poll results will bounce around from day to day simply because of this survey error. This occurrence complicates any analysis using aggregate polling data.

There are different types of survey error; see Groves (1989) for a very thorough classification. The most basic and familiar of these is random sampling error, the variation in results that reflects the subset of people included in the sample. With the use of random sampling, the subset of people differs from sample to sample. The properties are well known, and we can provide reasonably accurate estimates of this error.

We cannot literally separate survey error from reported preferences. By applying long-established principles of statistics, however, we can estimate the proportion of the variance of the observed preferences that is due to true preferences and the remaining proportion that is due to survey error. If we assume random sampling (or its equivalent) by pollsters, the answer is easy to compute. We start with the observed variance in the polls. The observed variance can be daily variation in observed preferences over a specific time period, for example, over the final 30 days of the 2008 campaign. Or it could be yearly variation in the observed preferences over a specific cross-section, for example, preferences in the final week of each election. Statistically, the observed variance is the mean squared deviation of poll results from the observed mean. Then we estimate the error variance—the mean squared error per survey. The true variance is simply the subtraction of the error variance from the observed variance. The surplus (observed minus error) variance equals the true variance of presidential preferences, discounting for survey error.

But how do we estimate the sampling error? Assuming random sampling, for each daily poll-of-polls the estimated error variance is $\frac{p(1-p)}{N}$, where p = the proportion voting for the Democratic candidate rather than the Republican. (Whether p designates the Democrat or Republican obviously does not matter.) Thus, when the size of the sample goes up, the estimated error variance goes down. When the race gets closer, the estimated error variance goes up. For instance, if the polls are 60–40 from a sample of 1,000 voters, we estimate error variance to be $.6(1 - .6)/1,000$, or $.00024$. If we use percents instead of proportions, the number would be 2.4 percent. If the result from a sample 1,000 is 50–50, we estimate error variance to be slightly larger, at $.00025$, or 2.5 in percentage terms. If the same result obtains from a sample of 2,000, we would estimate the error variance to be $.000125$, or 1.25 percentage points.

To illustrate, we focus only on polls conducted during the final 60 days of the campaign, or roughly from Labor Day to Election Day, when polling is most regular. For the value of p we take the observed Democratic proportion of major-party preferences in the poll. For N we take the number of respondents offering Democratic or Republican preferences. This gives us the estimated error variance for each daily poll-of-polls. The error variance for all polls-of-polls for the last 60 days in each election year is simply the average error variance. The total variance is observed from the variance of the poll results themselves. The estimated true variance is the arithmetic difference:

Estimated true variance = total variance – error variance.

The ratio of (estimated) true to total variance is the statistical reliability. The estimates for the final 60 days of fifteen campaigns are reported in table 2.2.

The table suggests that the true variance differs quite a lot across election years. Note first that in two election years—1960 and 1964—the observed variance is actually *less* than we would expect from random sampling and no true change. The 1960 contest was close throughout the last 60 days, perhaps never truly straying from the 50–50 margin ending in the outcome in which Kennedy defeated Nixon by a whisker. Quite plausibly, virtually all of the fluctuation in the 1960 horserace observed at the time was simply the result of sampling error. By similar reasoning, the 1964 horserace also was a virtually constant voter verdict—this time Johnson decisively defeating Goldwater. In these two contests, it is conceivable that few individuals changed their preferences during the fall campaign.

By our estimates, the largest true variance occurred in 1968, 1980, and 2000. In these elections, 75 percent or more of the observed variance was true variance. A true variance of 6.5 (2000) to 9.6 (1968) is indicative of a range of about 10 to 12 percentage points over the last 60 days of these

Table 2.2   Variance of daily trial-heat polls within 60 days of the election, 1952–2008

Election year	Error variance	True variance	Total variance	Reliability
1952	1.94	1.31	3.25	.40
1956	1.73	3.47	5.20	.67
1960	2.10	—	0.88	—
1964	1.72	—	0.59	—
1968	2.29	7.28	9.57	.76
1972	2.19	1.83	4.02	.45
1976	2.33	0.96	3.29	.29
1980	1.77	5.12	6.99	.75
1984	1.71	2.72	4.43	.61
1988	2.06	1.65	3.71	.44
1992	1.97	2.26	4.23	.53
1996	1.74	1.03	2.77	.37
2000	1.61	4.89	6.50	.75
2004	1.49	1.29	2.69	.45
2008	1.23	0.65	1.88	.34
Mean	1.86	2.30[a]	3.69	.45[a]
Median	1.77	1.65	3.71	.45

[a]For the calculations of means, the estimated true variance and reliability in 1960 and 1964 are considered to be 0.

campaigns. Clearly, the electorate's aggregate vote intentions changed considerably during these presidential campaigns.

It is tempting to speculate on different possible explanations for the variation from election year to election year in the actual volatility of the intended vote. One likely culprit is variation in voters' prior knowledge about the candidates. Where there is an incumbent, things should be less volatile. Where the challenger is well known, the volatility should be lesser still. Thus, the thinking goes, we should expect little change in the polls during 1996 because Clinton and Dole were seemingly known quantities. Indeed the imputed true variance in 1996 was slight. In contrast, 1980 should be volatile because voters were trying to figure out Reagan. And this was one of the most volatile election campaigns. By our reasoning, it is easy to explain the volatility of 2000, when nonincumbent Gore faced the relative newcomer Bush. This reasoning fails in other instances, however. In 2004, for instance, polls were very stable even early in the election year as voters were asked to decide between a known, President G. W. Bush, and a newcomer to the national scene, Senator John Kerry. Earlier, polls moved around considerably in 1956, when Eisenhower and Stevenson were well known, but did not in 1960 and 1976, when the voters were learning about Kennedy and Carter, respectively. Thus, we conclude that the degree of volatility is not easily explainable, at least given the conventional wisdom.[9]

It should be sobering that, on average, the reliability of fall polls is a mere .45. This means that a bit less than half (45 percent) of the observed variance in the polls during the fall campaign is real, and a bit over half is sampling error. Even this estimate probably is generous regarding the accuracy of polls. By assuming simple random sampling, we ignore design and house effects. Design effects represent the consequences of departing in practice from simple random sampling, due to clustering, stratifying, weighting, and the like. House effects represent the consequences of different houses employing different methodologies and can reflect a variety of factors.[10] Poll results vary from one day to the next in part because polls on different days are conducted by different houses (also see Wlezien and Erikson 2001). The point is that there is a lot more error in survey results than just sampling error.[11]

What is clear from our analysis is that the electorate's aggregate preferences typically do not vary much over the fall campaign. We can put a number on the likely range in true preferences over the course of the fall campaign. Statistically, the range (from high to low) around the mean will be approximately plus or minus two standard deviations. From table 2.2 we see that the estimated mean true variance is 2.30 percentage points, so the corresponding standard deviation (the square root of the variance) is 1.52 points. This implies that for the average fall campaign, the maximum range of aggregate preference has been about 6 percentage points. As we discuss further in chapters 4 and 5, only a small percentage of the vote is at play during the autumn in a typical election year.

2.3 The Changing Volatility of Voter Preferences over the Election Year

In assessing the variance of voter preferences, we are not limited to considering only the final 60 days of the campaign. In this section we examine the variance of the time series of voter preferences during earlier time segments of the campaign. Here we are interested in how the stability of preferences tends to vary with the point in the election cycle. Are preferences more changeable at some points than at others? Again, we adjust for sampling error. We subtract out variance owing to sampling error and assess the degree of (estimated) true variance in preferences in the different periods of each campaign. Then we "average" the variance by both period and election.

Table 2.3 summarizes this analysis, showing the median *sampling-error adjusted* within-election-year variance (across the fifteen elections) for a

Table 2.3 **Within-year variance of daily trial-heat preferences by 60-day moving averages over the election cycle, 1952–2008**

Days before the election	Median variance
1–60	2.00
31–90	2.61
61–120	7.73
91–150	8.46
121–180	1.34
151–210	1.68
181–240	2.75
211–270	3.84
241–300	5.15

Note: Table is based on the daily poll-of-polls and adjusted for sampling error. The higher variance within the periods 61–120 and 91–150 days reflects the turbulence of the convention season.

staggered series of 60-day time segments. The numbers in the table are what we find in a typical election year. Note the dramatic differences in the variances from one period to the next. The variance is lowest at 120 to 180 days before the election, the early summer lull before the conventions. The variance peaks in the period thereafter, or roughly the convention season, especially 90 to 120 days out, when the "out" party usually meets. The variance drops sharply after the conventions, during the final 60 days representing the fall campaign—the period we examined in detail earlier. Indeed, the change during this period is only trivially more than we see in early summer.

The pattern of declining (within-year) variance from summer to fall generalizes across thirteen of the fifteen elections, with 2004 and 2008 the rare exceptions. In other words, there almost always is less daily variation in the true preferences of the electorate during the fall campaign than during the preceding summer. This suggests that electoral preferences harden by the time the general election campaign begins in earnest after Labor Day.[12] The 2004 and 2008 exceptions are anomalies not because preferences varied more than usual during the fall campaigns for these years, but rather because the estimated variances over the summer campaigns (120 to 61 days before the election) were extraordinarily low. The estimated variance of the daily vote division during the summer of 2004 was a mere 0.14; for the summer of 2008 it was 0.27 percentage points. These near-zero estimates imply that the impacts of the long campaigns of 2004 and 2008 hardened voters early. In each year the summer polls varied scarcely more than they would have by sampling error alone if it were the case that preferences were constant throughout the period.

With the 2004 and 2008 exceptions noted, there can be no mistaking the message: the electorate's presidential preferences are more volatile during the summer of the election campaign (centered 90 to 120 days out) than during the heat of the fall campaign (1 to 60 days out).[13] Much of this represents the impact of the national conventions, which stimulate voters to attention. Still, the markedly higher volatility during the summer season may surprise if we fix on the plausible hypothesis that voters become increasingly attentive as the campaign progresses. The more they pay attention, the less they change their minds. There exists an explanation for the pattern: the more people pay attention, the more their preferences harden. We can imagine that at the campaign's start, voters are sufficiently malleable so that minor campaign events affect voter choice. Then, as the campaign progresses, voters become more polarized in their choices, making it difficult for events of the fall campaign to change many minds. From this perspective, there is a diminishing marginal effect of additional information, at least as regards shifts in dichotomous vote choice.

The variabile stability of aggregate preferences over the election cycle tells us that the electorate is more moveable at some times than others. Consistent with the conventional wisdom, we find that preferences churn the most during the convention season. Then, as the election approaches, preferences harden. This point is addressed further in chapters 4 and 5.

2.4 Cross-Sectional Variance: Compression over Time

So far we have examined the variance of preferences during the campaign within election years, observing choices over time within specific campaigns. An alternative perspective is cross-sectional analysis. Here, we observe the variance of preferences across elections for specific slices of time. These results are also revealing.

Suppose we could observe voter preferences for any specific time in the election cycle (e.g., 60 days out) for our set of fifteen elections, 1952–2008. As we vary this point in the timeline, how would the variance of cross-sectional preferences change? Our initial question would be, does the variance increase or decrease? An increase would mean that inter-election variation gets wider as time progresses, with electoral margins widening. A decrease would mean that inter-election variation narrows, with electoral

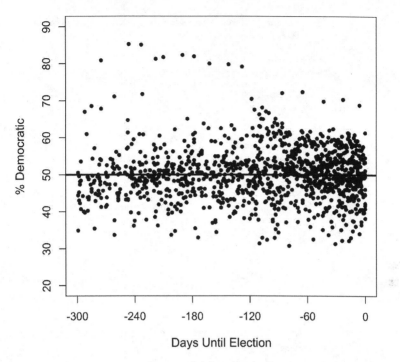

Figure 2.4. Voter preferences, all daily polls of polls, 1952–2008.

margins shrinking. Put simply, then, the question is whether the electoral division expands or contracts over the campaign.

Figure 2.4 provides the raw data. This graph pools all the poll data over the fifteen elections, mingling cases for different years. The pattern to observe through the jumble of observations is the decline in the vertical (between-election) variance over time. Clearly there is a declining dispersion of voter preferences as the election approaches, that is, the polls increasingly converge toward the 50–50 point. Our next task is to document this statistically.[14]

Because the electorate is polled only occasionally rather than on a daily basis, our first task is to average the daily polls by time-segment over the fifteen campaigns. We use 30-day increments. Table 2.4 displays the results. We observe an interesting pattern. Early in the election year, from 210 to 151 days before the election, the cross-sectional variance is slightly above 120 points. This translates to an 11-point standard deviation and an implied range of close to 50 percentage points between the most Democratic and the most Republican result in trial-heat polls. By the final 30 days of

Table 2.4   Between-year (cross-sectional) variance of major-party vote in trial-heat polls, for 30-day time intervals prior to the presidential election, 1952–2004

Days before election	Between-year (cross-sectional) variance
Actual election day	36.8
1–30	68.7
31–60	72.7
61–90	82.5
91–120	100.8
121–150	104.3[a]
151–180	126.2
181–210	130.4

Note: Each observation is based on a poll of all polls during the date interval. Variance estimates are corrected for measurement error.
[a]Based on 14 election observations; data are missing for 1952.

the campaign, the variance shrinks by almost half from its size at the beginning of the year—to 68.7. This translates to a standard deviation a bit under 7 points and an implied range across elections of about 25 percentage points. The variance shrinks again, by about another third between the last month's polls and the actual election.

We refer to the pattern shown in figure 2.4 and table 2.4 as variance compression. Starting with the conventions, election margins tighten as the campaign progresses. Clearly, large leads early in campaigns cannot be sustained at their early levels. The presence of variance compression adds a further bit of evidence as we try to solve the puzzles of the campaign timeline.

2.5 Modeling Presidential Polls as Rolling Cross-Sections

So far our brief tour of the presidential polling data has involved comparing variances (time series or cross-sections) in thick windows of time, 30 or 60 days at a time. To obtain further leverage, the ideal would be to exploit more fine-grained data, with presidential preferences measured for smaller time spans such as weeks or even days. The limitations of the observed data, however, give us pause. Time-series analysis of individual election campaigns is a challenge. Polling questions are asked irregularly, and the ratio of sampling variance to the true variance is too large to make time-series analysis feasible. The same goes for pooling the data as a multiyear panel with a fixed effect analysis. Our best answer is to treat the data as a series of rolling cross-sections, where, for specific time segments of the campaign, we analyze the cross-sectional variation in voter preferences. Measurement error is little problem for such an exercise; whereas sampling error variance swamps the variance from true change when observing within-election polls, sampling error is dwarfed by election-to-election differences in the cross-section. Measured across elections, the variance in the vote exceeds the error variance by a factor of 50 or more. For instance, when the vote is measured as 30-day cross-sections (as in table 2.3), the minimum of the estimated reliabilities is a whopping .98. This tells us that virtually all of the difference in the polls across elections is real. But whereas measurement error loses force as a problem in the cross-section, there remains the problem that presidential surveys are sometimes sparse and conducted at irregular intervals. For analyzing smaller time-bands than 30-day intervals, how do we avoid complications from excessive missing data?

For some of the analyses of the following sections, we measure the vote division for one-week or two-week intervals, where the data are from weekly or biweekly cross-sections at regular intervals in terms of distance from the election. For instance, in one analysis the dependent variable could be the vote division in each campaign as pooled from all polls conducted six weeks before the election. For some purposes, as we will see, this kind of pooling is useful.

For some analyses, however, we can go further and perform daily analysis, based on estimates of the vote division on specific dates of the campaign, such as day 44 before the election. Of course, we have no direct measures milled as finely as at the daily level, although we can and do interpolate daily voter preferences from available polls. For any date without a poll centered on that date, an estimate is created as a weighted average from the most recent date of polling and the next date of polling. Weights are in proportion to the closeness of the surrounding earlier or later poll. For instance, if the previous polls are three days earlier and the next polls are two days later, we interpolate the current voter preferences as .4 times the earlier polls and .6 times the later polls. By this device, we can obtain estimates of the vote division for each date within 219 days of the election for each presidential election of the years 1952–2008.

A potential drawback is that we no longer can correct for sampling error. For our preliminary analysis of the cross-sectional variance over time (see table 2.3), we presented results by 30-day intervals that were adjusted for sampling error in the manner described in section 2.2. The reality is that the estimated reliabilities were .98 and greater, making the adjustment trivial. Although we cannot directly estimate the error variance for the daily interpolated estimates, we can infer their upper bound to be low relative to the cross-sectional variance. Our estimate is that the reliabilities of the interpolated daily estimates of the vote division vary from .96 to .99 with an average of .98.[15] This result is more than satisfactory.

We illustrate the advantage of exploiting the interpolated daily vote division with the following example. Earlier, for table 2.3, we estimated the between-year variance of the vote division at staggered 30-day intervals. The estimates were corrected for sampling error. By assuming we can ignore the minimal sampling error, it is now possible to estimate the cross-sectional variance on a daily basis over the period of 200 dates. Figure 2.5 shows the results.

The data of figure 2.5 are consistent with the tabular results from table 2.4 but show a finer (daily) resolution. Consistent with our observation that the variance of the cross-sectional vote becomes compressed over the campaign, we observe a regular decline in the daily variance. (The daily variance takes on slightly higher values than those for 30-day intervals, which average out bumps and wiggles.) The variance decline is somewhat jagged, however, with an irregular pattern during the summer period. As

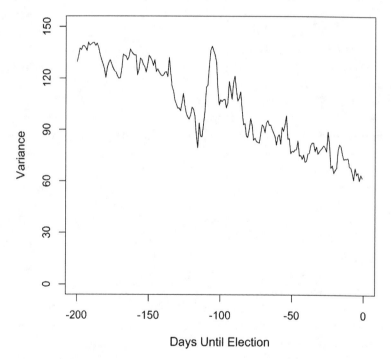

Figure 2.5. Cross-sectional variance of the daily vote division, estimated for each of 200 days before election day, 1952–2008.

Table 2.5   Variance of the weekly division of vote intentions in polls, at designated time points of the presidential campaign

April (ED-200)	Before conventions	After conventions	Final week
134.05	116.63	81.35	63.80

Note: N = 15. Each reading is a weekly poll of polls. Where no polling exists for the designated week, the most recent poll is substituted. An exception is the post-convention poll, where the subsequent poll is substituted for missing data. Before-convention polls are for the week ending the Monday before the first convention. After-convention polls are for the week beginning the second Tuesday after the second convention.

we will see, this irregularity is the result of the irregular scheduling of the party conventions, which shake up the vote at different times in different years.

We can test for the convention effect on the variance directly. Table 2.5 presents the weekly cross-sectional variance of vote intentions at four key points in the campaign: April, one week before the conventions, two weeks after the conventions, and the final campaign week. (We refer to these four benchmark time points throughout subsequent chapters.) Although the time gap between the pre- and post-convention readings is considerably less than the gap between April and the pre-convention reading or between the post-convention reading and the final week's reading, we see that the decline in the variance of the polls during the conventions period is twice what we see over the wider time intervals. The conventions thus shake up preferences but also bring them closer to 50–50. Overall, half of the decline in the variance occurs during the convention season. Still, as shown clearly in table 2.5 (and in tables and figures just above and below), the vote compresses at other times besides the conventions. Indeed, the decline in the aggregate variance persists as a modest linear descent outside the convention season.

Figure 2.6 shows the daily readings of the variance where time is now measured relative to the convention schedule. The figure shows the estimated variance at daily intervals between 14 and 80 days before the election and 14 to 60 days after.[16] (The 80- and 59-day marks are chosen to guarantee 15 cases for each data point.) Although not shown in the graph, the between-year variance spurts to 142 percentage points at the most volatile moment—in polls conducted between the two conventions. Outside the convention period, we can see that that the variance of the daily readings of vote intentions drops in a steady glide when measured relative to the convention season. To be sure, there already is substantial tightening of the race prior to the conventions. It also is clear from the figure that the

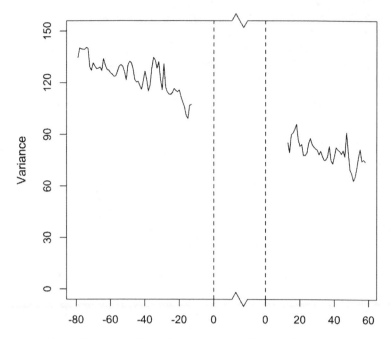

Figure 2.6. Cross-sectional variance of the daily vote division, estimated relative to the party conventions, 1952–2008.

rate of variance compression slows after the convention season. We will see in future chapters that the convention break in the time series is an important factor determining campaign trajectories, as one might expect. We also will see that the same is not true for another set of salient campaign events, namely, presidential debates.

2.6 Summary

This chapter answers the first of the two questions we posed in chapter 1: Do voters' preferences vary over the course of the campaign? The not-surprising answer to the question is a resounding yes. But there is a lot more to it than this. Preferences are more volatile in some election years than in others. Despite such differences across years, we observe that the volatility in the time series peaks in the late summer—about the time the political parties hold their national conventions—and then declines as the general election campaign begins. This holds true in virtually every year. Evidently, the more the mass media and the public pay attention, the less voters change their minds. Moreover, as preferences harden, the cross-sectional variance of preferences compresses. Poll margins late in the campaign are closer to average—about 50–50—than those from earlier in the year.

This chapter's analysis of the variance in the polls and in underlying electoral preferences is an important first step, if only a very general one. Beyond the volatility of the electorate's preferences, we are interested in the actual dynamics of electoral change. What we have observed so far is merely that net voter preferences do not stay constant over the course of a campaign. This could mean nothing more than short-term variance in responsiveness to campaign events, signifying little in terms of the final outcome. Or, shifts in preference could signify shocks that persist to Election Day. Our interest is in both the electoral shocks of campaign events and their persistence. It is not only a matter of whether voters are influenced by campaign events when they occur but whether the influence lasts to Election Day. This is the topic to which we turn next.

THREE

Thinking about Campaign Dynamics

The previous chapter documents an important fact: with some interesting variation across election years, the electorate's presidential vote intentions evolve over the course of a presidential campaign. We know this because poll results within an election year vary far more than would be expected by sampling error alone. But how should we model the dynamics of electoral preferences over the presidential campaign?

One possibility is that preferences start at some pre-campaign set point and then move unpredictably from that point on, driven by the unforeseeable actions of the two presidential campaigns. This would seem to be the strongest case for campaign effects. The electorate's opening verdict is some plausible starting point in terms of the relative strengths of the two candidates and then careens uncontrollably as a function of which campaign outperforms the other and by how much. The model is hardly attractive, particularly if one envisions the relevant effects to be a series of distortions, gaffes, and hoopla that can only serve to guide the electorate away from a choice determined by the "fundamentals." It also is not very credible, as we know that outcomes are, at least to some extent, predictable in advance. Is there another, more attractive, interpretation of how campaign effects work?

Most scholarly accounts of campaign effects are quite different from that of the previous paragraph. In these accounts, campaigns move the electorate *toward* an outcome driven by the fundamentals, not away. This is what Bartels (2006) calls the "priming" function of campaigns. Others refer to enlightenment or "learning." (We have already noted how priming and learning may be related.) The story goes that early in the campaign, voters allot minimal attention to campaign news and develop only superficial impressions for the pollsters to analyze when they monitor preferences. Then, as the campaign progresses, voters start to focus on the fundamentals of the campaign, which (recall from chap. 1) come in two different flavors—"internal" ones that are specific to individual voters and "external" ones that reflect the political and economic context of the election. The campaign effectively delivers these fundamentals to the voter rather than distorts the outcome away from what they would predict. The view that campaigns cause voters to attend to the fundamentals is an established perspective in the literature. Can we accommodate it within our conceptualization of the voter preference time series?

For now, we hold off regarding the content of these fundamentals and concentrate on the dynamics of aggregate vote choice over the campaign. We consider how voters might (or might not) be influenced by forces we depict as fundamentals. For instance, is the variation of the vote division during the election campaign nothing more than episodic and transient shifts that dissipate within days only to become extinguished by Election Day? Or does it represent an accumulation of (perhaps small) voter responses to the campaign, which carry the Election Day verdict far afield from what the polls show early in the campaign? Further, do shifts in preference respond to the same or different types of stimuli at different stages of the campaign?

The discussion must venture into the realm of time-series statistics. Time-series analysts take seriously the task of diagnosing the statistical properties of their data—for example, is the series stationary or integrated? These queries are typically motivated by statistical concerns that rarely interest the lay reader—for example, given the data characteristics, what kind of statistical methodology should be performed? Here, our interest is substantive, not statistical. In describing the time series of campaign preferences, we hope to capture substantive information about preference change during the campaign.

We can only tread lightly into the arena of time-serial statistical diagnostics. The data allow no more. Polls are conducted irregularly during campaigns, rather than at regular intervals such as every day or even every week. And, as we discussed in chapter 2, polls are subject to considerable measurement error. Furthermore, we must confront the fact that national aggregations of candidate preferences represent the composite of millions of individual-level time series describing individual voters.

3.1 Campaigns and the Individual Voter

We start by modeling the individual voter's decisions that comprise the national vote. Consider the voter's choice at some arbitrary starting point early in the campaign time series. Without the constraint of actually measuring it, we can consider this choice as the relative preference for Candidate A versus Candidate B, that is, the degree of attraction to A minus the degree of attraction for B. One could consider this score as an attitude—degree of relative liking—or as the voter's relative utility as an anticipated benefit from one candidate relative to the other. The exact conceptualization does not matter. We set the scale of hypothetical measurement so that high scores are pro–Candidate A and low scores are pro–Candidate B. The zero point is the threshold of vote choice. If the voter's momentary score is greater than zero, she votes for A; if less than zero, she votes for B.

Now let us imagine this voter's hypothetical time series of daily readings over the course of the campaign, starting with our earliest readings in April (or before). Early in the election year, a respondent in a trial-heat poll might not have given much thought to her relative preferences for the likely party nominees, but is able to retrieve sufficient information from memory to state a preference for one of the candidates. What would go into this choice?

For now, let us assume that the voter has a basic disposition of relative liking, built on partisan experience plus some contextual information regarding the current political times and the early information about the candidates. If the voter's choice is monitored regularly, this fundamental disposition anchors the voter's choice. Over time, on average, the best guess regarding our voter's relative preference is this disposition. But our voter's relative preference of the moment may depart from the disposition. From time to time, our voter might be swayed by new information in her political environment that compels at least a momentary departure from the basic disposition. This short-term variation might be due to personal discussions or information in the mass media or even the silent contemplation of political issues. We can think of these sources as a series of shocks or innovations to a person's thinking. The half-life of these shocks could be fleeting, or they could be long lasting. If they become a permanent part of the person's political memory, they not only change the short-term response but the voter's long-run disposition as well for Candidate A over Candidate B (or vice versa).

Consider next a collection of voters, as described, with individualized dispositions and short-term variation around these dispositions. If we could measure their individual scores on the Democratic minus Republican scale, we could monitor their average over time. If individual dispositions are constant and short-term variation is idiosyncratic to the individual, then the aggregate mean value would be nothing more than a constant. (The individual variation would cancel out.) Similarly, the proportions preferring the Democratic and Republican candidates, above and below the zero threshold, would be constant. To create aggregate change, therefore, the campaign innovations must move in phase, at least partially, with voters responding somewhat in tandem to common stimuli. In other words, events must affect individuals in such a way to produce a net partisan benefit rather than be neutral.

These common shocks then produce shifts in aggregate voter preferences over the campaign. If these common shocks or innovations are temporary in nature, their influence on the Election Day outcome is minimal, as what matters in the final analysis is the division of constant voter dispositions (plus late shocks). The campaign does have an impact on the outcome, but only at the end of the timeline. If, on the other hand, the campaign-induced shocks are long lasting or even permanent, their impact persists until Election Day. In this latter case the campaign matters continually, over the entire timeline.

Thus, we can conceptualize election outcomes as essentially a function of the collective voter dispositions present at the start of the campaign plus their change (if any) over the campaign. Of course, even with polls conducted regularly over the campaign, we cannot directly measure the march of voter predispositions. Viewed through a filter of survey error, the electorate's vote division reflects a combination of long-term voter dispositions plus short-term variation that may masquerade as meaningful change. And, of course, the polls do not measure the relative preferences themselves. They measure only the division of probable or likely voters by their presidential choice of the moment as Democratic or Republican. It is to the properties of this aggregate time series that our discussion turns next.

3.2 Bounces and Bumps

We start with the knowledge that because the electorate's vote division does sometimes change over the course of the campaign, campaign events (broadly defined) must be exerting some sort of impact. In the language of popular commentary about campaigns, the question is: Do these shocks from campaign events take the form of temporary "bounces" or permanent "bumps"? Figure 3.1 illustrates the distinction. Bounces dissipate with time, as depicted in figure 3.1A. They matter on Election Day (if at all) only when they occur late in the campaign. Bumps persist, as illustrated in figure 3.1B. Because they last until Election Day regardless of when they occur, they are more consequential.

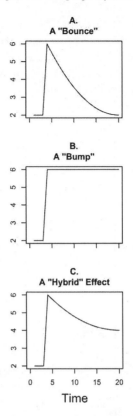

Figure 3.1. Bounces and bumps.

Bounces or bumps? The answer is important because it reveals the relevance of campaign shocks. As a series of short-term bounces, the campaign-induced shocks to the electorate's collective choice over the campaign have little net impact on the final outcome. As an accumulation of bumps, however, all campaign-induced shocks affect the outcome whether they occur early or late in the campaign. With only bounces, the election verdict is largely a reversion to a preordained equilibrium value rather than transient campaign events. With only bumps, the election verdict is the sum of campaign events, with no equilibrium. Of course the truth might be that campaign shocks generate both short-term ripples (bounces) and long-term waves (bumps). Figure 3.1C illustrates this hybrid. For practical purposes, long-lasting bounces may be indistinguishable from permanent bumps.

If campaign effects are bounces, over-time preferences must revert to an "equilibrium" mean value that represents in some way the "fundamentals" of the campaign. Here the final Election Day outcome is the simple sum of this equilibrium plus the effects of late events that have not fully dissipated by Election Day. If campaign effects are bumps, conversely, they persist and affect the outcome. In effect, the election outcome is the sum of all the bumps—perhaps small in size—that occur during the campaign. The answer may be that campaign events produce both bounces and bumps. It may be that some effects dissipate and others last. It is the bumps and not the bounces that matter in the long run. With both bumps and bounces, the accumulated bumps provide a moving rather than stationary equilibrium. The bounces are but short-term noise.

3.3 Modeling Campaign Dynamics

This section introduces a series of mental experiments in which we imagine that we can observe the actual time series of vote intentions over the campaign. Let us assume that we have trial-heat polls at regular intervals over the course of a campaign. Let us further assume that we have perfect polls, that is, no bias, sampling error, and so forth. Furthermore, let us assume that these perfectly measured readings are at regular intervals, perhaps daily, throughout the campaign. What would they show?

Consider the time series of the electorate's aggregate vote division (V_t) during the election cycle to be of the following form:

(3.1) $$V_t = \alpha + \beta V_{t-1} + u_t$$

where V_t is the vote percentage for Candidate A rather than Candidate B and u_t is a series of random campaign shocks.[1] That is, preferences on one day are modeled as a function of preferences on the preceding day and the new effect of campaign events, broadly defined. The specific events from one day could trigger a series of delayed shocks to voter preferences in subsequent days, as the media message reverberates. By the same token, the shock emitted on any given day could include the delayed reaction to events from earlier days. Equation 3.1 allows us to characterize different general models of campaign dynamics.

Equation 3.1 models a conventional AR1 autoregressive process. The definition of an AR, or autoregressive, process is that the variable of interest (e.g., the vote division) is a function of its value at the previous time period plus a new random shock for the new period. What makes it an AR1 model is that apart from its lagged value at $t - 1$, that is, the previous period, the variable's history does not matter. That is, if we know (without error) the preferences at the previous reading ($t - 1$), preferences at earlier dates

($t - 2$, $t - 3$, etc.) add no further useful information. Similarly, if we know (without error) the preferences further back in time at $t - m$, preferences at earlier dates (e.g., $t - m - 1$, $t - m - 2$, etc.) do not matter. (A convenient conceptualization, the AR1 assumption is relaxed below when we consider the vote as a composite of two separate time series.)

The variance of u_t reveals the typical magnitude of the daily shocks to voter preferences. As long as the u_t variance is nonzero, we know that campaigns affect voters, and the larger the variance the greater the immediate effects. The expectation that campaign effects are present in US presidential elections is standard, as discussed in chapter 1.

The existence of campaign shocks provides only half the story, however. We also want to know about dynamics. That is, are shocks permanent or do they decay with the progress of time? In theory, these dynamics are directly evident from the coefficient β in equation 3.1. If β is between 0 and 1, the process is what is called a "stationary series" in time-series parlance. Two features of a stationary series are a constant variance over time and a reversionary equilibrium value. If β equals 1.0, the process is not stationary but rather an integrated series, otherwise known as a "random walk." Two features of a random walk are a growing variance over time and the absence of a reversionary equilibrium. Whereas with a stationary series, expected change is in the direction of the long-term mean—the more off equilibrium, the greater the reequilibration—with a random walk the expected change is zero. That is, scores are as likely to go up as down.[2]

The distinction between stationary and integrated series matters for our understanding of campaigns. A stationary series is an accumulation of ever-receding bounces. An integrated series is an accumulation of bumps. If electoral preferences over a campaign form a stationary series, current preferences are largely a function of the reversionary equilibrium (long-term dispositions) value plus recent bounces. How disproportionately recent shocks matter compared to those from the more distant past is a function of the size of β. The closer β is to 0, the more only recent events matter. The closer β is to 1.0, bounces from the remote past continue to live. In extreme, when $\beta = 1.0$, the bounces become bumps and accumulate to form an integrated series, otherwise known as a random walk. If electoral preferences comprise an integrated series, current preferences are equally a function of campaign shocks past and present.

Consider first the possibility of a stationary series. With $0 \leq \beta < 1$, effects decay over time. As an "autoregressive" (AR) process, preferences tend toward the equilibrium of the series, which is $\alpha / (1 - \beta)$. If the division is greater than its equilibrium value, it will decline over time; if it is below the equilibrium value, it will increase. The equilibrium does not represent the final outcome, however. What happens on Election Day also will reflect late campaign effects that have not fully dissipated by the time voters go to the polls. The degree to which late campaign effects do matter is evident from β, which captures the rate of carryover from one point in time to the next. The smaller the β, the more quickly campaign effects decay and the less they matter on Election Day.

With aggregate preferences over a campaign behaving as a stationary series, predicting V_t from V_{t-1} one period earlier can be described by the following equation:

(3.2) $$V_t = V_t^* + \beta(V_t^S - V_t^*)$$

where V^* is the equilibrium or long-term mean. (Recall that V^* is $\alpha/(1-\beta)$, where α is the intercept in equation 3.1. With a further algebraic transformation, equation 3.3 sets the dependent variable to be the $t-1$ to t change in electoral preferences.

(3.3) $$\Delta V_t = (\beta - 1)(V_{t-1} - V^*) + u_t$$

where $\Delta V_t = V_t - V_{t-1}$. Note that preference change consists not only of the new shock u_t but also the lagged departure from equilibrium ($V_{t-1} - V^*$) *times* the requilibrating rate ($\beta - 1$), which will be less than 0. To be absolutely clear, when Democratic vote intentions at time $t-1$ are above (below) the equilibrium value, we predict a drop (rise) in Democratic vote intentions at time t. The smaller the β, the greater the requilibrating rate ($\beta - 1$), and so the larger the drop.

In the extreme, when β approaches 1.0 there is no reequilibration, leaving preference change as simply the new shock. The long-term electoral change then is the summation of accumulated shocks without reversion, or an integrated series in which all past shocks matter equally with no forgetting. With $\beta = 1$, equations 3.2 and 3.3 simplify to

(3.4) $$V_t = V_{t-1} + u_t$$

and

(3.4a) $$\Delta V_t = u_t.$$

Because shocks decay in a stationary series, the variance is a function of both the variance of the u_t shocks and also the autoregressive parameter β. Asymptotically (in the long run), the variance of a stationary series is constant, that is, "stationary":

$$(3.5) \qquad Var(V_t) = Var \sum_{k=1}^{t} (\beta^{t-k} u_{t-k}) = \frac{Var(u)}{1-\beta^2}$$

As β reaches 1, however, the long-run variance of V_t increases. Whereas the variance of a stationary series is constant, the variance of an integrated series continues to grow.

3.3.1 A Stationary Series or a Random Walk?

Should vote intentions in presidential campaigns be modeled as a stationary series or as a random walk? As we will see, the off-the-shelf application of either model is unsatisfactory, and further tinkering is required. Consider first the potential of modeling voter preferences over a series of presidential campaigns as a set of stationary series.

In general, if aggregate preferences follow a stationary series, predicting V_t from V_{t-m} at m days earlier can be described by the following equation:

$$(3.6) \qquad V_t = V^* + \beta^m (V_{t-m} - V^*).$$

To the extent that β is less than 1.0, and the $t - m$ time gap is large, the forecast for time t at time $t - m$ reverts to V^*, the constant term representing the fundamentals.[3] In a certain sense, then, the campaign does not matter until close to Election Day in this model. Meanwhile, since the Election Day outcome would become the natural baseline from which earlier forecasts are measured, there would be a natural tendency to mistake the outcomes as the fundamentals rather than a combination of fundamentals and late campaign effects.

As we have seen, to depict the campaign vote division as a stationary series is to depict campaign effects as a series of campaign bounces. The problem is that a stationary series maintains the equilibrium as a constant as if campaigns are governed by an underlying equilibrium value that is evident at the start of the series and never changes. It is not very plausible that the electorate's collective long-term dispositions are set in concrete by forces that are in place by the start of the campaign.

Now, consider the possibility that, rather than as a stationary process, the electorate's vote division moves throughout the campaign as a random walk. With $\beta = 1$, campaign effects actually cumulate. Each shock makes a permanent contribution to voter preferences. There is no forgetting. As a "random walk"—what also is referred to as an "integrated" process— preferences cumulate over the election cycle and become more and more telling about the final result. The actual outcome is simply the sum of all shocks that have occurred during the campaign up to and including Election Day.[4] An attractive aspect of conceptualizing campaign dynamics as a random walk is that it allows campaign effects to persist throughout the campaign, lending the final outcome a certain degree of unpredictability given the initial values.

There is, however, one feature of a random walk that appears to violate the nature of the actual data. With a random walk, the cross-sectional (between-elections) variance of the vote division must increase with time. The farther along in the campaign cycle, the farther apart are the divisions in different campaigns. Observed over many campaigns, we would see a tendency for races to become increasingly one-sided rather than tighten as the campaign progresses. This expansion of the cross-sectional variance is not consistent with the facts. In reality, as we saw in chapter 2, the cross-sectional variance has a tendency to compress over time. At first blush, therefore, it seems that aggregate electoral preferences could not evolve as a random walk.

3.3.2 Vote Intentions as a Random Walk with a Stationary Component

We must consider the possibility that vote preferences combine long-term bumps and short-term bounces. In other words, we can conceptualize the series as the addition of a random walk as the moving equilibrium (V_t^*) plus a short-term stationary series (V_t^S) around this equilibrium:

(3.7)
$$V_t = V_t^* + V_t^S$$

where

(3.7a)
$$V_t^* = V_{t-1}^* + u_t$$

and

(3.7b)
$$V_t^S = \beta V_{t-1}^S + e_t$$

The two parts can be combined in the following "error correction" model:

(3.8)
$$V_t = V_{t-1}^* + \beta (V_{t-1} - V_{t-1}^*) + e_t + u_t$$

where $0 < \beta < 1$ and e_t is introduced as the disturbance to $V_t = V_t^*$. In this model, some effects (u_t) persist—and form part of the moving equilibrium V_t^*—and the rest (e_t) decay. That is, the fundamentals move as a random walk, whereas short-term campaign forces create a stationary series of deviations from the moving fundamentals.[5] Some campaign effects persist and the rest decay.

If the time series of aggregated preferences is a combination of the two processes, the integrated component takes on greater importance than the short-term variation of the stationary series. Indeed, statistical theory (Granger 1980) tells us that any series that contains an integrated component is itself integrated in the long run. The intuition is that, because of its expanding variance over time, the integrated component will dominate when viewed over a long-term perspective.[6]

A combined integrated series plus stationary time series makes intuitive sense. By this process, the fundamentals (V^*) move toward their final evolution on Election Day. Meanwhile the vote division is also subject to short-term perturbations that may seem important at the time but do not last until Election Day. In fact our working assumption is a variation of this model. But for that to work, one important obstacle must be overcome. Since the hybrid model is dominated by the integrated series, as discussed earlier, its cross-sectional variance must expand with time, yet we observe that the actual variance contracts over time. Thus, as with a strict random walk, the hybrid model is seemingly incompatible with the fact that the variance of aggregate vote intentions declines over the timeline.

3.3.3 Time-Series Properties and Campaign Effects

These different models of campaign dynamics are not mere statistical musings. They formalize general arguments in the literature about the role of political campaigns. What we ultimately want to know, after all, is whether the campaign has real effects on electoral preferences and whether these effects matter on Election Day. We know that preferences do change over the campaign as new shocks (along with sampling error) create changes in the polls. But do these changes persist to Election Day?

We must ask, are there permanent campaign effects that last until Election Day, and, if so, are they of a magnitude to make a difference? If there are short-term effects, we must also ask, how large are they? And, do they persist long enough to matter on Election Day? In the extreme, all influences (apart from sampling error) on the polls from early in the campaign to the end are equally eventful, signifying a very consequential campaign. At the other extreme, all campaign-season influences are transient, whereby only the most recent campaign effects are lasting on Election Day.

Statistically oriented social scientists are often conditioned to view stationary series as the natural state of affairs, due in part to their familiarity and their convenient properties. But if we model the time series of electoral choice as a stationary series, awkward questions follow. With the campaign-induced time series of electoral preferences as a set of stationary series, variation in election outcomes would be due almost solely to cross-election variation in a set of equilibrium outcomes. Since these equilibria would be stable from the arbitrary starting point of the series onward to Election Day, election outcomes would be knowable from the early polls. This would beg the question of how different equilibria could emerge before each election season as a function of early political forces only to then remain stable throughout the actual campaign. As we have seen, modeling the vote division as driven by a random walk process (with perhaps short-term variation around it) presents its questions as well, since races actually tend to tighten, not get more one-sided as the campaign unfolds.

As we set up our questions about the nature of how campaign preferences evolve over the campaign timeline, we do not demand or expect a knife-edge diagnosis whereby campaigns matter a lot or matter not at all—or that all innovations in preferences are strictly permanent or ephemeral. We expect the presence of both a long-term sequence of small bumps and a short-term set of large but then receding bounces. Moreover, the bounces might persist with a considerable half-life. When stationary effects are so persistent (β approaching 1.0), and the series appears possibly integrated, the distinction between permanent and merely long lasting is of little practical consequence (see note 3). The surprise would be if campaigns produce nothing more than short-term effects that dissipate within days.

3.4 Shifting Dynamics over Time

So far our speculation about the nature of campaign preferences has ignored the role of temporal variation in the model, as if the dynamics of our various series have identical statistical properties both early and late in the election year. We could find differences over the campaign in the nature of the time series. For instance, we might find the variance of shocks increases (or decreases) as Election Day approaches. Further modification is needed, therefore, as the actual data clearly do not fit a strict stationary series, an integrated series, or their simple composite. Thus, some modifications are in order.

In this section, we consider two modifications. First, we consider the temporal implications of treating the underlying random walk in terms of aggregated voter utilities (or relative liking) rather than in the vote division itself. Second, we consider the possibility that the voters' considerations can change over the campaign, as if the function of the long campaign is to prime the voters to concentrate on certain fundamental information at the expense of other, less relevant considerations.

3.4.1 The Intensity Effect

As we have seen, a series that moves as a random walk (with or without short-term variation around it) would normally expand the cross-sectional variance of the vote division, as vote intentions from different years would increasingly diverge from one another as the campaign timeline progresses. How then can we modify our model to accommodate the fact that the cross-sectional variance of the vote division contracts rather than expands with time? One solution emerges from our understanding of how aggregate vote intentions evolve from individual voter assessments. The changing vote division represents the changing proportion that favors one candidate over the other, while cumulative campaign effects represent the aggregate change in voters' relative utilities. As voters accumulate their relative utility for the two candidates (perhaps as a random walk), the flow of campaign information intensifies voters' relative preference for one candidate over the other. As a result, the aggregate variance of individual preferences can expand at a faster rate than the variance of the aggregate mean preference. The consequence is a natural tightening of electoral contests. We call this the "intensification effect."[7]

Consider again that aggregate preferences are the sum of individual vote choices. And these individual choices are the function of voters' relative attraction to the two candidates. As a campaign evolves, with individuals' relative liking for one candidate over another themselves a series of random walks, the variance of these individual preferences will increase. The result of this campaign intensification is fewer voters being on the fence. As the campaign progresses, campaign events create fewer vote conversions because there are fewer voters on the fence available for conversion. More conversions that do occur will flow from the candidate who is ahead to one behind, than from the one behind to the one ahead. The result is a tightening of the vote division, counteracting the expansive properties of a random walk.

To see this, suppose we could observe individual voters' mean scores on a scale of relative liking for the parties—the degree of liking Party A minus the degree of liking of Party B—and that these relative preferences form a random walk. These random walks are largely idiosyncratic, but when they move in tandem to a common set of national-level stimuli, the mean shifts represent campaign effects. Aggregations of individual random walks must also behave as a random walk. We do not, however, observe these aggregations but rather the manifestation as a Democratic (Republican) percentage of the two-party vote (or some other variant of aggregating vote choice). Measured as an aggregation of dichotomous Democratic versus Republican choices, the prospective vote will not necessarily display the characteristics of a random walk when the variance of the underlying latent attitude is expanding.

Let us conduct the following mental experiment. Assume individual latent attitudes change in the manner of a random walk, but with no net effect (neither party gains). For convenience, suppose the latent attitudes are normally distributed with a standard deviation of 1.0. Figure 3.2 illustrates this change. Assume a vote threshold of 0.5 standard deviation units, as shown in the tighter of the two normal distributions. Voters scoring higher prefer candidate B; those with a lower score prefer candidate A. This breakdown yields 69 percent for A and 31 percent for B. Now suppose

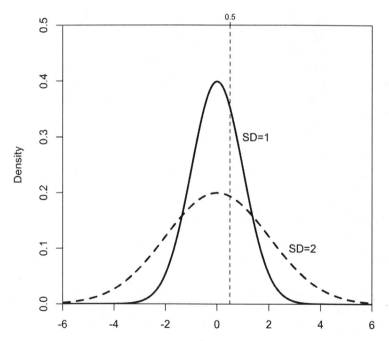

Figure 3.2. The changing distribution of the two-party vote as the standard deviation of voter relative utilities doubles.

that the campaign generates a further spread in latent attitudes to double the original standard deviation (increasing the variance by a factor of 4), as illustrated by the broader of the two normal distributions. If the mean attitude does not change, the threshold of 0.50 standard deviations on the original scale now shifts to 0.25 standard deviations on the expanded scale. With only 60 percent of a distribution being to the left of 0.50 standard deviations, the percentage voting for Candidate A drops from 69 percent to 60 percent, even though there is no net change in mean attitude.

Further, consider the result if the campaign generates a small perturbation in the threshold. The proportion of the voters who shift sides will be greatest with the tighter distribution. The broader the distribution of relative utilities for the candidates at the time, the less will be the observed effect of any campaign shock when measured in terms of vote proportions.

From this exercise one readily sees that growth in the variance of voter preferences over a campaign can depress the percentage for the candidate who is ahead. And each increment of aggregate attitude change yields a diminishing impact on the percentage for each candidate. Undoubtedly such a process contributes to a slowing of any growth in the cross-sectional variance of the vote, which we measure as the dichotomous vote division. Short-term effects might be particularly affected, so that bounces decline in amplitude over the campaign.

It is certainly plausible that the individual-level variance in relative utility expands over a campaign as preferences intensify. In reality, however, do individuals' relative preferences expand over a campaign as much as required to fully account for the declining cross-sectional variance? For a more complete accounting, we need to consider a related possibility, namely, "partisan mobilization."

3.4.2 The Partisan Effect

In chapter 1 we described the "fundamentals" of the election as a combination of campaign-induced "external" factors and voters' "internal" attractors, such as their unique partisan dispositions.[8] As voters strengthen their partisan leanings, further campaign events hold less sway over their vote choice. In terms of their dichotomous vote choice, strong partisans tend to be locked into their choices, whereas "independent" voters with no partisan leanings fluctuate in response to campaign news. Here is the important part. If, as many suggest, one function of campaigns is to reinforce voters' partisan predispositions, the preferences of even mildly partisan voters become stronger over the campaign. This partial strengthening has the effect of diminishing the cumulative effect of the campaign on aggregate vote choice.

Think of a typical voter starting out the campaign as a partisan, but not very mindful of its possible implications on vote choice. This voter's relative candidate preference will respond to the campaign news. As this information about the candidate choice accumulates, the cumulative effect on our voter's utility calculation (or candidate affect, if you prefer) will grow. So will the chance that our weakly partisan voter will vote for the candidate of the other party. In one sense, the voter is flirting with the other party.

The complication arises as the campaign also activates our voter's partisan identity, which pushes her candidate preferences increasingly toward her party's candidate. As this happens, the cumulative effect of campaign information, while still present in our voter's mind, becomes increasingly irrelevant to the vote decision. The voter becomes more committed to a candidate both because of increased campaign information and partisan activation. A crude approximation of this dual process for the individual voter is as follows:

$$U_{it} = U(E_t) + \varphi, U(I_t)$$

where U_{it} = the ith voter's relative utility for Candidate A minus Candidate B at time t,

$U(E_t)$ = the utility derived from the external fundamentals of the campaign at time t,

$\varphi, U(I_t)$ = the utility derived from the internal fundamentals from voter predispositions, and

φ_t = the salience of internal fundamentals (e.g., partisanship) at time t.

As the campaign progresses, the salience parameter (φ_t) increases.

Assuming this is the correct model at the individual level, the macrolevel effect is for the growing partisan activation to push the vote margin toward the center. Partisan activation compresses the cross-sectional variance of aggregate vote intentions, even as the growth of campaign effects expands it. A useful way of thinking about this is to consider a set of partisan voters and a set of independent voters over a campaign. The time series of our partisan voters (equally divided between Republicans and Democrats) will show little response to campaign events. It is not that they are unaware; it is just that the news rarely pushes their choice across the threshold of the partisan divide. Meanwhile the collective choices of the independents respond freely to the campaign news. Now, consider that over the campaign the electorate as a whole becomes less like the independents and more like the strong partisans. The net effect is that the contribution of campaign effects on the time series will decline. It will not, however, evaporate. The candidate favored by the campaign will win a greater vote share than if the outcome were a strictly party-line vote. The size of the advantage, however, will lessen over time.

In the vocabulary of the *American Voter* authors (esp. Campbell et al. 1966), the partisan fundamentals are the "normal vote." The cumulative campaign effects are the "short-term partisan forces," with "short-term" applying to the specific election year. The translation of our argument is that while the short-term forces grow over a campaign, the increasing "attraction" of the normal vote diminishes their cumulative effect on the aggregate vote choice. The advantages of this partisan model are that it fits our understanding of partisanship and solves the puzzle of why the cross-sectional variance of the vote division shrinks over the campaign timeline.[9]

3.4.3 Implications

According to our model of voter decision-making, voters learn two types of fundamentals during presidential campaigns. First, the electorate's net relative favorability of the two candidates is formed by the cumulative political news over the course of the campaign. Second, voters increasingly tilt in the direction of their partisan leanings.

In the aggregate we expect the following. Campaign effects accumulate over the long term (bumps), with declining additional shocks over the campaign. They are possibly accompanied by short-term changes due to campaign shocks of temporary impact (bounces). Overlaid on these processes, the growing intensity of voter preferences causes the vote to gravitate toward the electoral division based on partisan predispositions. The cumulative campaign shocks are still present at the end, but in diluted form.

This theorizing accounts plausibly for the declining cross-election variance in aggregate vote intentions over the campaign timeline. The net variance can compress from the growing pull of partisanship even as campaign shocks cause the variance to widen. Later, especially in chapter 7, we will see evidence that this is the correct model.

3.5 Conclusions

This chapter has addressed the dynamics of voter preferences over the course of a campaign. We imagine that we could perfectly observe the daily readings of the vote division and consider what the dynamics of this time series would look like. This exercise is designed to inform our examination of the actual evidence from polls, which follows.

We began by considering the vote division in terms of two standard time-series models from the statistical tool kit: a stationary series or a random walk. With a stationary series—campaign shocks as bounces—the vote division shifts around a steady equilibrium, which is in place throughout the campaign. That the campaign's basic equilibrium remains in place throughout the campaign with this model is a source of unease. With the vote division as a random walk—campaign shocks as bumps—there is no equilibrium, so the vote can be propelled in directions unpredictable in advance. That vote margins widen instead of tighten with this model is a source of unease. Allowing a random walk combined with a lesser stationary series admits both bounces and bumps but does not solve the problem of counterfactually projecting a growing cross-sectional variance.

It is possible to model countervailing forces that work to compress the cross-sectional variance over time. Taking into account that individual voters' attitudes intensify over a campaign helps further to slow the expansion of cross-sectional variance. The hardening of vote choices based on reinforced party identifications pushes the vote even more toward the fundamental partisanship of the electorate. The final verdict represents this partisanship plus, to a diminishing extent, the cumulative fundamentals of the campaign content.

One seeming oddity is that the cross-sectional variance of the vote is at its height at the earliest point of the campaign timeline for which we have poll data to measure it. Voters may not know much about the forthcoming presidential contest early in the election year. Presented with the two eventual candidates as choices in an early poll, however, voters can create diverse vote divisions in different elections based on minimal information at hand. Moreover, as we will see, the early information to some extent survives and forms part of the voters' net decision-making on Election Day.

The models presented in this chapter will be useful as we explore the actual time series of fifteen vote divisions during 1952–2008. Although at times we find the data to be frustratingly limited, they still allow us to go quite a long way. We turn next, in chapter 4, to our empirical analysis of the polls and what they tell us about the dynamics of vote divisions during presidential election campaigns.

FOUR

Vote Intentions over the Campaign Timeline

The previous chapter offered some speculation about the time-series properties of the vote division in trial-heat polls over presidential campaigns. The present chapter returns to our empirical analysis of presidential preferences in campaigns. Here we take a close look at the actual poll data that comprise the vote division in the presidential polls of 1952–2008. Then, in the next chapter, we examine how the vote division in the polls translates into the actual vote on Election Day.

In chapter 3, we framed the campaign dynamics question as a time-series issues: whether or not the time series of candidate preferences over the campaign is an integrated series, where shocks persist to Election Day. If, instead, candidate preferences form a stationary series, and especially one where shocks have a short half-life (e.g., not near-integrated), the shocks decay with the series evolving around a stable equilibrium. We posited that both processes could be at work: that an integrated series dominates as a slow-moving equilibrium, with a stationary series providing short-term variation around the moving equilibrium. That is, some campaign effects last and others decay.

In theory, competing hypotheses about the time-series process could be tested by simply analyzing the time-series data over many readings of the polls at different dates across each campaign. Unfortunately, as noted in chapter 2, this strategy is not feasible. Consider the handicaps:

- First, the reporting of poll data is sporadic, particularly in the earlier years of our analysis. The data are not sufficiently dense to allow the luxury of daily readings (or even near-daily readings) of the poll of polls throughout campaigns. We can of course obtain daily estimates of what the polls would show by interpolating missing data, and for some purposes, interpolation to obtain daily estimates provides useful leverage. But when we need to treat the data as independent observations, it is necessary to expand the time intervals of our survey readings. Accordingly, in this chapter, we often analyze aggregate vote intentions by measuring our poll of polls on a weekly or even biweekly basis. Even when measured in this way, there are occasions when we are left with missing data. Difficult as it might be to believe in our current age of seemingly constant polling, there have been times during past campaigns when pollsters go for two weeks or more without testing public sentiment about the presidential race. Thankfully, this was fairly rare, and so a basic analysis of polls across weekly and biweekly intervals is possible.

- Polls measure the vote division with error, as even the best surveys are prone to sampling error. To some degree we can control for sampling error by statistical adjustment. Over specific campaigns, the estimated error variance competes in size with the observed variance of the time series. When we pool the data across campaigns, however, the true variation tends to swamp the survey error.

- In theory, we could perform a time-series cross-sectional analysis, where we observe the within-election data across different campaigns. The data, however, are too infrequent and fragile for us to have any confidence in the results of such an analysis.

- We anticipate that the time series contain both long-term and short-term components, so that some campaign effects persist permanently throughout the campaign while others are transient. One implication is that the data will not follow a simple AR1 model, where (when modeling the vote division as a function of its previous values) the vote division is simply a function of its most recent values and not the earlier history. We show evidence, however, that the short-term effects dissipate quickly, lasting little more than a month. This allows some leverage in terms of an instrumental variable approach, to assess the integrated component of the vote division time series.

- As mentioned, the party conventions are important interventions in the time series. And the conventions do not arrive at the same time point in all campaigns. Over the half century we analyze, the convention season has drifted from July to late August and into early September. Thus, the major intervention does its intervening at different stages of the campaign time series for the different years—not always in the same weeks of the campaign. One solution to this problem is to measure time not only in terms of weeks or days to the election but also weeks or days before or after the convention season.

The limits the data impose cannot be exaggerated. The fifteen time series we deal with are irregularly spaced in time, measured with error, contain both long- and short-term components, and are interrupted by irregularly spaced convention-season interventions. Fortunately, we have available two alternative strategies to straightforward time-series analysis. First, we examine the poll data cross-sectionally, relating the polls' vote division at one campaign time-point to the vote division at another, where the units are election years. Second, although we lack the data to analyze time series in specific election years, we pool the data set across years for a rudimentary time-series cross-sectional analysis.

4.1 Cross-Sectional Analysis

Respecting the complications just discussed, we start not by venturing into the murky realm of time-series analysis but rather by observing the data as a series of cross-sections. For specific dates in the campaign calendar, we model the polls' vote division across the fifteen election years as a function of its lagged value. For this exercise it would be inappropriate to use interpolations of missing data. Thus, instead of daily readings, we use weekly readings—the poll of polls for each week. We measure each week Tuesday through Monday, allowing each year's series to end on election eve.

The weekly readings contain some missing data, but not enough to seriously hobble our analysis. The 29-week by 14-year grid marking the frequency with which poll data are available by week of the campaign and by year can be found in the appendix at the end of this book. As one would expect, we have more poll data later in the campaign than earlier. And we have more data from recent years than from early ones, as we showed in chapter 2.

4.1.1 The Polls: From Mid-April to Election Eve

As a starting point, consider what the polls show the vote division to be at date ED-200, or 200 days before the election. This places our start in mid-April, about 29 weeks before the election. As discussed in chapter 2, ED-200 is a useful benchmark because by then in most presidential years the eventual two presidential candidates are known, and in all years, pollsters have already conducted trial-heat races between the eventual candidates. For our fifteen elections, we trace vote intentions from the week centered on ED-200 to the last week of the campaign, ending on election eve (ED-1).

Figure 4.1 shows the relationship between the vote division at ED-29 weeks and ED-1 week as a scatterplot.[1] Its most obvious feature is the dom-

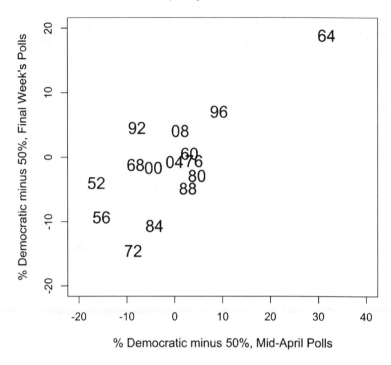

Figure 4.1. Scatterplot of the relationship between vote intentions in mid-April and vote intentions during the final week of the campaign. Mid-April polls are from week ED-29 (centered on 200 days in advance) or (if missing) the most recent national poll to that date. Correlation = +.77.

inance of one outlier—the observation from the 1964 Johnson–Goldwater contest. This case is an outlier in the sense that the Democratic candidate's lead is disproportionately large in comparison to leads in the other years. In mid-April 1964, Johnson held an unearthly 4–1 lead, which declined to slightly more than 2–1 in the last poll. (The margin shrunk again by Election Day, as Johnson won by "only" 61 percent to 39 percent.) With the 1964 observation in the database, the correlation between the early and late vote divisions in figure 4.1 is 0.77, meaning that the early reading can explain a bit over half the variance (adjusted R-squared = .56; 15 cases) in the final week's polls. Omitting the 1964 outlier, the correlation declines to 0.52, with early readings explaining only about one-fifth of the variance in the final readings (adjusted R-squared = .21; 14 cases). Clearly, although any presidential candidate would prefer to be ahead in mid-April of the election year, electoral prospects often change by the final polls before Election Day.

The regression slope predicting the final polls from week ED-29 is a mere 0.53 (0.41 without 1964). Thus, in mid-April, the leading candidate should expect her vote margin to shrink almost in half by election eve. As with the correlation evidence, the low regression coefficient over a span of 29 weeks seemingly suggests considerable instability over the campaign. We should, however, consider the following. If the weekly rate of shrinkage were constant over the 28 weeks (as with an AR1 model with constant parameters), we would expect that the regression of the weekly vote margin on the margin from the previous week would be .977. (That is, .977 to the 28th power equals the observed 0.53 slope predicting the election eve polls from the polls 28 weeks earlier.)[2] The long-term shrinkage would be largely invisible from week to week. Yet such a straight course from April to November is not guaranteed. The national "vote" in presidential trial-heat polls might bounce around more than with a straight AR1 model. And the process might be quite non-uniform, with more change at some points in the campaign timeline than others. To obtain a better understanding, it is time to look closely at the weekly readings of the vote division over our fifteen elections.

4.1.2 The Polls: Week by Week

With our weekly polls of polls, we can track the trajectory of shifting voter preferences week by week throughout the campaign. Figure 4.2 displays vote intentions in the weekly polls as a function of the prior week's polls. This figure pools together all weekly polls in which the electorate was polled in both the current and prior week over the final 28 weeks of the campaign, for all presidential elections of 1952–2008.[3] The figure shows vote intentions in one week to be very similar to vote intentions in the previous week, but with exceptions.

Table 4.1 shows the details of the regression equation depicted by figure 4.2. The lagged vote division accounts for 81 percent of the observed variance in the weekly vote division. Some of the unexplained variance is measurement error, of course. When the regression equation is adjusted for sampling error in both the dependent variable and the independent variable, the explained variance rises slightly to 84 percent.[4] Correcting for measurement error thus offers an improvement over OLS (ordinary least squares), but the difference is slight.

With or without the correction for survey error, the intercept of the equation is virtually zero—meaning that the lagged vote division where no change is expected is about "zero" on the scale. Recalling the scaling of

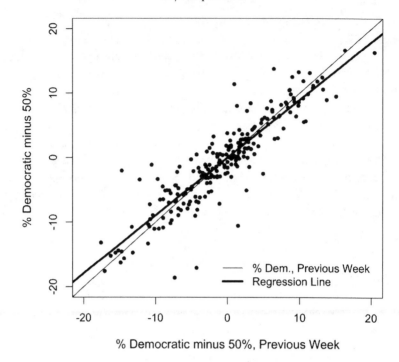

Figure 4.2. Weekly vote intentions and lagged weekly vote intentions in the final 28 weeks of the campaign, 1952–2008.

Table 4.1 Vote intentions by lagged vote intentions in the polls: Weekly readings, 1952–2008

	Intercept	b (slope)	Adjusted R^2	RMSE
OLS	−0.00 (0.20)	0.90 (0.03)	.81	2.97
Reliability-corrected[a]	0.00 (0.19)	0.91 (0.03)	.84[b]	2.81

Note: N = 231 weekly polls of polls, taken the last 28 weeks of the campaign, 1952–2008. Dependent variable = percentage Democrat (of two-party vote in polls) minus 50 percent. Intercepts near zero indicate that the vote division tends to be 50–50 when the lagged vote division is 50–50.
[a]Reliability estimate = .98.
[b]R^2 estimate, taking into account measurement error in both the independent and dependent variable.

the vote division as a deviation from 50 percent, zero means an expectation that the Democratic percentage will neither decline nor grow when the vote is already evenly divided. The regression coefficient of 0.90 or 0.91 suggests that any lead one week will shrink by about 10 percent of its value the following week. (We will see shortly, however, that pooling the data from weeks at all points in the campaign timeline exaggerates the rate of weekly change.) The residual variance (RMSE, or root mean squared error) is about 3 points. This means that the surprise component unexplained by the lagged vote is a distribution with a standard deviation of about 3. One implication is that, when using this equation to predict the vote from last week's vote division, the error will be six or less percentage points (two standard deviations) about 95 percent of the time.

By pooling across dates, figure 4.2 deceptively masks all variation from week to week in the relationship between the vote division and the lagged vote division. Analyzing the cross-sectional week-to-week variation separately by the number of weeks to the election is more informative. Figure 4.3 displays the lag-1 relationship separately for each of the

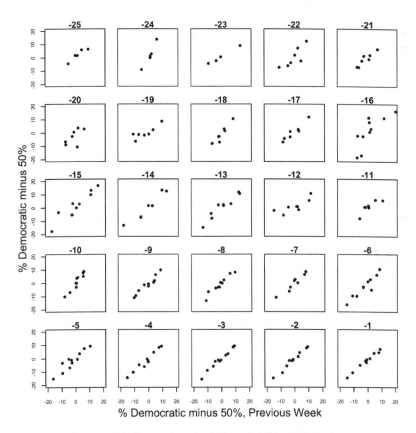

Figure 4.3. Weekly vote intention by lagged weekly vote intentions, by campaign week, over the final 25 weeks of the campaign. Weeks are coded as the number of weeks until the election.

final 25 weeks of the campaign. (There are too few cases over weeks ED-28 to ED-26 for meaningful analysis.) As the slope of the relationship varies slightly from week to week, figure 4.3 shows a greater degree of stability when each week of the campaign timeline is treated separately.

Most evident from the figure is the extreme stability in the lower panels representing the final weeks of the campaign. By the final weeks, electoral verdicts are sticking with little change. To highlight this result, figure 4.4 shows in greater detail the lag-1 relationships for each of the final four campaign weeks, that is, over the final five weeks. The figure clearly shows that during the heat of the campaign in October into early November, very little happens to change the national verdicts. We must look earlier in the campaign season for major campaign effects. Indeed we see from the

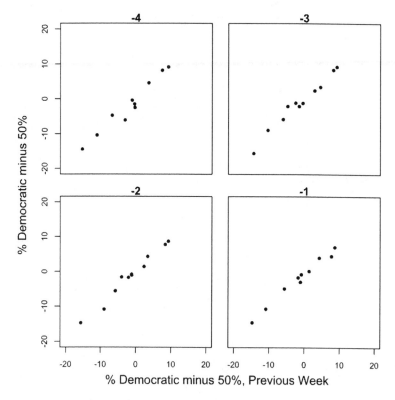

Figure 4.4. Weekly vote intention by lagged weekly vote intention, by campaign week, over the final four weeks of the campaign. Weeks are coded as the number of weeks until the election.

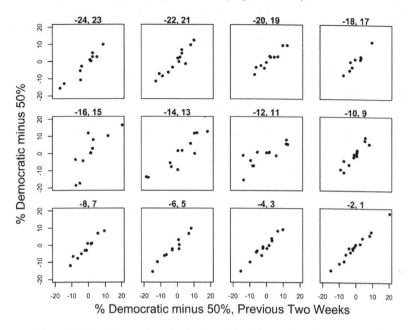

Figure 4.5. Biweekly vote intention by lagged biweekly vote intentions, over the final 24 weeks of the campaign. Weeks are coded by the second week of the biweekly set, for example, −1 = weeks 1 and 2 before the election.

twenty-five graphs of figure 4.3 that the volatility of the voter preferences is greatest in the middle period, centered on the convention season.[5]

Seasonal patterns are even more apparent if we divide the campaign by biweekly periods (fortnights) instead of weeks. The fortnight-by-fortnight autoregressive functions are displayed in figure 4.5. The top row of panels shows considerable stability before the convention season; the middle row shows a pattern of relative instability during the summertime convention season; and the final row shows tremendous stability during the fall campaign season.

Table 4.2 presents the weekly vote-by-lagged-vote equations for the final 8 weeks of the campaign. The first set of columns display the observed OLS regression equations week by week. They show some remarkably tight fits. From the adjusted R-squareds and the regression coefficients (both approaching 1.00) and the RMSEs, one might even think that only sampling error keeps us from perfect prediction. That is, one might imagine a near "perfect" relationship with virtually no error, except for the contribution of sampling error in both the independent variable (the lagged vote division)

Table 4.2 Predicting weekly vote intention from lagged weekly vote intention, by campaign week

Weeks before election	N	OLS			Reliability corrected			TSLS		
		b (SE)	Adj. R^2	RMSE	b (SE)	Adj. R^2	RMSE	b (SE)	Adj. R^2	RMSE
1	10	0.89 (0.04)	.98	0.95	0.89 (0.04)	.98	0.90	0.90 (0.06)	.98	0.96
2	11	0.97 (0.05)	.97	0.98	0.98 (0.04)	.99	0.75	0.96 (0.05)	.97	1.19
3	11	0.97 (0.05)	.97	1.25	0.98 (0.05)	.99	0.89	0.96 (0.06)	.97	1.26
4	10	0.97 (0.07)	.95	1.63	0.98 (0.06)	.98	1.16	1.03 (0.10)	.95	1.72
5	11	0.89 (0.11)	.86	2.77	0.89 (0.11)	.90	2.35	0.96 (0.16)	.85	2.82
6	10	1.01 (0.13)	.87	2.93	1.03 (0.12)	.91	2.40	1.41 (0.36)	.72	4.30
7	9	0.91 (0.10)	.91	1.83	0.92 (0.09)	.96	1.23	0.94 (0.25)	.91	1.84
8	10	0.97 (0.09)	.93	1.64	0.98 (0.08)	.97	1.08	0.82 (0.12)	.91	1.92
1–8	82	0.95 (0.03)	.93	1.81	0.96 (0.03)	.95	1.51	0.99 (0.04)	.92	1.83

Note: The dependent variable is the weekly poll of polls. Time units are weeks, Tuesday through Monday. The estimated R^2 and RMSE for the reliability-corrected equations are adjusted for the estimated measurement error in the dependent variable. For the TSLS analysis, the instrument for V_{t-1} is V_{t-9} or the poll of polls 9 weeks before time t and 8 weeks before time $t-1$.

and the dependent variable (the current vote division). If so, this would mean that aggregate preferences are stagnant over the final eight weeks before the election—the very period when the formal presidential campaign is supposed to matter.

Fortunately, it is possible to transform the equation that describes the observed data to estimates of the underlying equation in the true variables. One simply adjusts for the estimated reliabilities of the variables. For each week's readings, the reliability of the independent variable (the lagged vote division) and the dependent variable (the current vote division) was estimated under the assumption of simple random sampling. The reliability-adjusted equations were first estimated to take into account the error in the independent variable by using the standard "eivreg" STATA program. Then, the adjusted R-squareds and RMSEs were reestimated to take into account the error in the dependent variable. The results of these exercises are shown in the second set of columns in table 4.2. (The discussion of the third set of columns is reserved for the next subsection.)

The reliability-corrected equations differ only modestly from their OLS counterparts because there is little unreliability to begin with—the estimated reliabilities are in the range of .96 to .99. The reason for these high reliabilities in the face of sampling error is that, with cross-sectional data (as opposed to time series), the sampling error variance is swamped by the observed cross-election variance. Still, the reliability-corrected equations display a further shrinkage in the root mean squared error—the estimated standard deviation of the weekly shocks. Especially late in the campaign, the RMSE is in the range of one point or less, indicating that the degree of true change in the vote division from week to week is quite small.

Whether or not they are corrected for sampling error, the coefficients in table 4.2 tend to be larger than those based on the pooled analysis in table 4.1, often approaching or exceeding the value 1.00. Typically they are in the high 0.90s. Together with low RMSEs, the large coefficients suggest very little week-to-week change during the final eight weeks of campaigns, apart from a very slight shrinkage in the size of leads.[6]

4.1.3 *Evidence of Long-Term Equilibrium*

Chapter 3 suggests that the way to model voting during campaigns is as short trends (bounces) revolving around year-specific equilibria that would themselves be moving (in response to permanent bumps). To get evidence of the existence of separate long-term equilibria for different years, we can apply the statistical technique known as two-stage least squares (TSLS). Figure 4.6 provides the intuition. We would like to model the weekly vote at time t as a function of its equilibrium value at time $t - 1$. The observed vote division at time $t - 1$ is a combination of the lagged long-term equilibrium, the lagged short-term bounce, and measurement error. But we can separate out the long-term effect by use of a further lagged variable as the instrument. In this case, we use the lagged vote division nine weeks earlier as the instrument for the lagged vote from the previous week. The assumption that gives us leverage is that the vote division at lag-1 is unaffected by the earlier short-term effects at lag-9, which would by then be largely extinguished. Yet the lag-9 division will reflect the long-term equilibrium. By theory, the lag-9 vote division predicts the current vote division only through its connection to the lag-1 equilibrium value.

The TSLS procedure is to first predict the lag-1 vote from the lag-9 vote as the first stage. The second stage is to predict the time t vote from the predicted lag-1 vote. This produces a consistent estimate of the lag-1 equilibrium effect because the coefficient represents the ratio of the slope from

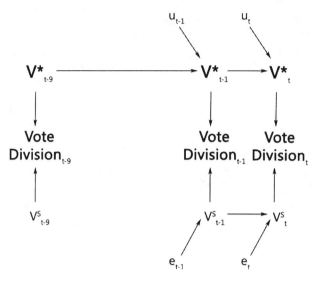

Figure 4.6. Schematic causal model for testing the effect of the lagged equilibrium vote division on the current vote division, with the lag-9 measure used as the instrument. The TSLS estimate of lag-1 V^* effect is the ratio of the two regressions predicting the current and lag-1 vote divisions from the lag-9 vote division. The key assumption is that the short-term effects (V^s) at lag-1 and lag-9 are unrelated.

regressing the time t reading on the lag-9 reading to the slope from regressing the time $t - 1$ reading on the lag-9 reading.[7] If the lag-9 reading predicts the two future readings with identical coefficients, there is no decay from time $t - 1$ to t, and the $t - 1$ slope parameter for the $t - 1$ equilibrium vote will be 1.0. If the lag-9 reading predicts the $t - 1$ reading with a greater slope than it does the time t reading, the estimated slope for the time $t - 1$ equilibrium vote will be less than one.[8]

We can see the TSLS estimates in the previously ignored third set of columns in table 4.2. The key results of interest are the estimated coefficients. These wobble a bit, as the TSLS estimates represent the ratio of two observed coefficients. They clearly are very high, however, with the median (and modal) value of 0.96. Moreover, pooling all weekly polls of polls for the final eight campaign weeks yields a coefficient of 0.99. Since the TSLS estimate represents the prediction from only the equilibrium portion of lagged vote intentions, this coefficient approximates nicely the prediction (1.00) if the trajectory of the vote margin is governed by a random walk.

Also of interest in the TSLS equations are the imputed standard errors of the disturbances (RMSEs). These are similar to or larger than even the

OLS estimates. This is because these equations are designed to estimate the equilibrium portion of the vote division only—V^* in the terminology of chapter 3. The RMSE captures the (square root of the) variance from all other sources. Here, besides sampling error in the dependent variable, the "error variance" is specified as the sum of the variance of the disturbance (u_t and e_t in equation 3.11) to the equilibrium equation plus the variance of the error correction of the short-term component V^s at time t.

If we model the vote from the lagged vote over a longer lag than one week, the decay of the short-term component for the lagged week increases. For observations over the final eight weeks of the campaign, table 4.3 models weekly vote intentions as a function of prior vote intentions at various lags from one to eight weeks, by use of both OLS and TSLS. The OLS coefficients are attenuated somewhat because they reflect both the lagged short-term and long-term components. In theory, the TSLS estimates incorporate only the long-term component. With one minor exception, the TSLS estimates are larger—approaching the theoretical limit of 1.00. As expected, the OLS–TSLS "gap" increases with the lag length.[9] The TSLS coefficients generally decline slightly with each increase in the lag. This is expected, given our knowledge of the growing compression of the cross-sectional variance in the vote over the campaign (chap. 2) and our theoretical discussion of its implications (chap. 3). We also see, from the adjusted R-squareds and the RMSEs, that the unexplained variance increases—but in small increments—when the time gap is stretched. This is verification that

Table 4.3   OLS and TSLS equations predicting vote intentions from the lagged vote at various lags, over the final 8 weeks of the campaign

Lag length (in weeks)	N	OLS				TSLS			
		b	SE	Adj. R^2	RMSE	b	SE	Adj. R^2	RMSE
1	82	0.95	0.03	.93	1.81	0.99	0.04	.93	1.83
2	73	0.94	0.03	.92	1.86	0.96	0.05	.92	1.86
3	67	0.94	0.03	.92	2.09	0.97	0.05	.92	2.10
4	51	0.89	0.05	.86	2.45	0.97	0.08	.86	2.50
5	41	0.87	0.06	.83	2.65	0.86	0.09	.83	2.65
6	30	0.89	0.07	.85	2.75	0.96	0.10	.85	2.80
7	19	0.95	0.12	.74	3.01	1.03	0.20	.70	3.22
8	13	0.78	0.16	.69	3.11	0.86	0.23	.68	3.15

Note: The instrument for the lagged vote = the vote division in polls 8 weeks earlier than the lag week (or even earlier, if otherwise missing). Because lag periods overlap in some instances, the standard errors should be treated only as suggestive. The window of weeks for the dependent variable is the final 8 weeks of the campaign. The window of lagged weeks is 1 week earlier.

even the long-term (equilibrium) component of aggregate vote intentions do change over the late campaign. The change, however, is clearly gradual.

4.2 The Conventions

We have seen that the greatest stability of the vote division in the polls is during the late fall campaign—in the final weeks of October leading into November. One might think then that the least stability would be in the spring, when polling and the early campaign start in earnest, but this is not the case. Rather, the least stable period is in the middle of the campaign timeline—in the summer. The key political feature of the summer campaign, of course, is the intervention of the two major-party conventions. First the out-party holds its convention during one week of the summer, followed by the presidential party holding its convention in the following week or weeks. In this section, we take a closer look at convention effects as they can be inferred from our cross-sectional data.

On the basis of our analysis so far, the convention effect remains vague because the party conventions occur at different times in different years. In this section, we try to remedy this difficulty by rescaling the campaign timeline in terms of time relative to the two party conventions. Instead of measuring weeks as time until the election, here we measure them as time before and after the two conventions.

As a start, figure 4.7 displays three graphs representing what the polls show to be the trajectory of the vote division over four benchmark dates—29 weeks (roughly 200 days) before the election, two weeks before the first convention (pre-convention), two weeks after the last convention (post-convention), and the last week.[10] Figure 4.7 graphs the vote in the polls by the lagged vote in the polls from week ED-29 (mid-April) to the pre-convention period to the post-convention period to the final week. The average time gap between the two convention readings is 51 days; the average gap from the post-convention reading to the final reading is 59 days; and the average gap from the 200th day (29 weeks) to the pre-convention reading is 90 days.

A notable feature of these graphs is that the smallest correlation from one time to the next is between the pre- and post-convention observations. The polls change more during the short interval between conventions than during the 90 (or so) days before the convention season or the 59 (or so) days after. Table 4.4 presents the full interperiod correlations.

To put in perspective the relative shifting between conventions versus the stability at other times, consider the following:

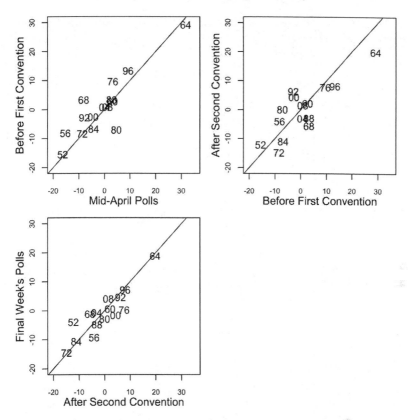

Figure 4.7. Vote intention by earlier vote intention, from mid-April to before and after the conventions and the final week. Vote division is the percentage Democratic minus 50 percent in the weekly polls. See the text for a description of time periods.

- The correlation sequence of successive readings—0.88 for week ED-29 to before the conventions, 0.85 before to after the conventions, and 0.91 post-convention to final week—highlights the relative instability between conventions. The correlation is lowest from before to after the conventions, even though the time between the two readings is, on average, about two-thirds the length of the comparison time intervals before and after the conventions.
- As an indicator of the post-convention stability, the April and pre-convention readings each correlate about the same with the final poll readings as with the earlier post-convention readings (0.77 versus 0.78, and 0.82 versus 0.84, respectively).
- Most remarkably, the correlation between readings in mid-April and the

Table 4.4 Correlations among trial-heat readings of the intended vote at four benchmark points in the campaign, 1952–2008

	Mid-April	Before conventions	After conventions	Final week
Mid-April	1.00			
Before conventions	.88	1.00		
After conventions	.80	.85	1.00	
Final week	.77	.82	.91	1.00

Note: The vote division is measured as percentage Democratic. See the text for exact description of time periods.

Table 4.5 Predicting Democratic vote intention at benchmark points over the campaign timeline from lagged vote intention, OLS and TSLS

	Pre-convention		Post-convention		Final week	
	OLS	TSLS	OLS	TSLS	OLS	TSLS
Early April	0.83	0.71				
	(0.12)	(0.14)				
Pre-convention			0.69	0.73		
			(0.13)	(0.14)		
Post-convention					0.79	0.85
					(0.11)	(0.13)
Intercept	1.22	0.42	−0.75	−0.83	0.77	−0.77
	(1.31)	(1.40)	(1.33)	(1.35)	(0.96)	(0.97)
Adj. R^2	.78	.80	0.67	.66	.78	.78
(RMSE)	(5.09)	(4.82)	(5.21)	(5.22)	(3.73)	(3.75)
N	15	12	15	15	15	15

Note: Readings are for week ED-29 (mid-April), 2 weeks before the first convention (pre-convention), 2 weeks after second convention (post-convention), and the final week. Missing values were obtained by stretching the weekly windows as described in the text. The instruments for the TSLS analyses are weekly readings from 9 weeks earlier. Standard errors are in parentheses.

final week is almost as large (0.77) as the interconvention correlation between the readings before and after the conventions (0.85).

Taking the four benchmark readings, table 4.5 shows equations predicting the vote division at each time point from the previous reading. Included are TSLS estimates, using earlier lag-9 readings of the independent variables as instruments. The coefficients for the lagged vote division from the previous benchmark period are somewhat below 1.00 in all cases, and the smallest predicting post-convention vote intentions from the pre-convention reading.[11]

Figure 4.7 illustrates the modest slope for the convention season, where in 12 of 15 elections, the party trailing going into the convention season gained during the convention period. (The Democrats' weak showings in 1972 and 1984 are major exceptions. The 2008 election technically is a slight exception as the financial crisis was taking its toll on McCain by the time of our post-convention reading.) This shrinkage of the lead is accompanied by shrinkage of the cross-sectional variance during the convention season, as documented in chapter 2. Thus, our analysis confirms that conventions add a special jolt to electoral preferences.

4.2.1 Convention Effects: Bounces or Permanent Bumps?

Next, we peer inside the "black box" of the convention season to observe the separate effects of the Democratic and Republican conventions. Since the "out-party" always moves first, holding its convention ahead of the presidential party, it is helpful for this analysis to flip the vote division variable and measure it not as a Democratic percentage but as percentage for the president's party. We measure the in-party vote at three stages: before and after the conventions as previously, and at the middle of the convention season.[12]

Figure 4.8 shows two graphs. In the first panel, we see the in-party mid-convention-season vote division as a function of the pre-convention vote division. With most observations below the 45-degree line, it is clear that in most campaigns, the in-party support deflates after the first convention as the opposition gains a short-term boost. Then, as the second panel shows, with most observations above the 45-degree line, the presidential party gains a boost. When the smoke clears, the average result is a wash. Over the fifteen elections, the in-party gains 0.1 points from pre- to post-convention, which by no accounting is statistically significant.

The first two columns of table 4.6 display the two linear OLS equations modeling the data in figure 4.8. With vote intentions now measured as the in-party vote, the two intercepts represent short-term convention effects when the lagged vote division is at 50–50. Conveniently, the two intercepts are virtually identical except for opposite signs, suggesting parity—that both the in- and out-party are boosted by about four points following their convention. The slope is higher for the out-party convention effect than the in-party convention (0.97 versus 0.66). (A shallow slope indicates *less* continuity from pre- to post-convention.) The shallower slope for in-party conventions reflects the fact that some of the greatest convention boosts were for in-party candidates who were trailing, for example, Carter in 1980, Bush in 1988, and Gore in 2000.

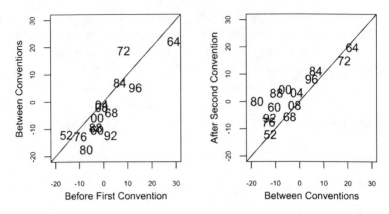

Figure 4.8. Incumbent presidential party vote division from before to after the conventions. Here, the vote division is measured as the percentage for the incumbent presidential party, to highlight the successive out-party and in-party gains. Exact descriptions of time dates are given in the text. There is no midconvention reading for 1956.

Table 4.6   Effects of conventions on support for the presidential party in trial-heat polls

	Between-conventions intended vote	Post-convention intended vote	Final week intended vote	Final week intended vote
Intercept	−4.06 (1.75)	3.73 (1.28)	1.52 (0.92)	1.99 (1.57)
Pre-convention	0.93 (0.16)		0.75 (0.11)	0.72 (0.10)
Between conventions		0.66 (0.11)		
Δ Post-pre-convention			0.58 (0.19)	
Δ Mid-pre-convention				0.68 (0.19)
Δ Post–between conventions				0.50 (0.21)
Adjusted R^2	.71	.73	.78	.80
RMSE	6.47	4.66	3.47	3.35
N	14	14	15	14

Note: For this table, the intended vote is measured as a percentage for the incumbent presidential party, to highlight the successive out-party and in-party gains. In the first two equations, convention effects are seen in intercepts. Exact descriptions of time dates are given in the text. There is no midconvention reading for 1956. Standard errors are in parentheses.

We must ask, of course, whether convention effects are bounces or permanent bumps. To obtain better purchase, the last two columns of table 4.6 show two equations predicting the final week's incumbent-party vote in the polls as a function of the incumbent's pre-convention vote, the incumbent's vote shift from pre-convention to after the first (out-party) convention, and the incumbent's vote shift from after the first convention to post-convention following the second (in-party) convention.[13] The test is whether the pre-convention vote division and the convention season shifts have equal slopes predicting the final week's vote. If they do, each increment of shocks due to the conventions lasts as long as increments in the pre-convention polls.

The answer is a qualified yes. When the convention-season shift is treated as one composite variable, as in column 3 of table 4.6, convention-induced shifts have about the same impact at the end as do shifts of equal increment before the conventions—0.58 and 0.75 ($p = .30$). When the two convention effects are separated, as in column 4 of the table, the earlier out-party convention seemingly has more impact than the later in-party convention. This difference, however, should not be taken too seriously, as it is not statistically significant.

A much simpler test is to see how much of the post-conventions shift carries to the final week's polls. The party that gains pre- to post-convention on average improves by 5.2 percentage points as measured from our pre- and post-convention benchmarks. On average, the party that gains from before to after the conventions maintains its gain in the final week's polls. In other words, its poll numbers do not fade but instead stay constant post-conventions to the final week.

This is an important result. Although the convention season is the time for multiple bounces in the polls, one party ends up with an advantage when the dust clears. And this gain is a net convention bump rather than a bounce.

4.2.2 The Convention Season versus the Early and Late Campaign

The ready interpretation is that the major-party conventions play a major role in reshuffling the electorate's vote preferences. This of course is not startling news, but rather a demonstration of the conventional wisdom about conventions. Our analyses clarify the nature of the effects and their impact. They also highlight the striking contrast between the scrambling of preferences during the convention season and stability of the polls during the earlier and, especially, later campaign periods.

Table 4.7 documents this stability. It shows the OLS and TSLS equations predicting the division of vote intentions from lagged vote intentions at various lags, where time is now measured relative to the conventions instead of days until Election Day. The time periods cover the eight weeks immediately before the conventions and the eight weeks starting three weeks after the conventions. Like the TSLS coefficients from table 4.3, table 4.7's

Table 4.7 OLS and TSLS equations predicting vote intentions from the lagged vote at various lags, for the final 8 weeks of the campaign and the final 8 weeks before the conventions

Post-convention

Lag length (in weeks)	N	OLS				TSLS			
		b	SE	Adj. R^2	RMSE	b	SE	Adj. R^2	RMSE
1	76	0.95	0.03	.93	1.84	1.00	0.04	.93	1.87
2	67	0.93	0.03	.93	1.79	0.94	0.04	.93	1.79
3	59	0.93	0.03	.93	2.10	0.97	0.05	.93	2.12
4	46	0.86	0.05	.86	2.52	0.90	0.08	.86	2.53
5	34	0.88	0.06	.85	2.54	0.93	0.10	.85	2.58
6	23	0.91	0.07	.81	2.65	0.90	0.09	.85	2.65
7	14	0.84	0.11	.81	2.66	0.81	0.17	.81	2.67
8	6	0.84	0.18	.84	2.51	1.19	0.77	.61	3.55

Pre-convention

Lag length (in weeks)	N	OLS				TSLS			
		b	SE	Adj. R^2	RMSE	b	SE	Adj. R^2	RMSE
1	53	0.85	0.08	.69	3.25	0.99	0.11	.67	3.35
2	54	0.93	0.04	.94	2.51	0.95	0.05	.90	2.54
3	49	0.88	0.06	.79	3.26	0.85	0.08	.79	3.26
4	35	0.89	0.07	.84	2.34	0.88	0.08	.84	2.34
5	32	0.90	0.08	.81	4.03	0.89	0.10	.89	4.03
6	18	0.77	0.09	.81	2.35	0.76	0.14	.71	2.35
7	14	0.84	0.08	.90	2.99	0.81	0.08	.90	3.01
8	7	0.91	0.10	.92	1.66	1.00	0.12	.92	1.78

Note: The instrument for the lagged vote = the vote division in polls 8 weeks earlier than the lag week (or even earlier, if otherwise missing). Because lag periods overlap in some instances, the standard errors should be treated only as suggestive. The window of weeks for the dependent variable is the final 8 weeks of the campaign. The window of lagged weeks is 1 week earlier. Standard errors are in parentheses.

TSLS coefficients approach 1.0 but decay somewhat with the time lag between the lagged and current vote division. In sum, the post-convention pattern from table 4.7 mirrors that for the final eight weeks (table 4.3), which should not surprise since the time intervals overlap greatly.

For the pre-convention period, the explained variance tends to be somewhat lower (and the RMSEs somewhat higher) than for the post-election period. Perhaps because of the irregularly timed pre-convention readings, the equations are more difficult to interpret. Since the explained variance does not shrink systematically with the lag length, the explained variance does not seem to be the result of sizable permanent shocks. The TSLS slopes do not tend to be any larger than their OLS counterparts, which would be the expected pattern with lots of short-term variation. In sum, the pre-convention pattern from table 4.7 indicates slightly more volatility in aggregate vote intentions than the post-convention period, but the data do not lend themselves to further generalization.

4.3 Presidential Debates

So far, this chapter has ignored the impact of presidential debates. If party conventions get voters' attention sufficiently to alter their vote choices more than usual, the same might be true about presidential debates. The first televised presidential debates in 1960 were each viewed by about 60 percent of US households.[14] Subsequent debates—in all presidential campaigns of 1976–2008—have drawn far fewer, but even the least watched debates (three each in 2000 and 2004) drew the attention of about 30 percent of households. With the public so closely focused on debate performance, one would think televised debates cause many prospective voters to switch sides based on what they see.

The common wisdom, however, is that debates do *not* change many minds (see, e.g., Abramowitz 1978; Miller and MacKuen 1979; Lanoue 1991). Instead, by the time of the debates in late September or October, most voters have made up their minds. They watch to root for their preferred candidate and to confirm their choice. Voters seem to have little difficulty proclaiming one candidate the "winner" of a debate and then voting for the opponent, whom the voter had favored all along (Holbrook 1996). For instance, in 2004, by consensus of the public (in polls) and media critics, Democrat John Kerry "won" all three presidential debates with President George W. Bush, yet he gained little in the polls as a result.

According to political lore, there are exceptions when debates make a difference. Some say that John Kennedy's narrow victory over Vice President Richard Nixon in 1960 would not have occurred without his show of readiness in the first presidential debates. (The scarcity of polling during the campaign makes this statement hard to verify.) In 1976, commentators said that President Gerald Ford "lost" his foreign-policy debate with soon-to-be president Jimmy Carter with his gaffe of surprisingly insisting that Poland was not a Communist nation. (Carter's downward slide during the fall campaign seems to belie that this debate gaffe did much lasting harm.) The biggest debate effect might have been in 1984 when President Ronald Reagan wandered during his final statement in the first of two debates. Within days he had lost half of his eighteen-point lead against former vice president Walter Mondale. Reagan recovered, however, when in the final debate he joked that he was not going to use as an issue his opponent's "age and inexperience." Evidently this was sufficient to restore Reagan to his equilibrium position in the polls.

Here, our fresh look at debate effects is to examine them globally in the following way. We observe the net effect of each debate season (from the first to the last debate) by comparing the polls centered during the week after the final debate with the polls centered during the week before the debate.[15] The graph in figure 4.9 shows a fairly strong degree of continuity from before to after the debates. To readers of this chapter, this should not surprise. Except for 1976, when Carter's support was in steady decline during the fall (but not enough to cost Carter the election), vote inten-

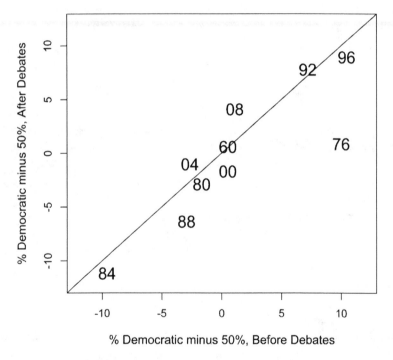

Figure 4.9. Vote intentions one week after the final debate compared to vote intentions one week before the first debate, 1960, 1976–2008. The diagonal line represents perfect continuity, before–after.

Table 4.8   Predicting post-debate vote intentions from pre-debate vote intentions

	All elections with debates: 1960, 1976–2008	Excepting 1976
Regression coefficient	0.83 (0.18)	1.05 (0.13)
Adjusted R^2	.71	.89
RMSE	3.33	2.12
Variance (independent variable)	39.66	34.08
Variance (dependent variable)	37.22	41.75
N	(10)	(9)

Note: Vote intentions pre- and post-debates are measured for the week immediately before the first debate and for the week immediately after the final debate.

tions the week after the debate closely matched those the week before the debate.

A closer look, however, shows more volatility during debate periods than is normal for the fall campaign. Table 4.8 displays the equation predicting the post-debates polls from pre-debates polls. It does so with and then without the 1976 outlier included. We can ask: What would we expect compared to a normal campaign interval without debates to get voter attention? Since the average number of days between before-debates and after-debates readings is 30 days, a rough comparison is the regression of vote intentions on vote intentions lagged 4 weeks, pooling all weeks during the final weeks of the campaign. Referring to table 4.3, we observe the adjusted R-squared to be .86 and the RMS to be 2.45. Over the ten debate periods, the comparable figures are .71 and 3.33. So the evidence is that before the debates, it is harder to predict the verdict after the debates than is normal for this length of time during the fall campaign. Debates seem to make at least a bit of difference.

Out of curiosity, we can see what happens when we omit the 1976 outlier, as in the final column of table 4.8. Now, vote intentions are slightly more stable than normal during the debate period. In fact the coefficient of about 1.00 suggests the best prediction from the debates is the initial verdict before the debates. Clearly, any claims about debate effects from our exploration are fragile. It is clear that debates do not have major impact to the same degree as party conventions. What is not clear is whether they have more effect than other events during the fall campaign. Although vote choices appear to be slightly more volatile than would be the case if the debates did not take place, this mild generalization becomes tentative given the limits of the data.

4.4 Conclusions: Where We Stand So Far

This chapter has examined changing vote intentions across presidential campaigns as revealed in the available weekly poll readings over the final 29 weeks of the fifteen presidential election campaigns since 1952. We have seen that the polls in the final week bear only a partial resemblance to those at the start of our series in mid-April. The transformation from mid-April polls to the final polls is a function of small weekly increments rather than wild fluctuations.

The one anomalous period that stands out is the convention season, when presidential preferences are scrambled, with more change during that period than either the pre-convention or the post-convention periods. With the convention season excluded, we see evidence that aggregate vote intentions are a function of year-specific equilibria. These equilibria, however, are more than mere "year" effects. They are not constant over the campaign. They move in small but important increments, obscured by short-term variation around them. Preferences change throughout the campaign, and some of the change lasts.

Thus far, our story has focused entirely on poll results, and we have completely ignored the vote. Although the evolution of poll results is revealing, we want to see how the shifting vote division revealed in campaign polls converts to the actual vote. This is what we turn to next.

FIVE

From the Campaign to Election Day

The previous chapter examined the vote division during the campaign as it is revealed in the polls. The present chapter turns to the actual Election Day vote, to see how well it can be predicted from the polls. We examine the precision of the vote prediction from the polls as a function of the date in the campaign timeline. But the purpose goes beyond the assessment of our ability to forecast elections from trial-heat polls. Our analysis allows us to make further inferences about the nature of campaign vote intentions as they evolve over the campaign timeline. Specifically, the relationship between the trial-heat polls and the vote informs us about whether campaign effects last to impact the final outcome.

5.1 Late Polls and the Election Outcome

We begin at the end of the campaign timeline by seeing how well the final polls predict the vote. Figure 5.1 displays the Democratic vote as a function of the final week's vote division in trial-heat polls. (Here and throughout this chapter, we measure the Democratic vote as the deviation from the 50 percent baseline.) From the figure we can see that the polls at the end of the campaign are a good predictor of the vote—the correlation between the two is a near-perfect 0.98. Still, we see considerable shrinkage of the lead between the final week's polls and the vote. The largest gap between the final polls and the vote is in 1964, when the polls suggested something approaching a 70–30 spread in the vote percentage (+20 on the vote −50 scale) for Johnson over Goldwater, whereas the actual spread was only 61–39.

It is informative to flip the scales and repeat the vote-by-last-polls graph in terms of the incumbent presidential party vote instead of the Democratic

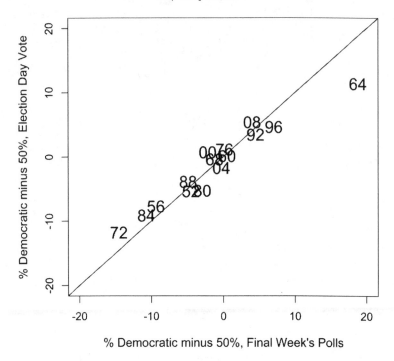

Figure 5.1. Democratic party vote for president as a function of the democratic vote in the final campaign week, 1952–2008. The vote and poll vote divisions are reported as percentages of the two-party vote. The diagonal line represents a projection of the poll results on the y-axis. The closer a figure is to the line, the less the deviation of the vote from the final week's vote division.

vote, as in figure 5.2. This figure shows a clear tendency for the late polls to exaggerate the support for the presidential party candidate; that is, most of the observations are below the line of identity relating the polls and the vote. From the figure it also is clear that the underlying reason appears to be that leads shrink for whichever candidate is in the lead (usually the incumbent party candidate) rather than that voters trend specifically against the incumbent party candidate. When the final polls are close to 50–50, there is no evident inflation of incumbent party support in the polls.

Table 5.1 extracts further statistical information regarding the vote-by-last-poll relationship. The details of the regression equation appear about the same whether we perform OLS, reliability correction, or TSLS and whether we predict the Democratic vote or the incumbent vote. In all instances, the coefficient for the polls is in the range of the mid-0.70s. All equations show a small negative intercept of about half a percentage point, suggesting that with the forecast of a close election, Democratic and incumbent party candidates perform slightly worse than projected. The deviations from zero are tiny and far from statistically significant, however. Thus, the final week's presidential polls do not appear to be systematically biased.[1]

Of special interest are the reliability-corrected equations since these presumably correct for sampling error. Assuming perfect polls *plus* no intervening events between the last polls and Election Day, the RMSE in the reliability-corrected equations should approach zero. Instead, we see a standard error slightly greater than 1.0. We can ask, is this small but nonzero error a sign of inefficient polls? Or is it due to the quite plausible hypothesis that the "error" represents last-minute vote shifts between the polls and Election Day?

As a test, we can analyze the vote-by-last-polls equation separately for

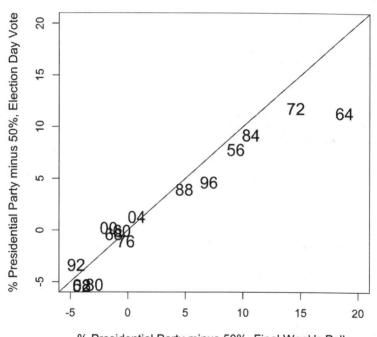

Figure 5.2. Incumbent presidential party vote as a function of the incumbent presidential party vote in the final campaign week, 1952–2008. The vote and poll vote divisions are reported as percentages of the two-party vote. The diagonal line represents a projection of the poll results on the y-axis. The closer a figure is to the line, the less the deviation of the vote from the final week's vote division.

Table 5.1 Predicting the Election Day vote from the polls in the final campaign week, 1952–2008

	OLS	Reliability corrected	TSLS
Dependent variable = Democratic percentage of two-party vote			
Intercept	−0.52	−0.51	−0.51
	(0.41)	(0.36)	(0.41)
Final week polls	0.74	0.75	0.75
	(0.05)	(0.05)	(0.06)
Adjusted R^2	.94	.96[a]	.94
RMSE	1.56	1.38	1.56
Dependent variable = incumbent presidential party percentage of two-party vote			
Intercept	−0.52	−0.55	−0.49
	(0.44)	(0.40)	(0.45)
Final week polls	0.78	0.79	0.77
	(0.06)	(0.05)	(0.06)
Adjusted R^2	.93	.96[a]	.93
RMSE	1.57	1.40	1.57

Note: The instruments for the TSLS equations are the post-convention vote divisions. Reliabilities are .988 for the percentage Democratic and .985 for the incumbent-party vote. Vote divisions in the polls and the vote are in terms of the percentage of the two-party vote minus 50. Standard errors are in parentheses.
[a]Estimated R^2.

the seven earlier elections (1952–76) and the seven later elections (1984–2008). We omit the middle year, 1980, which is known to have considerable late movement in the final week's polls. In the seven earlier elections, the N's for the final week of polling are all below 5,000, with a median of 1,502. In the seven later elections, the N's in the final week are all above 10,000, with a median of 22,944.[2] Clearly the N's are sufficiently large to imply little meaningful sampling error for the latter half of elections.

Our expectation is that if inefficient polling is responsible for the mild prediction error, we should see the greatest error for the early half of the series with smaller N. Instead, we find the largest errors for the later years. With reliability-corrected equations, the RMSE is 1.29 in the later years with heavy polling and only 1.07 in the earlier elections with sparser polling. Thus, the more recent elections with their increased wealth of late polling were slightly more difficult to predict from the late polls. This suggests that insufficient sample sizes are not the culprit behind the imperfect prediction. Rather, it seems that voter shifting is the source of late "error" and, since this error has increased over time in the face of more polling, that late electoral shifting has been on the increase over the span of our study.

Why do leads shrink during the final run-up to the election? One possibility is that the attenuation of leads in the final election verdict results from short-term influences that are tracked by the late polls but evaporate by Election Day. Estimation using TSLS provides a test. We ask: As instrumented by vote intentions measured eight weeks earlier, does the coefficient predicting the vote from the final polls increase? To the extent this is so, the OLS coefficient is depressed by inconsequential short-term influences on the polls that serve as the equivalent of measurement error. We consult the TSLS equations from table 5.1. The TSLS estimate is based on using the post-convention vote division as the instrument for the final polls. The idea, as in the TSLS analysis of polls in chapter 4, is to interpret the TSLS result as the estimate of the effect of the equilibrium portion of lagged vote intentions—here the intentions the week before the election in the trial-heat polls. Whereas the OLS coefficient reflects the equilibrium value of lagged vote intentions but is biased downward by short-term effects, the TSLS coefficient should represent only equilibrium effects.

The TSLS estimate predicting the actual vote from the presumed equilibrium value of the final week's polls is virtually identical to the OLS estimate.[3] Thus, even in terms of the equilibrium value, leads shrink between the final polls and the vote. This similarity of coefficients suggests that the presence of short-term campaign effects late in the campaign is not a major factor depressing the coefficient for the late polls.[4]

We can increase the parameter estimate for late polls by excluding the extreme 1964 case (when the Democratic landslide was even stronger in the final polls than on Election Day). This pushes the OLS coefficient (predicting the Democratic vote) all the way from 0.74 to 0.84. We can also recalculate the error correction adjustment without 1964. This nudges the coefficient to 0.86. We can conduct the TSLS version without 1964, and the coefficient advances to 0.88. As a final step, if we switch the prediction from the Democratic vote to the presidential party vote, again ignoring 1964, we gain just one more digit, with a coefficient of 0.89 (standard error = 0.07).

There is another possible influence on the coefficients that must be considered. By our construction, the preferences of undecided voters have been ignored. As the campaign evolves, the proportion of those who claim to be undecided shrinks. By modeling vote intentions as the two-party vote, we in effect assume that the undecideds' split is identical to that of the decideds, an assumption that is certainly wrong (also see Campbell 2008a). Even if we allocate undecideds differently, however, the resulting coefficients reveal essentially the same pattern.[5] Ultimately, then, the results imply an underdog effect, where the projected loser gains support at the very end of the race.

We are left with the simple possibility that most of the late switching goes to the disadvantaged party, though not by an amount that affects who ultimately wins. Conceivably, the shrinkage of leads could also be fueled by the polls' failure to capture the full measure of support for the disadvantaged party. This could be a by-product of an often-hypothesized "spiral of silence" effect—by which those who support the likely loser feel sufficiently isolated or ashamed that they resist revealing their true preferences to interviewers (Noelle-Neumann 1984).

Chapter 7's analysis of individual survey respondents provides clues that can be previewed here. Relatively few voters switch their vote choice late in the campaign. Relatively few undecided voters during the campaign end up voting, and those who do split close to 50–50. Moreover, there is no evidence that partisans "come home" to their party on Election Day (although this phenomenon occurs earlier in the campaign). Yet chapter 7 highlights one additional factor that explains why late leads shrink. Many survey respondents tell pollsters they will vote but then do not show up. These eventual no-shows tend to favor the winning candidate when interviewed before the election. Without the preferences of the no-shows in the actual vote count, the winning candidate's lead in the polls flattens.

Knowing how well the final week's polls predict the presidential vote provides an important end-of-campaign benchmark. Of course, the late trial-heat polls are silent about how the Election Day result comes into focus over the campaign. For this, we must assess the predictability of the vote from polls at earlier points in time. To this interesting topic we turn next.

5.2 Predicting the Vote from the Polls over the Campaign Timeline

While attention normally centers on the accuracy of the final polls, we give further attention to the earlier polls, which for many elections are found as early as 300 days before the election. We consider how well polls from different points in the campaign timeline predict the Election Day vote. The pattern of predictability furthers our understanding of the dynamics of the vote division throughout the long election campaign.

For this section, we measure vote margins in the polls not weekly as in the previous chapter and the previous section, but on a daily basis. We do this by simply interpolating the daily vote division from the polls in nearby days. When (as is often the case) a date has no poll, we assign the average of the vote division from the previous poll and the vote division from the next poll, weighting the two components by the closeness of their dates to the polls.[6] For the last dates before the election, we score the vote division from the final poll.[7]

First consider the scatter plot of the relationship between poll results at various points of the campaign cycle and the actual vote. We illustrate with figure 5.3, expanding our database temporarily to include all dates within 300 days of the election. In the upper left-hand panel of the figure, using only elections in which polls are available 300 days before the election, we see that there is little relationship between these early polls and the actual vote. As we turn toward increasingly current polls, moving horizontally

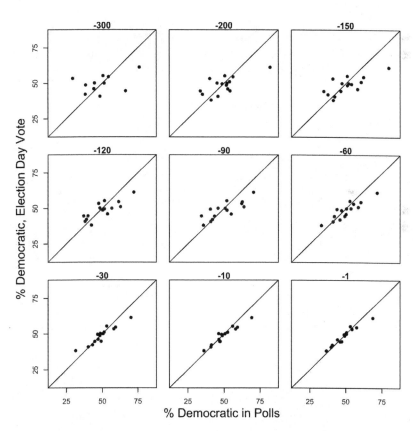

Figure 5.3. Vote by vote division in polls at various dates from 300 days to one day before the election, 1952–2008. Daily polls are interpolated where missing.

and then vertically through the figure, pattern emerges; simply, the later the polls, the greater the focus. That is, the points line up. The closer we get to the election, the more the polls tell us about the outcome.

Consider basic summary statistics focusing on the last 200 days, by which point we have polls in each election year. At 200 days before the election, reported poll results and the final vote differ quite a lot, by 6.4 points on average.[8] At the 100-day mark, about the time of the national party conventions, the average difference between the polls and the ultimate vote is 4.9 points. By the very end of the campaign, the average difference is a mere 1.8 points.[9] It thus is clear that the polls tell us more and more about the outcome as the campaign unfolds. This is not especially surprising, but it is a useful validation of conventional wisdom.[10]

To systematically examine the degree to which the polls at different dates predict the vote on Election Day, we generate a series of daily equations predicting the vote in the fifteen elections j during 1952–2008 from vote intentions in the polls at date T in the campaign timeline.

$$VOTE_j = a_T + b_T V_{jT} + e_{jT}.$$

Using the statistics from these equations, we first present and interpret the dynamics of how the variance explained by the polls (R-squared) varies over the campaign timeline. Second, we present and interpret the changes in the regression coefficient (b_t) as a function of the date.[11]

5.2.1 The R-Squared

The R-squared statistic tells us how much of the variance of the dependent variable (here, the Election Day vote) is accounted for by the independent variable(s), here the date's vote division in the polls. An important aspect of understanding the campaign timeline is the day-to-day trend in the R-squared predicting the final vote from the current polls. In the following section, we review some statistical theory regarding what the R-squared might tell us about the underlying time series. Readers without a strong statistical bent may prefer to skim or skip it, turning to the section that follows, which examines patterns in the data.

Theory

In terms of a formula,

$$R^2 = \frac{Explained.Variance}{Total.Variance}.$$

In chapter 3, we posited that the vote division is a combination of an integrated series or random walk, V^*, plus a short-term component V^S. Statistically, these series components can be described for elections j as follows:

$$V_{jT}^* = \sum_{t=1}^{T} u_{jt}$$

and

$$V_{jT}^S = \sum_{t=1}^{T} \beta^{T-1} e_{jt}$$

where the u_{jt} and e_{jt} error terms are the sources of V_{jT}^* and V_{jT}^S, respectively, following the terminology of chapter 3. For the moment, we conveniently assume that u_{jt} and e_{jt} are uncorrelated with each other and have constant variances over time.[12] We also ignore the election eve compression of the vote variance, as the vote margin shrinks by about 25 percent from the final polls to the actual vote.[13] With these assumptions and allowances, we can interpret the R-squared for any given campaign date T as follows:

(5.1)
$$R_T^2 = \frac{Var(V_T^*) + \beta^{ED-T} Var(V_T^S)}{Var(VOTE_{ED})}.$$

The moving parts in the equation are all in the numerator. The model's random walk assumption requires that the equilibrium variance $Var(V_T^*)$ grows with time T. Meanwhile, the short-term component of the explained variance $\beta^{ED-T} Var(V_T^S)$ also grows larger as the campaign progresses. We are interested in the description of the potentially nonlinear slope describing the change in the R-squared predicting the vote as the campaign timeline increases from day to day, and what it might tell us about campaigns and voters. To develop some expectations, we see that the slope at time T is the first difference between the vote margin at time T and at $T-1$:

Explained $Var(V_{T-1}) = Var(V_{T-1}^*) + \beta^{ED-T-1} Var(V_{T-1}^S)$

and

Explained $Var(V_T) = Var(V_{T-1}^*) + Var(u_T) + \beta^{ED-T-1} Var(V_{T-1}^S) + \beta^{ED-T} Var(e_T)$

By some algebra, the one-period change in the R-squared, therefore, is

(5.2)
$$\Delta \text{Explained } Var(V_T) = Var(u_T) + \beta^{ED-T} Var(e_T).$$

Let use consider some simple examples of how the net R-squared would look over time, based on equation 5.2. Clearly the explained variance

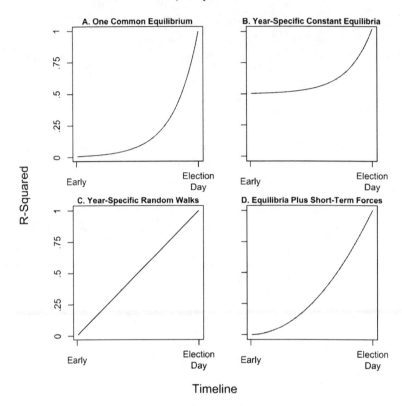

Figure 5.4. Four models of the R-squared predicting the vote from polls at various dates over the campaign timeline. Each model assumes shocks of constant variance over the timeline.

should go up with time, but the functional form will depend on the proper model of the two components. Figure 5.4 displays four possible idealized models, varying as a function of the relative contribution of the two components.

The upper left-hand panel (A) presents the path of an R-squared from a baseline model in which the vote is a function only of short-term effects, with all campaigns in different years sharing one common equilibrium value for V^*. By this model, the vote division in different years at the same time T during the campaign reflects variation around a common mean. In the long run—if campaigns were extended indefinitely—the early vote division would provide no information regarding the vote at the end of the process. This is because any difference between early polls and the common mean would decay by Election Day, leaving V^* as the expectation in each year. Late polls would provide information, however, as they reflect campaign effects that do not fully decay by Election Day. The result in terms of R-squared is the nonlinear temporal pattern shown in panel A, as the R-squared starts at zero on its path toward 1.0.

Next, consider panel B in the upper-right corner of figure 5.4, which shows the path of the R-squared if the vote is a function of both V_{jT}^S and V_{jT}^*. Here, the equilibrium term varies by year j but does not move over the campaign timeline. This model represents a set of stationary series varying around different yearly means, as discussed in chapter 3 (see fig. 3.2). The result in terms of R-squared bears the form of the nonlinear pattern shown in panel A, reflecting late-arriving campaign effects. But here in panel B, reading backward in time from Election Day, the curve trends toward a nonzero constant. This constant represents the contribution of the equilibrium values V_Y^*, which do not change during campaigns.

Next, consider panel C, which shows the results if campaign vote divisions were the result solely of a random walk over the campaign timeline. Here, the R-squared evolves linearly over time with the accumulation of shocks with no decay. Of course, the linearity is a function of the assumption of shocks with constant variance over time. If shocks are larger at some points in the campaign timeline, the slope of the R-squared regression line would be steeper for those intervals.

Finally, panel D presents the R-squared panel expected with both a random walk and stationary component. Here, the long-term component drives the results, as short-term variation around equilibrium is relevant for the actual vote only when it occurs late in the campaign.[14] The R-squared-by-time function would take a form that effectively combines the curves in panels A and C. As shown in panel D, there would be a linear trend that curves upward toward the end under the influence of late short-term forces, as late events have most sway on the vote.[15]

Which, if any, of these graphs should we expect as an accurate portrayal of the R-squared? Our hypothesized model has both a long- and short-term component to the poll margins, so that would seem to push us to model D. We must, however, be open to campaign shocks of uneven impact throughout the campaign. With the reality of a net decline in the cross-sectional variance of the vote division and the assumption of a random walk component, it may be that the short-term shocks do decline in magnitude over time. Suppose this is true, and $Var(V_T^S)$ declines toward zero. Suppose also that the rate of change of the R-squared also changes as a function of declining permanent u_t shocks.

Figure 5.5 presents one example where the variance of the short-term

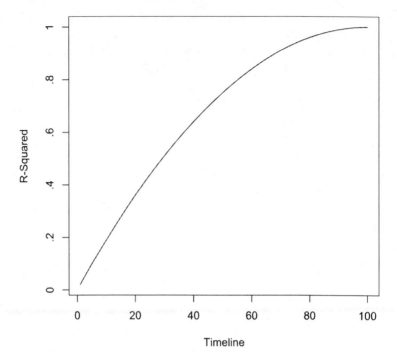

Figure 5.5. Model of R-squared where the vote is governed by year-specific random walks over the campaign timeline, with the variance of shocks declining linearly over the timeline, ending at zero on Election Day.

forces (V_T^S) declines linearly from time 1 to zero at time ED, while the u_t shock variance declines in such a fashion that it becomes inconsequential by Election Day. Given this input, figure 5.5 shows a rising R-squared with a slope that declines with time.

Which (if any) model provides a fit with the actual change in the adjusted R-squared over the campaign timeline? Let us see what the data reveal.

Data

How does the R-squared change predicting the vote from the polls change over the course of the campaign season? When comparing the R-squareds at different points in the campaign timeline, it is crucial to compare regressions with the identical set of years. If we were to vary the years from one date to the next, the R-squared would vary with the variance of the vote. Including landslide Republican and Democratic years would expand the variance and the R-squared; to concentrate on close elections would have the opposite result. Fortunately, trial-heat polls were already in place by January in 11 of our 15 presidential election years. We start with date ED-300, that is, 300 days before Election Day. For each date in this sequence, we regress the vote on the polls, interpolating for the many date-year combinations for which actual polls were not available. The four election campaigns we must omit for this exercise are 1952, 1968, 1972, and 1976. In January of these years, the pollsters evidently saw little chance that Stevenson (1952), Nixon (1968), McGovern (1972), or Carter (1976) would be party standard-bearers, even though two from this list went on to victory in November.

Figure 5.6 presents the result, using the statistically appropriate *adjusted* R-squared, which is the more conservative estimate of fit that takes into account the sample size. Much like the hypothetical graph in figure 5.5, the adjusted R-squared starts at near zero, increases rapidly, and gradually

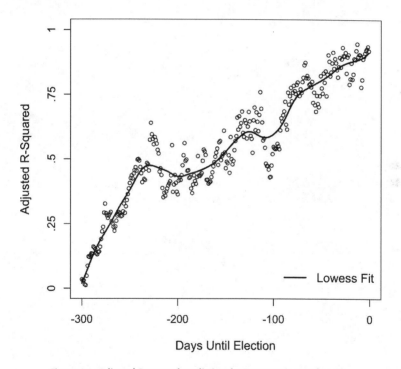

Figure 5.6. Adjusted R-squared predicting the Democratic vote from the Democratic vote division in the polls, by the date in the campaign timeline starting 300 days before Election Day. For eleven elections with polls going back 300 days, 1956–1964, 1980–2008. Daily polls are interpolated where missing. Lowess fit is with a bandwidth of .20.

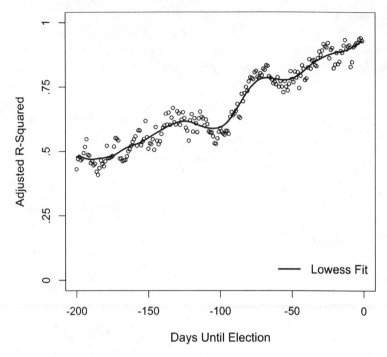

Figure 5.7. Adjusted *R*-squared predicting the Democratic vote from the Democratic vote division in the polls, by the date in the campaign timeline starting 200 days before Election Day. For fifteen elections, 1952–2008. Daily polls are interpolated where missing. Lowess fit is with a bandwidth of .20.

levels off on its march toward 1.00. Judging from the modesty of the increments, it would seem that the battle lines shift very little during the late campaign. In terms of our model, election shocks would start big and end up small. During the first 100 days of the election year, there apparently is a lot of learning about the campaign. Permanent shocks to the vote are increasing, while the seemingly large short-term effects (evident from the large cross-sectional variance of the vote) begin to burn off.

Figure 5.7 displays the cross-sectional *R*-squared from regressing the vote division on the poll division for each date starting 200 days before the election, when we have polls in all fifteen election years. Focusing on the final 200 days highlights a substantial growth in the *R*-squared in midsummer, where another bout of voter learning occurs. The figure reveals an interesting pattern: polls from 100 to 200 days before Election Day increase gradually in prediction accuracy. They also contain important information, as the *R*-squared hovers between 0.50 to 0.60. In effect, we have half the Election

Day story six months before the election and gain relatively little in the ensuing three months. The largest improvement in predictability comes from about 100 days out to about 70 days out (typically the convention period), as a midsummer spurt. Thereafter the slope of the R-squared flattens out and increases only incrementally. That is, the polls add an equal amount from day to day, on average, and peak at the end of the campaign, where the R-squared for the vote-on polls regression reaches a healthy .93.

Figures 5.6 and 5.7 teach us quite a lot. At the start of the election year, polls are taken but they are virtually meaningless for election forecasting purposes. In January of election year (measured here by polls on day ED-300), the polls involving the eventual major-party presidential candidates can explain a mere 4 percent of the variance in the ultimate vote margin. Still, a candidate would rather be ahead than behind at the early date. The leader in January won the election in eight of the eleven contests for which we have polls at that early date in the campaign timeline.

By April, the primary season is under way and, in most recent years, practically over. The candidates running paired in our trial-heats are no longer hypothetical choices. Rather, they are heavy if not prohibitive favorites to win their nominations. And by this time, the trial-heat polls between the eventual candidates can account for 43 percent of the variance in the vote. Further learning slows as the conventions approach. From day ED-200 to ED-100—approximately mid-April to mid-July—predictability from the polls improves by an additional 16 percent.

As the campaign moves into the summertime phase, campaign shocks grow with a lasting effect on the outcome. We know this because the predictability of the election outcome increases strongly through the summer months. From 100 days to about 70 days before the election, the adjusted R-squared jumps 22 points. As we will see, this is a function of the party conventions held during this period. By date ED-70 (late August), the convention spurt has ended. From this point until Election Day, the R-squared increases by its final 12 percentage points. The fall campaign leaves an imprint on the vote, but no more than that during the April-to-July interregnum, and certainly less than during the primary season or the convention period. By the beginning of the fall general election campaign, the result is almost hardened in place.[16]

5.2.2 The Regression Coefficient

Our next set of clues are the regression coefficients over the campaign timeline—the regression coefficients predicting the vote from the polls over the final 200 days of the campaign. Below we show the series of regression coefficients predicting the vote from the polls, for each date going back 300 days (for eleven years) or 200 days (for all fifteen years) from the election. As with our discussion of the R-squareds, we first present some theory. The less statistically inclined can skim or else skip to the data section just below.

Theory

The observed b_T represents the expected proportion of the observed vote margin that will survive to Election Day. But what about the equilibrium portion of the vote division? Let us define λ_T as the unobserved parameter representing the effect of V_T^*—the equilibrium portion of the vote division on the vote. The estimate b_T is not λ_T but rather a complicated compound incorporating the combined V_T^* and V_T^S effects (λ_T and β^{ED-T}). Specifically,

$$(5.3) \qquad b_T = \frac{\lambda Var(V_T^*) + \beta^{ED-T} Var(V_T^S)}{Var(V_T^*) + Var(V_T^S)}.$$

To understand how b_T varies with time, let us mentally divide the timeline into two segments. In the early segment, the short-term shocks do not last to Election Day, that is, β^{ED-T} approaches 0, leaving only the first component of the numerator of equation 5.3. But the short-term component is present in the denominator, functioning as if it is measurement error in the calibration of the equilibrium component. During this period, the b_T estimate of λ is biased downward in proportion to the size of the short-term variance V_T^S in relation to the equilibrium variance V_T^*. In the absence of short-term shocks, that is, where $V_T^S = 0$, equation 5.3 simplifies to the equilibrium effect (i.e., $b_T = \lambda_T$ for all segments of the timeline).

Now consider the later segment of the timeline. Here the short-term component matters and the second term of the numerator of equation 5.3 is greater than 0. In contrast with the first segment, therefore, the b coefficient will surge in size. The surge will depend on the extent to which the late, short-term variance (V_T^S) affects the vote.

Data

Figures 5.8 and 5.9 present the b_T coefficients over the campaign timeline. The size of b_T reveals, as an expectation, the proportion of the time T lead that will survive until Election Day. The central fact that stands out from figures 5.8 and 5.9 is the low but growing magnitude of the coefficients. The expectation is that poll margins at any point in time will shrink by

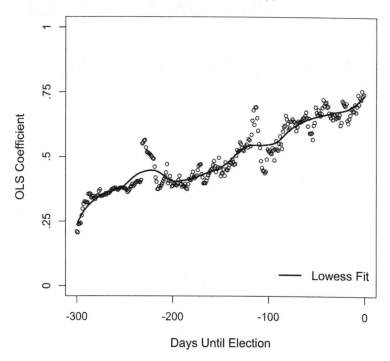

Figure 5.8. OLS regression coefficients predicting the democratic vote from the Democratic vote division in the polls, by date in the campaign timeline, starting 300 days before Election Day. For eleven elections with polls going back 300 days, 1956–1964, 1980–2008. Daily polls are interpolated where missing. Lowess fit is with a bandwidth of .20.

Election Day, and the farther from the election, the greater the shrinkage. Leads in January (300 days out), for instance, will shrink (as an expectation) up to 80 percent by Election Day (b_T about 0.20). At about 100 days out (midsummer) the shrinkage level is about half. And as we saw earlier, even the poll margins of election eve trim by 25 percent on Election Day.

Taking a close look at the full scan of 300 days (fig. 5.8), we observe a curve whose highlights mimic the R-squared curve of figure 5.6. The b_T starts out as low as 0.20 but quickly zooms up during the early months of the campaign. To observe the continued rise toward 0.75, we turn to the 200-day picture of figure 5.9. The trend appears fairly linear. Yet we can discern two more periods of steep growth in an otherwise wiggly line with a linear trend. One such period is the convention season around midsummer. The second is at the very end of the campaign. Whereas short-term

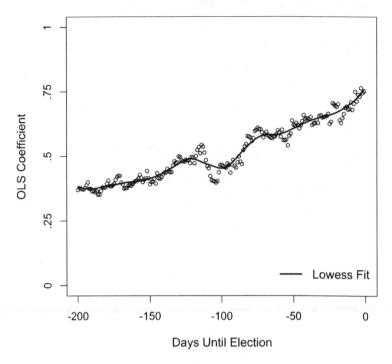

Figure 5.9. OLS regression coefficients predicting the Democratic vote from
Democratic vote division in the polls, by date in the campaign timeline
starting 200 days before Election Day. For fifteen elections, 1952–2008. Daily
polls are interpolated where missing. Lowess fit is with a bandwidth of .20.

campaign effects generally dissipate before the election, those that arise
near the campaign's end can and do affect the vote.

What can we add regarding our understanding of the dynamics of vote
intentions from figures 5.8 and 5.9? If we assume a constant λ—the effect
of the equilibrium component of preferences—of about .75, the growth of
b_T would be a signal of an ever-decreasing shrinkage of the variance of the
short-term forces. But the λ term could also be changing. The equilibrium
component could be an integrated series as we have posited, yet still show
further compressions of its metric similar to that from the late polls to the
vote. One such compression we saw from chapter 4 occurs at conventions
time, when the TSLS regression of the post-conventions vote division on
the pre-conventions vote division is about 0.70 instead of approaching
1.00. Can we do more with our slopes predicting the vote from the polls to
estimate the λ parameter?

We can obtain some purchase by once again applying TSLS. In chapter 4 we ran several TSLS regressions predicting the vote division from the lagged vote division, using the vote division lagged 9 weeks. The idea is that vote intentions at lag-9 comprise a good instrument for the lag-1 long-term component V_{T-1}^*, as it is relatively free of the short-term forces present at lag-1, 8 weeks later. We can use the equivalent instrumentation—the interpolated vote division at lag-8 as an instrument for vote intentions at time T in a regression predicting the vote from V_T^* at time T.[17]

We present the results graphically in figure 5.10. For the final 160 days of the campaigns, the figure compares the daily slopes from our OLS analysis (from fig. 5.9) with the TSLS estimates.[18] Both early in this segment of the election cycle and toward the very end, we see the two series tracking each other. In the middle—the convention season—the two series diverge with the TSLS estimate larger. This gap continues and actually widens some, and then slowly closes after the convention season is over.

The TSLS estimate is intended as an estimate of how much of the long-

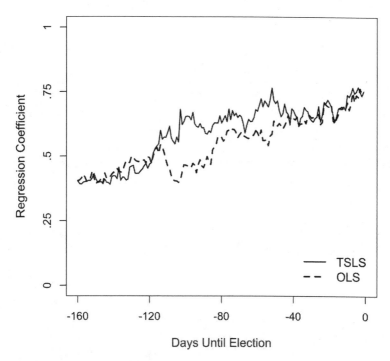

Figure 5.10. OLS and TSLS regression coefficients predicting the Democratic vote from the Democratic vote division in the polls, by the date in the campaign timeline starting 160 days before Election Day. For fifteen elections, 1952–2008. Daily polls are interpolated where missing.

term component (λ_T), of the vote division persists to Election Day. We see it hold remarkably steady at about 0.65 from about 100 days out until the final week. The implication is that, for this time period, if we knew which portion of the poll results is the long-term component rather than short-term effects or measurement error, about 65 percent of the lead would hold, as an expectation, until Election Day. The gap between the TSLS estimates and their OLS counterparts is evidence of short-term forces. Where OLS underestimates λ_T, the culprit would be short-term forces acting as the equivalent of measurement error dampening the observed statistical estimate.

It seems logical for strong short-term forces to be present during the convention season and for a little while thereafter, as the convention bounces wind down. It is plausible that there would be no appreciable short-term effects at campaign's end (when the OLS–TSLS gap closes). It is somewhat of a surprise, though, to find evidence that short-term forces are virtually absent in the period leading up to the convention. We return to this puzzle in the next section, where our analysis fixes on the convention period and how it compares to times immediately before and after.

5.3 Conventions and the Vote

In chapter 4's analysis of the vote division over time, we saw that the conventions were a period of interruption in an otherwise stable pattern in which each year's vote division holds fairly steady week by week. Here we examine the convention effect on the Election Day vote. Following our procedure for examining convention effects in chapter 4, this section models the vote as a function of the incumbent party vote rather than the Democratic vote. And we measure time not in terms of days before the election but rather as days before and after the two major-party conventions.

Our first step is to repeat the analysis of adjusted R-squareds and regression slopes over time, where the timeline is relative to the conventions. Figure 5.11 shows the results of the OLS analysis. The figure should not surprise. We see gradual increases in the observed R-squareds and b slopes as the timeline progresses. The coefficients are well behaved as mildly sloping linear lines, with an evident break during the convention period.[19] We leave a big window on each side of the convention period where we present no coefficients, because during these intervals the interpolated estimates are for some years "contaminated" by heavy weighting of data from surveys within the convention window. We include only dates for which estimates can be obtained using data from all fifteen elections.

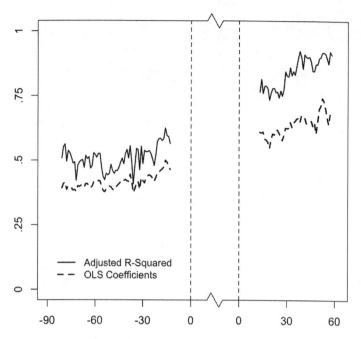

Figure 5.11. Adjusted *R*-squared and OLS regression slopes predicting the vote by
date of the vote division in the campaign timeline relative to party conventions,
1952–2008. Negative dates indicate the number of days before the first convention,
from −82 to +14. Positive dates are the number of days after the second convention, from +14 to +59. The date scale compresses the time gap between −14 and
+14. The average period from the start of the first convention to the end of the
second convention is 31 days. Daily polls are interpolated where missing.

For greater understanding, we turn to TSLS estimates of the regression
slopes. Here, the goal is to obtain estimates of the equilibrium effects (λ_T)
free of the influence of the measurement error due to short-term forces.
Figure 5.12 shows the results—a comparison of the OLS estimates (from
fig. 5.11) with TSLS estimates for dates pre- and post-convention. The
TSLS estimates are quite level, both before and after the conventions, but
at different heights. After the conventions, the TSLS slopes average 0.67,
as if about two-thirds of the presumed fundamentals from a date of the
late campaign carry over to Election Day. This average is close to the ceiling of 0.75 observed at election eve. Before the conventions, the average
slope is 0.46, or roughly two-thirds of the post-convention slope of 0.67,
which mirrors the slope of about 0.67 (from chap. 4) predicting the post-
convention vote division from pre-convention values.[20]

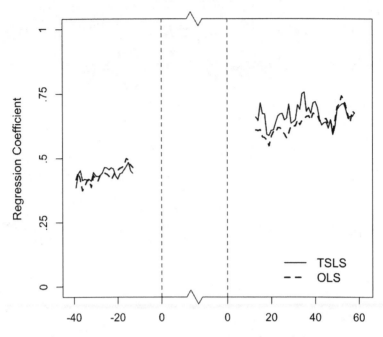

Figure 5.12. OLS and TSLS regression coefficients predicting the Democratic vote from the Democratic vote division in the polls, by the date in the campaign timeline relative to the party conventions. Negative dates are the number of days before the first convention, from −40 to 14. Positive dates are the number of days after the second convention, from +14 to +59. The date scale compresses the time between −14 and +14. The average period from the start of the first convention to the end of the second convention is 31 days.

In figure 5.12, the gap between the OLS and TSLS estimates should serve as a rough estimate of the degree of short-term forces biasing the OLS estimates at different time points relative to the conventions. These results help clarify the patterns shown in figure 5.10. Both before and after the conventions, the OLS slopes virtually match the TSLS slopes. Prior to the conventions, the two sets of slopes each average 0.46. Following the conventions we see a tiny OLS–TSLS gap, although the discussion that follows suggests it is probably not meaningful. Whereas the average slope post-convention (14 to 59 days after the second convention adjourned) was 0.67 estimated using TSLS, it is 0.64 estimated using OLS.

The similarities between the two sets of slopes offer some convenience. If short-term sources of variation in vote intentions do not matter much, then the OLS estimates should be good enough to estimate the relationship between the results of the polls and the eventual vote. The stable slopes within the pre- and post-convention time frames suggest that most influences on vote intentions during these periods leave permanent imprints that survive to Election Day.

5.3.1 The Polls from within the Convention Season and the Vote

At this point, we can gain a firmer foothold by turning to the relationship between what the polls show *during* the convention season and the Election Day vote. Figure 5.13 shows scatterplots, where the vote is measured as support for the presidential party. The statistical details are in table 5.2.

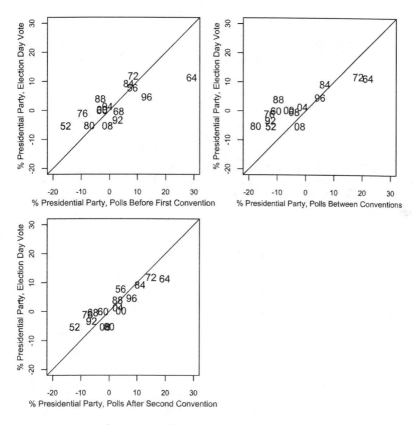

Figure 5.13. Incumbent party vote by incumbent party vote division in the polls before, between, and after the major party conventions, 1952–2008. (There is no midconvention reading for 1956.) The diagonal lines represent projections of the poll results on the y-axis. The closer a number to the line, the less the deviation of the vote from the final week's vote division.

Table 5.2 Predicting the Election Day vote from polls before, during, and after the major party conventions

	From pre-convention polls		From midconvention polls		From post-convention polls	
	Dependent variable = Democratic vote					
	OLS	TSLS	OLS	TSLS	OLS	TSLS
Intercept	−1.56	−1.60	−1.08	−1.18	1.08	1.08
	(0.97)	(0.98)	(1.05)	(1.15)	(0.75)	(0.73)
Regression coefficient	0.46	0.46	0.39	0.52	0.60	0.65
	(0.09)	(0.10)	(0.09)	(0.14)	(0.86)	(0.10)
Adjusted R^2	.63	.62	.58	.50	.77	.77
RMSE	3.73	3.79	3.94	4.29	2.91	2.91
	Dependent variable = presidential party vote					
	OLS	TSLS	OLS	TSLS	OLS	TSLS
Intercept	1.05	1.12	2.61	2.63	0.64	0.56
	(1.04)	(1.06)	(0.83)	(0.85)	(0.82)	(0.83)
Regression coefficient	0.42	0.41	0.43	0.44	0.59	0.56
	(0.10)	(0.11)	(0.07)	(0.09)	(0.09)	(0.11)
Adjusted R^2	.56	.55	.74	.74	.73	.73
RMSE	3.94	4.00	3.05	3.05	3.07	3.06
N	15	15	14	14	15	15

Note: The instrument for the TSLS analyses is the vote division in early April, week ED-200. The pre-convention polls are the weekly polls for the week ending the Monday before the first convention. The post-convention polls are the weekly polls for the week beginning the second Tuesday after the second convention. There is no midconvention reading for 1956. Vote divisions in the polls and the vote are in terms of the percentage of the two-party vote minus 50. Standard errors are in parentheses.

The table shows the predictions of the vote before, between, and after the conventions—both in terms of the support for the Democratic candidate and for the incumbent presidential party.

The upper-left panel of figure 5.13 shows the in-party vote as a function of pre-convention vote intentions, our benchmark measure from chapter 4. Note the shallow slope. The stronger the in-party showing in the pre-convention polls, the greater will be its decline by Election Day. The pre-convention polls correlate at a modest 0.77 with the final vote.

The upper-right panel shows the in-party vote as a function of the between-conventions vote division. The prediction tightens, as the correlation zooms from 0.77 (panel 1) to 0.87 (panel 2) in just a few short weeks.

This shows that the first (out-party) convention produces real learning on the part of the voters of the sort that survives to Election Day.[21] Still, the out-party gain is usually offset by the impact of the second convention, as the in-party usually outperforms its between-conventions polls on Election Day (see the positive intercept in table 5.2).

The bottom panel of figure 5.13 shows the in-party vote as a function of the post-convention polls, measured the second week after the final convention as in chapter 4. The slope now steepens as the variance of the polls compresses from the between-conventions to post-convention periods. And the inflation of the out-party vote evident between the convention vanishes. (In table 5.2, the intercept returns to near zero.) The polls-vote correlation grows no further between the periods.[22]

Thus, consistent with all expectations, the vote division first shifts toward the out-party after its convention and then back toward the in-party after its event. In effect, the conventions produce substantial bounces. It should be emphasized that the net convention effect is more of a bump than a bounce for the party that walks away from the conventions with the net vote advantage. We saw in chapter 4 that the party that increased its vote support from pre- to post-conventions on average gains 5.2 percent of the vote, a margin that persisted to the final polls. Here, we note that this gain persists and actually increases slightly (to 5.5 percent) by Election Day.[23] When a candidate leaves the convention season with a net gain in the polls, the gain persists not only in subsequent polls (as shown in chap. 4). It persists to Election Day.

5.4 Conclusions

This chapter has documented the relationship between the vote division throughout the election year and the Election Day vote. At the beginning of the year, vote intentions tell us little about the final outcome. Rapid learning takes place during the presidential primary season and, by the end of the nomination process, the electorate's preferences begin to take shape. They still are only half-formed at this point in time. The conventions stimulate further learning, and preferences are largely crystallized entering the general election campaign. Surprisingly little changes from the conventions to the final week of the campaign. At that point we observe the last minute shifts from trial-heat polls to the vote, described at the outset of this chapter.

Along the way of our analysis, we have distinguished between the long-term component of the vote—the permanent accumulation of electoral shocks—and the ephemeral short-term variation around it. The latter may be of little significance except at the very end of the campaign. The former clearly evolves over the election year.

It is striking that in early January (300 days until the election), the reported vote intentions in trial-heat polls vary quite a bit from one election year to another, yet do a poor job of predicting the Election Day vote. On the basis of our analysis, the events that influence aggregate electoral preferences before the election year even begins must have no real impact on the Election Day result. Since they ultimately do not predict the vote, they are short-lived, and do not stand the test of time.

Meanwhile, as the election year begins, the fundamental forces of the campaign are beginning to take shape. Left to be discussed is the nature of the fundamental forces that drive this long-term component of the vote in each presidential election. That is the focus of the next chapter.

SIX

Sources of Change over the Campaign Timeline

Previous chapters have modeled aggregate vote intentions over the campaign timeline as a time series modified by the accumulation of shocks, as voters absorb the evolving news about the presidential race. The present chapter explores the content of these shocks. It asks: What variables predict how vote intentions evolve over the election year, and at what points in the campaign timeline do they affect voter decisions?

Two different models are explored here. The first follows the familiar paradigm whereby aggregate vote choice is a function of economic conditions, actual or perceived. As we will see, the economy affects presidential approval, which in turn is a strong predictor of the presidential party's degree of electoral success. This "economic" model is largely based on voter retrospections—as if voters ask themselves how well the current administration has performed and reward or punish the presidential party accordingly. Of course, it does not mean that voters are not thinking about the future on Election Day. Rather, it is to say that they decide to stay the course or change based on the performance of the sitting president.

A second model is drawn from *The Macro Polity* (Erikson, MacKuen, and Stimson 2002). This "political" model is based on three political variables—the electorate's net party identification (macropartisanship), its liberal-conservative policy mood (Stimson 1999, 2004), and the ideological orientation of party positions as measured using party platforms (Budge et al. 2001). The latter two represent the two components of the electorate's relative ideological proximity to the Democratic versus Republican parties. Ideological proximity is mood relative to platforms of the parties. Because mood and platforms are measured in different units, we treat them as separate variables. The intent is to model preferences as a function of the same variables that dominate voting choice at the individual level—partisanship and relative proximity to the candidates on issues. To the extent voters are driven by mood and party positions (reflected in platforms), they are seemingly forward looking, as if the electorate evaluates the future policy choices of the parties.

It is already known that presidential election outcomes can be predicted from the variables in these models. Much less is known about how these effects crystallize over the campaign. For each model, we explore how well the variables predict vote intentions at various points in the campaign timeline. In addition, we explore how the economic and the political models together account for the vote outcome as the campaign evolves. We will see that the two models represent separate aspects of the electoral decision that actually are related.

6.1 Economic Variables and the Vote

It now is conventional wisdom that elections are influenced by the economy, as if voters reward or punish the party of the president based on the degree of prosperity. Expectations among scholars vary, from those who see elections as driven mainly by economic conditions at the expense of political variables (e.g., Fair 2002) to those who see the economy as a central concern but one whose effects can be modified by the behavior of candidates and their campaigns (Vavreck 2009). The exact voter psychology by which voters respond to the economy remains unclear (Erikson 2009), and we do not attempt to settle it here. Rather, we model the evolution of economic effects during presidential election campaigns.[1]

6.1.1 Measuring the Economy over the Campaign Timeline

When election modelers predict elections based on economic conditions, they choose a measure of the economy and also a time frame over which the economic variable is measured.[2] A typical choice is to measure the economy as either GDP growth or income growth over one or more quarters of the election year (e.g., Abramowitz 2008; Campbell 2008b; for an early example, see Tufte 1978). A more sophisticated method is to incorporate growth throughout all four years of the presidential term, discounting the earlier periods by giving greater weight to the growth in quarters closer to the election (Hibbs 1987; Wlezien and Erikson 1996; Bartels and Zaller 2001). The argument is that voters are more attentive to late growth than to growth early in the term.

There can be two quite opposite rationales for why voters would weight recent quarters more heavily. One is that voters are myopic, irrationally ignoring or forgetting the economy as it stood in the early quarters of an administration (Bartels 2008). The other is that rational voters are attentive to recent quarters' growth as a signal of the presidential party's competence in the months ahead (Rogoff and Sibert 1988). Hibbs (1987) has shown that the best predictions come when weighting each quarter of an administration .80 of the weight of the quarter that follows.

We follow the Hibbs approach here. Our objective economic indicator is the cumulative weighted quarterly real per capita disposable income growth, calibrated as an annual rate. To be absolutely clear, the measure is calculated by, first, taking the price-adjusted quarterly income growth; second, calculating the percentage change for each quarter of the election cycle; and third, reducing the weight of growth in each quarter by .8 going back in time, that is, increasing the weight for each quarter by 1.25 going forward.[3] In further discussions of this variable, we shorten its label to (capitalized) Income Growth. The measure is a general one, as it nets out taxes and inflation, adjusts for the size of the population, and takes into account the full election cycle but discounts early quarters.[4]

In addition to the objective economy as measured by Income Growth, we also consider the subjective economy—the state of the economy as voters see it—and its relation to the vote. Since the early 1950s, the University of Michigan's Survey of Consumers has measured the US public's beliefs about the economy. The central measure is the well-known Index of Consumer Sentiment, a composite based on answers to several survey questions about the US economy. The questions involve beliefs about the performance of the recent economy and about the economic future. The Survey of Consumers also ascertains peoples' beliefs about their own family's finances and, generically, whether the respondents have heard mainly good or bad news about the economy.

A partial list of these questions is presented in table 6.1. On each item, respondents can answer negatively (bad, worse, or unfavorable, depending on the question), positively (good, better, or favorable), or neutral. Negative scores are subtracted from the positive scores and averaged for the national sample. National scores on each item are recalibrated to a 200-point scale, where zero would mean all responses are negative and 200 would mean all positive (good, better, or favorable). Aggregate scores are generally in the midrange close to the neutral value of 100.

Our objective economic measure, cumulative income growth, is measured quarterly, for all fifteen administrations leading up to our fifteen elections. The subjective assessments were measured quarterly (with some

Table 6.1 Variables in the University of Michigan Survey of Consumers

Variable	Type	Time horizon	Question wording
Business expectations— good/bad	Business conditions	Year ahead	Now turning to business conditions in the country as a whole—do you think that during the next 12 months we'll have good times financially, or bad times or what?
Business expectations— better/worse	Business conditions	Year ahead	How about a year from now. Do you expect that in the country as a whole business conditions will be better, or worse than they are at present, or just about the same?
Personal expectations	Personal	Year ahead	Now looking ahead—do you think that a year from now you (and your family living there) will be better off financially, or worse off, or just about the same as now?
Business retrospections	Business conditions	Year ago	Would you say that at the present time business conditions are better or worse than they were a year ago?
Personal retrospections	Personal	Year ago	Would you say that you (and your family living there) are better off or worse off financially than you were a year ago?
Economic news heard	Business conditions	—	During the past few months, have you heard of any favorable or unfavorable changes in business conditions?

Note: All questions were asked quarterly (irregularly in early years) since 1954 (except News Heard, which was first asked in 1956). Starting in 1978, results are reported monthly.

gaps) since the early 1950s and monthly since 1978. When we use these subjective measures, our time series must start with the 1956 rather than the 1952 election.

Actually, we present *daily* estimates of these objective and subjective economic measures. We do so through interpolation. For quarterly measures, we first assign the quarterly scores to the middle dates of the four midquarter months. For monthly measures, we first assign the monthly scores to the middle dates of the twelve months. In each instance we then fill in the blanks by interpolation, connecting the dots if you will, much as we did to obtain daily readings of trial-heat polls.[5] As an example, consider the 31 days between July 16 and August 16, dates designated for the monthly readings. For these 31 days, we impute a weighted average of the July 16 and August 16 scores. The weights are determined by the date's relative closeness to the two monthly observations. For example, on July 23 the economic score for July 16 receives three times the weight of the score for August 16.[6]

6.1.2 The Objective Economy, Vote Intentions, and the Vote

To begin, we track the relationship between Income Growth and the vote. Over the fifteen elections, the correlation between income growth through the fifteenth quarter of the election cycle (the third quarter of the election year) and the presidential party vote is +.76. Thus, statistically, cumulative income growth just prior to the election by itself explains 54 percent of the variance in the vote.[7] We ask: How does this relationship build over the campaign?

Figure 6.1 displays the correlation between Income Growth and the vote over the campaign, in two ways. For each of 200 days of the cam-

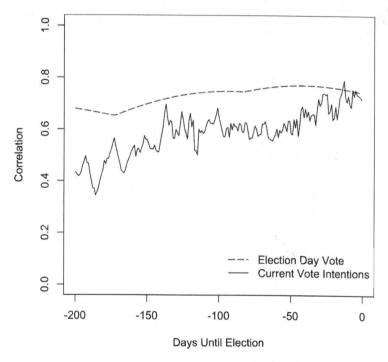

Figure 6.1. Correlations between cumulative per capita income growth and current vote intentions and the Election Day Vote. For fifteen elections, 1952–2008. Daily readings over the campaign timeline. Current vote intentions and the final vote are measured as the presidential party's share of the two-party vote. Cumulative per capita income growth is weighted so that each quarter counts 1.25 times the previous quarter. Daily data are interpolated.

paign, it shows the correlations of imputed Income Growth with both the concurrent daily (imputed) vote intentions and the Election Day vote. The first reading is at ED-200 in mid-April, when for some elections the likely major-party candidates' names are just becoming apparent. Cumulative income growth at the time already correlates at +.68 with the Election Day vote. Since this correlation evolves only a few extra digits over the campaign timeline, we can say that one can predict the actual vote from the current income growth about as well in April as in November. By April, the economic cake is largely baked.[8]

Perhaps even more interesting from figure 6.1 is the movement of the correlation between Income Growth and vote intentions for the same date in the timeline. This correlation shows a steep climb from April to November. The correlation at ED-200 is +.44, suggesting that voters in April are beginning to take the current economy into account when asked how they would vote. However, a +.44 correlation with 15 cases explains only 13 percent of the vote division variance (adjusted $R^2 = 0.13$) and is not statistically significant at even the .10 level.

Figure 6.2 illustrates the evolution of the economy's effect by presenting the scatterplots for the fifteen electoral observations. The first panel shows

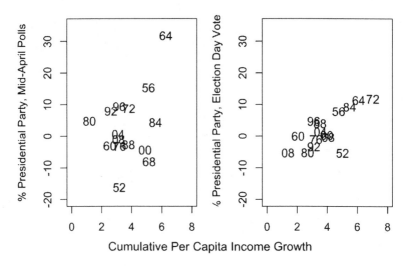

Figure 6.2. Scatterplots showing the relationship between (interpolated) cumulative per capita income growth (income growth) and vote intentions (mid-April, ED-200) and the Election Day Vote. The ED-200 vote intentions are measured for the week (as per chaps. 4 and 5) and are not interpolations. The right panel shows a profoundly negative economy for 1960, which may surprise. The explanation is that fig. 6.2 interpolates to include a decline in income growth in quarter 4 of 1960.

the very slim relationship between interpolated Income Growth 200 days before the election (ED-200) and vote intentions at the same date. Note that the correlation is positive *only* because of the 1964 outlier.[9] The second panel shows the final relationship between Income Growth (interpolated) at Election Day and the actual vote. By this measure, the economy changes slightly over the campaign, whereas voter choices gravitate toward Income Growth as a measure of economic performance.

Figures 6.1 and 6.2 provide the first direct evidence of an important fact: when asked as early as the spring of the election year how they will vote for president, survey respondents rarely factor in the economy when they cast their provisional "vote." It is the campaign itself that somehow primes and/or enlightens voters about the economy, which they increasingly incorporate into their vote decisions. Note that the climb of the correlation of Income Growth with the trial-heat poll results is gradual, not subject to interruptions. It is not, for instance, a function of the conventions steering people to give special thought to the economy. The data show no jump-shift in the correlation from before to after the conventions.

We conclude, then, that the objective economy increases its effect on electoral preferences as the campaign progresses and that the growth is gradual. But what about the subjective economy in people's heads? We turn to that next.

6.1.3 The Subjective Economy, Vote Intentions, and the Vote

Earlier, in table 6.1, we introduced measures of the subjective economy based on the University of Michigan's Survey of Consumers. Measuring the economy from subjective perceptions of poll respondents has the advantage of measuring actual beliefs about the economy, even if these beliefs depart from reality. A second advantage is that it presents no need to concoct a complex measure with different weights for different times in the presidential term. What people say at the moment should be sufficient without needing to also consider perceptions in previous months.

Which aspect of consumer sentiment is electorally the most important? Survey analyses suggest that voters respond more to national economic conditions than the state of their own pocketbook (Fiorina 1981; Kiewiet 1983).[10] For four separate questions from the Survey of Consumers, figure 6.3 displays the correlations with daily vote intentions, based on interpolated data over the final 200 days of the fourteen campaigns of 1956–2008. The correlations generally show the expected increase over time. Notably, all the correlations begin surprisingly close to zero at day

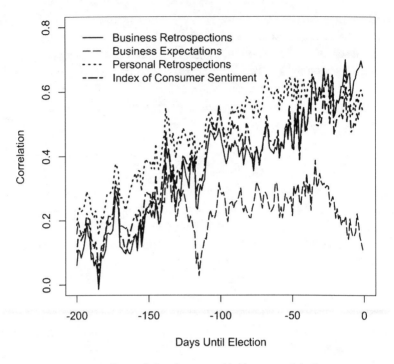

Figure 6.3. Daily correlations between subjective economic indicators
and vote intentions, 1956–2008.

ED-200 before they begin their rise. This suggests that in April of the election year, voters' beliefs about the economy have not yet affected their vote intentions.

We also see that, although three of the four sets of correlations continually rise over the timeline, those involving expectations of future business conditions (better/worse) stand out as different. That set of correlations first rises like the others, but then plateaus and finally plunges toward zero. Although this may seem mysterious or counterintuitive, there is an obvious explanation. Expectations are partially "politicized" by *future* government control following the election (Ladner and Wlezien 2007). Consider two scenarios for positive expectations at election time. When the economy is prospering and voters increasingly expect the incumbent party to be re-elected, expectations remain positive. When the economy is in crisis, however, voters increasingly expect the incumbent party to be defeated, leading to an expectation of better economic times ahead. Because both incumbent victories and defeats can produce positive expectations, there should be little correlation between economic expectations and vote intentions leading up to Election Day.

By a slight margin, the best predictor of the presidential party vote in late polls and on Election Day is Business Retrospections, or the relative perception of the quality of the economy over the prior year. There also is a second attribute of Business Retrospections that works in its favor as the choice for a subjective economic measure. It is the subjective measure that, by far, correlates the most strongly with the objective economy as measured by Income Growth.[11] For the final 200-day period, the correlation reaches its nadir of +.65 on day ED-174, rises to a peak of +.84 on day ED-80, and settles at +.73 on Election Day.[12]

Business Retrospections, therefore, is our chosen measure of the subjective economy going forward, under the new and simpler label of Economic Perceptions.[13] Figure 6.4 displays its correlation with vote intentions

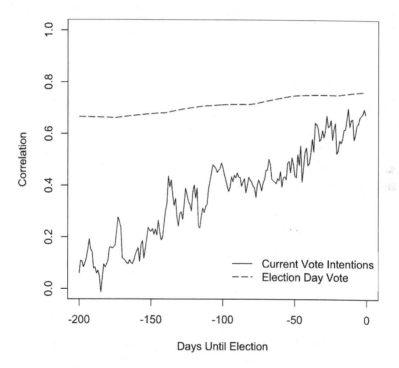

Figure 6.4. Correlations between the perceived economy and current vote intentions and the Election Day vote. For fourteen elections, 1956–2008. Daily readings over the campaign timeline. Current vote intentions and the final vote are measured as the presidential party's share of the two-party vote. Daily data are interpolated.

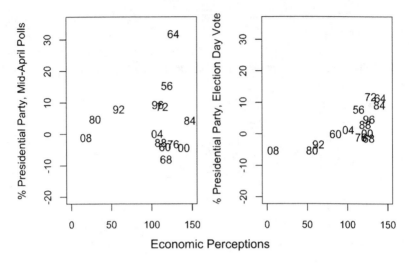

Figure 6.5. Scatterplots showing the relationship between the (interpolated) perceived economy (business retrospections) and vote intentions (mid-April, ED-200) and the Election Day vote.

over time, along with its correlation with the final Election Day vote. Note (again) the remarkable fact that 200 days before the election, perceptions of the economy over the past year (from the Survey of Consumer polls) are unrelated to vote intentions as measured in trial heat (from political polls). The perceived economy in the spring does, however, correlate with the actual vote. Thus, if we wish to forecast the November vote in the spring, we could pay attention to voter perceptions of the economy, even though voters have not yet factored it into their calculations. As we will see, the subsequent campaign brings the economy to the attention of the voters.

The scatterplots in figure 6.5 show the progression of the connection between the subjective economy and vote intentions. Much as for Income Growth, the first panel shows the absence of a relationship at ED-200, mid-April, while the second shows a strong relationship on Election Day. One can see three cases in particular drive the change. In 1980, 1992, and 2008, the economy was perceived to be in poor shape, yet the presidential party candidate was performing reasonably well in the early polls. On Election Day, they were all decisively defeated. The campaigns in these years somehow brought home the economy to the voters. In each instance the voters knew the economy was bad in April, but somehow they did not yet decide that the challenger party's candidate should lead the nation. As when measuring economic conditions using the objective measure, the trajectory of voter learning was gradual, without any clear evidence of an added boost from the conventions. Again, the data indicate that economic learning takes place throughout the campaign year, as the campaign delivers the message about the economy to the voters.

6.1.4 Introducing Presidential Approval

When voters react to economic conditions, the obvious mediating variable is the electorate's view of the current administration's performance. That is, one can readily imagine that the degree of prosperity affects the degree of presidential approval, which helps determine the vote. The evidence in support of this simple model is strong (Mueller 1970; MacKuen 1983; MacKuen, Erikson, and Stimson 1992). As we will see, when controlling for presidential approval, the economy makes no independent contribution. In other words, the effect of the economy on vote intentions is completely mediated by approval.

For the measure of presidential approval, we rely on Gallup's measure of presidential approval, which extends back to the 1940s. Gallup's question is, "Do you approve or disapprove of the way President _____ is handling his job as president?" We start with monthly averages of Gallup approval ratings and then assign the monthly score to the middle date of the month. For months without Gallup measures of approval, we interpolate. Then we interpolate the daily scores in the same manner as for the economic variables.

Figure 6.6 shows the daily correlations over the campaign timeline involving presidential approval and electoral preferences. The top curve presents the correlation of the daily approval level with the Election Day vote. The bottom curve represents the correlation between approval and vote intentions at the moment. At every time point, presidential approval predicts the eventual vote slightly better than it does the vote intentions recorded in the polls at the time.

Importantly, presidential approval by itself predicts both vote intentions and the final vote better than any of the economic indicators we have considered. We model the Election Day vote as a function of the trial-heat polls and presidential approval in the same equation for each of the 200 final days of the campaign timeline. Figure 6.7 summarizes the results. Here we see that, as estimated by the size of its regression coefficients, presidential approval is the superior predictor, though decreasingly so, until midsummer. Then, over the final 100 days of the campaign, trial-heat polls dominate, and increasingly so leading up to Election Day. This comparison

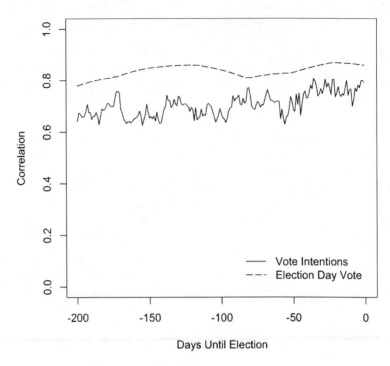

Figure 6.6. Correlations between presidential approval and vote intentions and the Election Day Vote, 1952–2008. Daily readings over the campaign timeline.

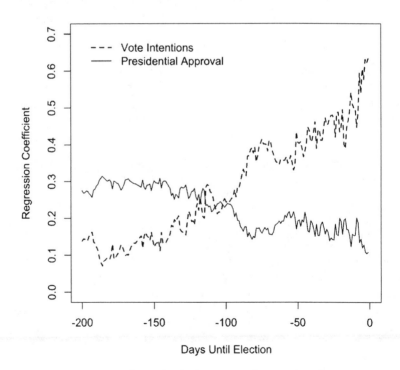

Figure 6.7. Predicting the Election Day vote from vote intentions in trial-heat polls and presidential approval over the campaign timeline, 1952–2008. Observations are regression coefficients.

of coefficients somewhat understates the predictive strength of presidential approval, as the date when trial-heat polls become the more statistically significant predictor turns out to be exactly three months before Election Day, that is, between ED-92 and ED-93.[14]

6.1.5 The Economy, Presidential Approval, and the Vote

The next step is to model the vote intentions and the final vote both as a function of presidential approval and our measure of the economy in the same equation. As we will see, approval dominates these equations in the sense that the predictive contribution of the economy drops once the approval level is taken into account.

Table 6.2 presents regression equations predicting the presidential party vote intentions and the Election Day vote itself from presidential approval and the current economic indicator for the four key time points of the campaign used in chapters 4 and 5: ED-200 in April, before the first convention, after the second convention, and during the final week. The findings for cumulative income growth are shown in the top half. Findings

Table 6.2 Predicting vote intentions at various time points and the vote from economic variables and presidential approval

	Trial-heat polls				Election results
	April (ED-200)	Before first convention	After second convention	Final week	
Objective economic model					
Cum. per capita	−1.27	6.31	7.98	9.24	6.91
income growth	(9.19)	(7.72)	(5.54)	(3.15)	(1.82)
Presidential	0.56	0.42	0.34	0.29	0.28
approval	(0.23)	(0.21)	(0.14)	(0.08)	(0.05)
Adjusted R^2	.32	.40	.53	.73	.86
Subjective economic model					
Perceived	−0.22	−0.00	−0.01	0.04	0.04
economy	(0.08)	(0.10)	(0.07)	(0.06)	(0.04)
Presidential	1.00	0.42	0.42	0.33	0.27
approval	(0.25)	(0.30)	(0.22)	(0.17)	(0.11)
Adjusted R^2	.51	.18	.33	.52	.68

Note: Before-convention polls are for the week ending the Monday before the first convention. After-convention polls are for the week beginning the second Tuesday after the second convention. $N = 15$ for Income Growth; $N = 14$ for Business Retrospections (1952 excluded). The dependent variable is the presidential party's percentage of the intended two-party vote. Intercept terms are not shown. Standard errors are in parentheses.

for economic perceptions are shown in the bottom half. We start with the top half.

With approval statistically held constant, cumulative income growth does not show a statistically significant effect on the vote until the final days of the campaign and then on Election Day itself. For all but this period, cumulative income growth seemingly affects the vote by affecting collective attitudes toward the president rather than independently. The evidence is even clearer for Economic Perceptions, shown in the bottom half of the table. With approval held constant, perceptions show no independent effect, even at the very end. Clearly, beliefs about the economy translate into attitudes toward the sitting president, which affect vote choice.

Table 6.2 does show one coefficient for Economic Perceptions that is statistically significant—for 200 days before the election—but in the "wrong," negative direction. There is a technical (and a bit complicated) interpretation for this anomaly: (1) economic perceptions affect how people evaluate the president, and (2) voters have not yet linked the economy to the presidential race. In April, that portion of presidential approval that does not involve the economy affects vote intentions, but the part due to the economy is not yet electorally activated. Thus, when controlling for approval, the equation discounts the economic part.[15]

Ultimately, then, economic conditions affect peoples' vote intentions by influencing their attitudes toward the sitting president. This may seem an obvious result, and it does comport with the existing literature (Erikson, MacKuen, and Stimson 2002). The evidence also is strong.

6.1.6 Forecasting the Vote from Economic Conditions

Although the economy is not a very good predictor of trial-heat polls early in the campaign, the early economy does help to account for the evolution of electoral preferences and predict the final vote. From early in the campaign to Election Day, the public increasingly factors in the economic news when forming its collective vote intention. The electorate responds over the campaign not only to fresh economic shocks but also to the state of the economy from early in the campaign. This makes the economy an early leading indicator of the vote to come, long before it actually influences voters.

To assess the predictability of the Election Day vote from presidential approval and the economy at different stages of the campaign, table 6.3 shows equations modeling the final vote at our four key time points of the campaign. In the top set of equations, the independent variables are

Table 6.3 Predicting the Election Day vote from presidential approval and economic variables measured at various time points

	Presidential vote predicted from variables at			
	April (ED-200)	Before first convention	After second convention	Final week
Objective economic model				
Cum. per capita income growth	6.11 (3.58)	5.88 (2.73)	7.83 (2.37)	6.91 (1.82)
Presidential approval	0.26 (0.09)	0.27 (0.07)	0.24 (0.06)	0.28 (0.05)
Adjusted R^2	.63	.76	.81	.86
Subjective economic model				
Perceived economy	0.03 (0.05)	0.03 (0.03)	0.04 (0.04)	0.04 (0.04)
Presidential approval	0.27 (0.14)	0.29 (0.10)	0.26 (0.11)	0.27 (0.11)
Adjusted R^2	.50	.66	.63	.68

Note: Before first convention = 7 days before the start of the first convention; after second convention = 17 days after the end of the second convention; final week = final day of the campaign. $N = 15$ for Income Growth; $N = 14$ for Business Retrospections (1952 excluded). The dependent variable is the presidential party's percentage of the two-party vote. Intercept terms are not shown. Standard errors are in parentheses.

presidential approval and cumulative per capita income growth (Income Growth). In the bottom set, they are approval and Economic Perceptions.

The first thing to notice is that, for any time point, even 200 days before the election, either set of two variables can account for at least half of the variance in the final vote. Collectively, they predict the future vote on Election Day better than they predict current vote intentions from the contemporary trial-heat polls. (Cf. tables 6.2 and 6.3.) Second, as expected, the predictive power of the economy and presidential approval increases the closer the measurement is to Election Day. In other words, tangible developments during the last 200 days of the campaign influence the final vote. Third, the equations themselves stay fairly constant over the timeline—changing little from April to election eve. The inference is that as the campaign progresses, other factors beyond those captured by the measured independent variables are decreasing in importance. We know this because the unexplained variance in the vote declines over the campaign timeline, whereas the equation remains essentially the same.

Table 6.3 also illustrates differences in the predictive power of our objective and subjective economic measures. Even with the control for approval, early readings of Income Growth predict the vote, with Income Growth's

Table 6.4 Predicting the Election Day vote from trial-heat polls and economic variables measured at various time points

	Presidential vote predicted from variables at			
	April (ED-200)	Before first convention	After second convention	Final week
Objective economic model				
Cum. per capita	9.11	7.69	6.75	1.31
income growth	(3.20)	(2.89)	(2.39)	(1.69)
Trial-heat polls	0.27	0.28	0.42	0.73
	(0.09)	(0.10)	(0.10)	(0.08)
Adjusted R^2	.61	.69	.83	.93
Subjective economic model				
Perceived economy	0.10	0.07	0.06	0.03
	(0.02)	(0.02)	(0.02)	(0.01)
Trial-heat polls	0.26	0.32	0.46	0.65
	(0.08)	(0.10)	(0.09)	(0.07)
Adjusted R^2	.74	.70	.84	.95

Note: Before-convention polls are for the week ending the Monday before the first convention. After-convention polls are for the week beginning the second Tuesday after the second convention. $N = 15$ for Income Growth; $N = 14$ for Business Retrospections (1952 excluded). The dependent variable is the presidential party's percentage of the two-party vote. Intercept terms are not shown. Standard errors are in parentheses.

contribution becoming statistically significant after the conventions. With the control for approval, however, the Economic Perceptions measure has virtually no independent predictive power. Again, this is evidence that subjective economic perceptions affect the election almost exclusively through assessments of presidential performance.

Although the equations involving the economy and approval are informative, even more important and interesting are the forecasting models, presented in table 6.4, involving the economy and the trial-heat polls. Does knowing the state of economic conditions increase the forecasting ability beyond the information from the trial-heat polls? The answer is yes, especially if the question is asked early in the campaign. From chapter 5, we saw that trial-heat polls in April predict no more than 40 percent of the variance in the November vote. Adding knowledge of the April economy increases the explained variance to over 60 percent. For later periods in the campaign timeline, trial-heat polls and the economy together predict increasingly well, with the polls increasingly being the major factor. This makes sense because vote intentions increasingly absorb the effect of the economy—the later in the campaign, the more the economy is factored into voter decisions.

What might seem odd is that when trial-heat polls are the control, the stronger economic indicator for predicting the election is now the subjective rather than the objective economy. In fact, in April, Economic Perceptions comprise a stronger predictor than even the trial-heat polls. The measure contains a large amount of electorally relevant information that is not yet reflected in the trial heats. As the campaign progresses, the trial-heat polls absorb the economic effects.

6.1.7 The Economic Model—A Summary

We have seen that the electorate gradually incorporates information about the economy as the campaign timeline progresses. Subjective economic evaluations are an important source of the current president's degree of popularity, but early in the campaign they do not have much impact on vote intentions in the upcoming presidential race. The campaign brings the economy to the voters' attention and in a gradual way.

We defer until later further discussion and speculation regarding the mechanisms by which the economy affects individual voter decisions during the campaign. It is important to keep in mind that, as important as the economy is, it leaves much of the variance in vote outcomes unexplained. To fill the gaps, we turn to some familiar political variables.

6.2 The "Political" Model: Party Identification and Issue Proximity

If our starting point for predicting elections was our microlevel knowledge about what motivates individual voters, our immediate interest would not center on the economy. Rather, our first consideration would be that voters are influenced by their party identifications. Second, we would consider the role of policy issues and ideology in campaigns, because voters tend to select the presidential candidate who is closest to their own views. For explaining individual voting decisions, party identification plus some measure of issue proximity perform well.

Here, we are trying to explain a macrophenomenon—*aggregate* vote intentions over the campaign. Until the late 1980s, political researchers tended to treat aggregate-level party identification as something closer to a constant rather than a variable, since voters tend to stick to the same party over time. More recent research and the march of history have shown that aggregate partisanship does change more than previously thought (Mac-Kuen, Erikson, and Stimson 1989). Still, when attempting to explain presidential election results, analysts have been slow to turn to the relative mix of Republican and Democratic *identifiers* as having much to do with the partisans division in terms of how people *vote* for president.[16]

Similarly, until recently, political scientists largely ignored the role of the electorate's ideology when accounting for presidential election outcomes. It had been thought that aggregate policy preferences or aggregate ideological leanings do not move much over time, and therefore are of no consequence for electoral change. The view changed with the introduction of James Stimson's (1991, 1999) measure of policy "mood"—the electorate's liberalism-conservatism extracted from the responses to multiple survey questions about public policy. Stimson's "mood" research finds that the electorate's policy preferences do meaningfully shift from election to election.

It also is common knowledge that major-party presidential candidates vary in their ideological orientations from election to election. These shifts also can be measured, for example, from the content of party platforms. As a result, we can test the possibility that changes in the relative closeness of the major-party candidates to the voters can affect macrolevel vote choice of the type examined here.

In the book *The Macro Polity*, Erikson, MacKuen, and Stimson (2002) show that presidential election outcomes can in fact largely be accounted for using aggregate partisanship and ideological proximity. They measured aggregate party identification as their index of "macropartisanship," the share of partisans who identified themselves as Democrats in Gallup polls in October of election year. They measured proximity with two variables: (1) Stimson's public "mood," generated from trends in opinion from surveys across the years, while adjusting for question content; and (2) Budge et al.'s (2001) measure of platform ideology. The electorate's relative issue proximity to the Democratic and Republican candidates is reflected by the degree to which the electorate is in a liberal mood relative to party platforms. Although mood and platforms are measured on different scales, they can be included as separate variables. Liberal mood predicts Democratic voting, while liberal platforms predict Republican voting. (Liberal platforms imply Republican moderation.)

Unlike *The Macro Polity*, in this volume we estimate the political model to predict vote intentions over the campaign timeline, and not just the Election Day verdict. We also add three elections and their data points. Whereas *The Macro Polity* covered only the twelve elections between 1952 and 1996, we extend the analysis through 2008, for a total of fifteen elections. Our primary interest is in how partisanship and issue proximity predict vote intentions throughout the election year.

6.2.1 Measurement

Our measurement of the three variables in the political model is similar to the original but differs in some details.

Macropartisanship

We measure macropartisanship from all available poll readings of party identification that are from surveys that (1) employ personal interviews (in-person or telephone) and (2) sample the universe of adults (rather than registered voters).[17] Then we calculate the percentage Democrat among Democratic and Republican identifiers.[18] For each reading of macropartisanship, we set its timing as the survey's midpoint. Where readings from more than one survey house are available for a day, we take the average, or poll of polls. Then, to ensure reliability, we take an average of available daily readings going back 28 days. As a final step, we interpolate the results where necessary, to obtain a daily reading of recent partisanship.

Even measured as a moving average over a 28-day bandwidth, macropartisanship is far from constant over the campaign timeline. In terms of autocorrelation, macropartisanship reveals *less* stability than presidential approval. Approval on Election Day correlates at a whopping +.94 with approval in April, at ED-200, whereas macropartisanship correlates at +.77 with itself over the same period.[19]

Policy Mood

Policy mood is James Stimson's composite estimate of the US electorate's relative liberalism or conservatism, derived from the degree of change in responses to multiple survey questions. While the measure is reported in several flavors, we use Stimson's annual (one-dimensional) measure 1952–2008. From the annual scores, we create a quasi-moving average using (where possible) readings from the previous year or the following year. We center the scale on July 1 as if it were the date of the year's mood score. For all other dates, mood is prorated to incorporate some of the following year's mood (post–July 1) or the previous year's mood (pre–July 1). For instance, a date 1/6 of the way through the year will be scored with a weighted average of 1/3 the previous year's mood and 2/3 the current year's mood.

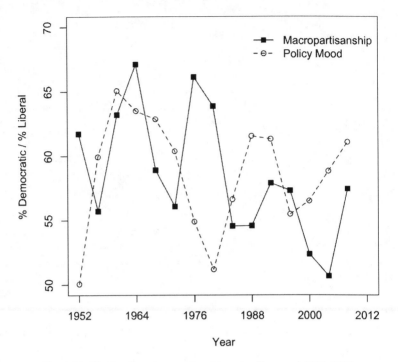

Figure 6.8. Election Day macropartisanship and policy mood, 1952–2008.
Measurement of the variables is described in the text.

There are alternative ways of encapsulating mood, of course. We could use the variant of Stimson's mood calculation that includes a second dimension. We could skip the prorating, leaving mood as a constant for each year. The choice of variant makes very little difference to the results.[20]

The Election Day values of macropartisanship and mood are shown in figure 6.8. Note that Democratic strength and liberal policy mood are statistically unrelated. In fact they show a slightly negative correlation ($-.07$). Over time and in the aggregate, how Democratic or Republican the public is at any point has been unrelated to its liberal or conservative tenor.

Platform Ideology

We measure party/candidate positions during the campaign by borrowing the updated scores of US parties from the Comparative Manifesto Project (Budge, Robertson, and Hearl 1987; Budge et al. 2001). The manifesto team coded party platforms for ideological content and scored them on a scale representing percentage liberal minus percentage conservative. We do not argue that voters actually read platforms or that the Budge et al. measure of platform ideology is a perfect indicator of parties' positions, of course. Rather, our expectation is that the platform scores provide a proxy for the positions of the presidential candidates as seen by the voters.

Figure 6.9 graphs the ideological trends of the Republican and Democratic platforms for the presidential election years 1952–2008, as calculated by Budge et al. (2001).[21] While the Democrats always score more liberal than the Republicans, as we would expect, both parties have moved in the conservative direction over time. As the Democrats become increasingly conservative—moving toward the position of the median voter—they increasingly gain an advantage in terms of ideological proximity to voters, which offsets their slipping edge in terms of partisanship. Similarly, the Republican Party gains by moderating with a move toward the center. As either party approaches the ideological middle from its ideological flank, it gains votes. It follows that the more liberal (conservative) either party becomes, the more the Republicans (Democrats) gain.[22] Accordingly, in the

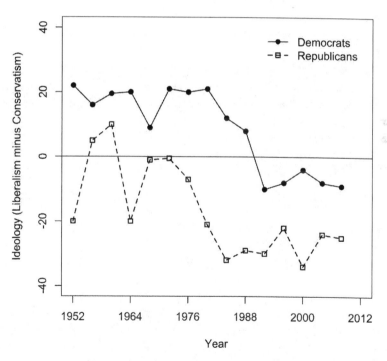

Figure 6.9. Party platform ideology by year, 1952–2008.
Measurement is described in the text.

analysis that follows, we summarize party platforms as the mean of the Republican and Democratic platform scores.[23]

Platform ideology is only weakly related to the public's policy mood but correlates positively with macropartisanship. The correlation is strongest—at a hefty +.79—just before the conventions and declines to an average of +.52 after the conventions. One can make the case that parties are more likely to take stands that appeal to their ideological base when they have the comfort of being relatively strong in terms of party identification.

6.2.2 Testing the Political Model over the Campaign

To test the political model, the equations of table 6.5 predict Democratic vote intentions, over our four key time points of the campaign, plus the final vote. For comparison, the table also shows predictions of presidential approval over the timeline from the same political variables. Approval is measured as approval minus 50 percent for Democratic presidents and 50 percent minus approval for Republican presidents.

First, consider vote intentions over the campaign timeline. The coefficients for our three political variables are fairly stable over the timeline. Following expectations, Democratic voting is a positive function of Democratic partisanship, liberal mood, and a negative function of platform liberalism. In April and (particularly) just before the conventions, however, these variables' contributions appear very wobbly, with large standard errors. The model does not predict vote intentions very well before the conventions, apparently because other, seemingly short-term, factors sway voters at that point in time.

After the conventions, predictive power increases markedly—with each variable becoming statistically significant. The model predicts a large share of the variance, similar to that of the approval plus economy model of the previous section. By Election Day, the political model accounts for 70 percent of the variance. Though considerable, the statistical performance is below the level reported earlier in *The Macro Polity*, based on fewer elections and a slightly different operationalization of mood and macropartisanship.[24]

The regressions predicting presidential approval from the political variables are interesting as well. In a result that should surprise, until the final reading of the four time periods, the three political variables predict a greater share of the variance in approval than of vote shares in the trial heats. One interpretation is as follows. Even early in presidential election years, people respond according to political considerations when asked

Table 6.5   Predicting vote intentions and presidential approval at various time points and the vote from macropartisanship, policy mood, and platform ideology

	Dependent variable = trial-heat polls % Democratic				
	April (ED-200)	Before first convention	After second convention	Final week	Election results
Macropartisanship	2.14	1.41	1.49	1.49	1.04
	(0.70)	(0.84)	(0.33)	(0.28)	(0.21)
Policy mood	0.90	1.25	0.82	0.68	0.63
	(0.54)	(0.59)	(0.34)	(0.27)	(0.21)
Platform ideology	−0.78	−0.60	−0.51	−0.54	−0.43
	(0.30)	(0.37)	(0.15)	(0.11)	(0.09)
Adjusted R^2	.37	.17	.60	.71	.70

	Dependent variable = % approve the president minus 50% × party (1 = D, −1 = R)			
	April (ED-200)	Before first convention	After second convention	Final week
Macropartisanship	1.96	2.20	1.53	1.54
	(0.50)	(0.62)	(0.42)	(0.52)
Policy mood	1.61	1.66	1.49	1.44
	(0.39)	(0.43)	(0.40)	(0.50)
Platform ideology	−1.25	−1.46	−1.08	−1.07
	(0.22)	(0.27)	(0.19)	(0.21)
Adjusted R^2	.75	.72	.73	.66

Note: Vote intentions are measured as the Democratic percentage of the two-party vote. As a dependent variable, presidential approval is measured as the deviation from 50 percent if a Democratic president and as 50 percent minus approval if a Republican president. Before-convention polls are for the week ending the Monday before the first convention. After-convention polls are for the week beginning the second Tuesday after the second convention. Intercept terms are not shown. N = 15. Independent variables are described in the text. Standard errors are in parentheses.

how they rate the president. These considerations are less salient, however, when people are asked early in the election year for which of the two candidates they would vote for president. This result is parallel to the impact of economic information. Early in the election year, the economy influences presidential approval but has not yet had much impact on choices for the next president in trial-heat polls.

Unlike with the economic model, the political model shows marked evidence of voter learning from the conventions. This makes perfect sense because, although the economy's performance is not contingent on the conventions, the party platforms and issue alignments should be. From before to after the conventions, the coefficients predicting vote intentions from political variables do not change markedly, but they are accompanied by a sharp increase in the explained variance. This result, clear in table 6.5, suggests that a function of the conventions is to make partisanship and policy more salient to voters when deciding on a presidential candidate. More superficial sources of the vote become less important following the conventions.

6.2.3 Predicting the Election Day Vote

Except for macropartisanship, the independent variables of the political model do not change much over the campaign. Thus one might expect that the three variables would predict the Election Day vote about as well when measured for any date on the campaign timeline. However, this is not so. As a forecasting equation, the model performs well only after the conventions. Table 6.6 shows the details.

Figure 6.10 helps explain this pattern. It shows the correlations between the three indicators, measured at different times, and the Election Day vote. The platform ideology correlation is a constant since there is but one measurement for each election year. The mood correlation is virtually a constant, given mood's construction. Only the macropartisanship correlation shows variation, and it increases markedly in the wake of the conventions—naturally it is at its maximum when measured at the time of the vote. Evolving macropartisanship is what mostly accounts for differences in the predictability of the vote during the election year.

The results also highlight the importance of model specification. Figure 6.10 shows that none of the independent variables correlates strongly

Table 6.6 Predicting the Election Day vote from macropartisanship, policy mood, and platform ideology, measured at different times in the campaign

	April (ED-200)	Before first convention	After second convention	Final week
Macropartisanship	0.54	0.90	0.88	1.04
	(0.42)	(0.44)	(0.10)	(0.21)
Policy mood	0.51	0.59	0.64	0.63
	(0.32)	(0.31)	(0.23)	(0.21)
Platform ideology	−0.37	−0.52	−0.39	−0.43
	(0.18)	(0.19)	(0.23)	(0.09)
Adjusted R^2	.17	.30	.59	.70

Note: Before-convention polls are for the week ending the Monday before the first convention. After-convention polls are for the week beginning the second Tuesday after the second convention. $N = 15$. The dependent variable is the Democratic percentage of the two-party vote. Intercept terms are not shown. Independent variables are described in the text. Standard errors are in parentheses.

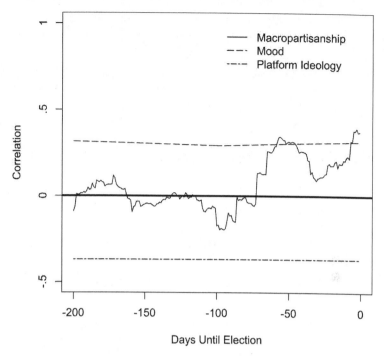

Figure 6.10. Correlations between macropartisanship, policy mood, platform ideology, and the Election Day vote, 1952–2008. Macropartisanship is measured as percentage Democratic, while mood and platform ideology are measured in terms of liberalism. See the text for details. The vote is measured as the Democratic percentage of the two-party vote.

with the vote. It takes the three of them together to provide a useful model of presidential elections. In table 6.6, the effects of mood and platform ideology on the Election Day vote are clearest when measured late in the campaign. Their effects are revealed by controlling for party identification measured near Election Day. Among other purposes, the macropartisanship control helps to minimize the extraneous variance from other variables at the end of the campaign.[25]

6.3 Comparing Models

We can explain over half the variance in the vote from the economy alone, and more (70 percent) when presidential approval is added. Voters choose based on how the economy is performing plus how much they like the president. A second, political model accounts for the same amount (70 percent) of the variance in the vote from macropartisanship and ideological proximity. Voters chose based on their partisanship plus which candidate they are closest to on issues. One could imagine that if we put the two models together, we could predict virtually all the variance in the vote. It is not that simple, however, because the two sets of predictions overlap. To some extent the economy influences the three political variables of the political model. That is, when the economy is relatively good, the president's party gains adherents, the presidential party's ideology (e.g., liberal for Democratic presidents) gains supporters, and the party risks a platform favorable to its ideological base. For details, see Erikson, MacKuen, and Stimson (2002).

To explore further, we take the predictions from both models and then model the vote as a function of the "economic" and "political" predictions. First, we model daily presidential party vote intentions from cumulative income growth alone, take the predictions from this model, and convert them to predictions of the vote for the Democratic candidate. Second, we model daily vote intentions from our three political variables and produce predictions of the Democratic vote. Then, we include the two sets of predictions in the same equation of the vote. (Alternatively, we can rerun the political model but adding as an independent variable the prediction from the economic model.) For this exercise we do not use presidential approval because it is a good absorber of both the economy and the political variables.[26] We ignore Economic Perceptions as the economic indicator because we would lose one precious case for which it is not measured—the 1952 election.

Figure 6.11 documents the degree to which the Election Day vote can be predicted both from cumulative income growth and the political model. Not only do the two models predict the vote fairly well, but they also predict each other. The two predictions correlate throughout the campaign timeline—starting at a very modest .27 in April (ED-200) and progressing to .62 by the final week. The data suggest that the growth of this correlation over the campaign may be due to the economy affecting partisanship: the correlation of macropartisanship and the economy-based prediction stands at a negligible .01 in April but rises to .47 on Election Day.

Table 6.7 shows the results when the predictions from the two models are combined in one equation. For each of our key time points, the equations in the top panel predict vote intentions. The two model predictions combined result in increasing variance explained over time, with coefficients that change little. Although the three-variable model makes the greater statistical contribution, the economic prediction (based solely on

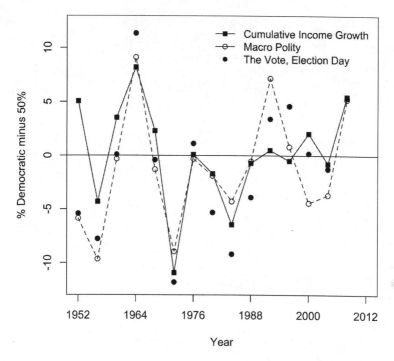

Figure 6.11. Predicting the Election Day vote from two regression models of the vote. the economic model is based on cumulative income growth alone. The political model is based on macropartisanship, policy mood, and platform ideology.

income growth) holds its own. Of special interest is that the coefficients all are under 1.00, dampened predictably because of the correlation between the two predictors.

The top panel of table 6.7 may be the clearest evidence yet that the fundamentals increasingly govern the election as the campaign progresses. Early in the campaign, the combined economic and political variables leave the vast bulk of the variance in vote intentions unexplained. Early trial-heat polls reflect mainly short-term factors that are statistically independent from the fundamentals that govern the late polls and the final outcomes.

The bottom panel of table 6.7 shows the results when the predictions of the two models are pitted against each other in the same equation to predict the Election Day vote. Here, the economic model is the clear leader until the end of the campaign. By the final week, the political model has crystallized.[27] The progress of the campaign first brings home economic conditions to voters, which continues through Election Day. As the cam-

Table 6.7 Predicting vote intentions at various time points and the Election Day vote from the predictions of the economic and the political models

	Dependent variable = trial-heat polls				Dependent variable = election result
Model	April (ED-200)	Before first convention	After second convention	Final week	
Economic	0.63	0.52	0.63	0.51	0.51
	(0.39)	(0.38)	(0.33)	(0.19)	(0.16)
Political (3 variables)	0.89	0.73	0.75	0.71	0.71
	(0.25)	(0.39)	(0.34)	(0.18)	(0.18)
Adjusted R^2	.56	.39	.71	.80	.84
Correlation between economic and political variables	.27	.52	.47	.62	.63

	Dependent variable = Election Day vote			
	April (ED-200)	Before first convention	After second convention	Final week
Economic	0.71	0.62	0.60	0.39
	(0.22)	(0.19)	(0.11)	(0.15)
Political (3 variables)	0.21	0.32	0.39	0.57
	(0.14)	(0.19)	(0.09)	(0.13)
Adjusted R^2	.51	.64	.87	.81
Correlation between economic and political variables	.27	.52	.47	.62

Note: Before the first convention = 7 days before the start of the first convention; after the second convention = 17 days after the end of the second convention; final week = final day of the campaign. For the election results equation, the independent variables are measured for the final day of the campaign. $N = 15$. The dependent variable is the Democratic percentage of the two-party vote. Intercept terms are not shown. The economic model prediction is the presidential party's vote or vote intention prediction based on cumulative income growth and converted to a prediction of the Democratic vote. The political model prediction is based on macropartisanship, mood, and platform liberalism. All model predictions are for the day of the date in question, not the final vote. Standard errors are in parentheses.

paign progresses, economic considerations become absorbed by the political variables, particularly macropartisanship. Late campaign shifts in partisan identity then help predict the vote.

6.4 Conclusions

This chapter has made some progress in tracing the causes of change in voter intentions over the campaign timeline. Early in the election year, aggregate vote intentions are difficult to predict from the economy or the political variables reflected in the *Macro Polity* model. However, economic conditions early in the election year have a strong bearing on how people will vote on Election Day. By some mechanism, the campaign season gets voters to focus increasingly on the economy when choosing a presidential candidate. The same is true of political variables, although they come into focus for voters later, toward the end of the campaign. The campaign does not merely prime and enlighten, however—the fundamentals themselves evolve over the timeline. Indeed, this may help explain the differences we observe in the effects of the economic and political fundamentals

Although our analysis reveals a lot, it would be a mistake to think that our various vote equations succeed in capturing the vote equilibria at different times in the campaign. Consider our "prediction of predictions," the composite prediction of the two models in table 6.7. If these ultimate predictions truly capture the equilibrium of vote intentions, we would expect the observed vote division to follow the predictions over the timeline. For most elections, this is the case. Vote intentions either hover around the predictions or at least catch up to the predictions by Election Day. For four of the fifteen campaigns, however, the predictions systematically overpredict (1968, 2008) or underpredict (1964, 1996) the Democratic vote for all 200 readings of the campaign. This is a humbling reminder that we do not know all the fundamentals. Other factors beyond those we model— some of them intangible—are present throughout presidential election campaigns. This makes election forecasting a hazardous enterprise.

SEVEN

Campaign Dynamics and the Individual Voter

Previous chapters have dealt solely with the aggregate vote intentions over the campaign timeline. In this chapter we zoom in to focus our microscope on individual voters. We seek to assess the degree of vote choice stability at the individual level that underlies the net aggregate stability we have observed. How stable are the individual vote decisions that comprise the aggregate change? And who changes? Further, we seek to understand further how the structure of vote choice varies across the campaign timeline. Are different voter motivations activated at different times? Can we gain further understanding of the changes in the cross-sectional aggregate vote intentions over the campaign timeline?

The wealth of available survey data from sources such as the Inter-University Consortium for Political and Social Research (ICPSR) and from the Roper Center's iPoll presents a host of opportunities. We focus first on the American National Election Studies (ANES) presidential polls available from ICPSR. For each presidential year included in our analysis, the ANES interviews a panel of respondents both before and after the election. We assess the differences between the pre-election vote intentions of the panelists and their post-election reports of their vote decisions between 1952 and 2008.

The ANES pre-election interviews are concentrated in September and October of the election years. We also model individual voters from Gallup polls at or near the four key time points of the campaign identified in earlier chapters—April (around ED-200), just before the first national party convention, a week after the second convention, and the final poll of the election season. This represents voters in 4 surveys × 15 years for 60 polls altogether. From these cross-sectional surveys we are interested particularly in the growth of voters' reliance on their personal fundamentals. That is, we want to see whether and how the structuring effects of partisanship and demographic variables change over the campaign timeline.

7.1 Vote Shifts by Individual Voters

Observers often write about voters as if they are very malleable and subject to persuasion from the latest political information that reaches their attention. Yet, we have seen that in the aggregate (and when adjusting for sampling error), vote intentions from one period to the next in a campaign tend to be very stable. Suggestive though this is, the aggregate stability does not necessarily require a similar degree of stability among individual voters. For instance, suppose that over one week the Democratic candidate gains 2 percent of the vote (which would be a major change in the scale of things). This net change of two percentage points could come in many combinations of Republican voters shifting to the Democratic candidate and some Democratic voters shifting to the Republican candidate. It could result from a mere 2 percent of the voters switching from Republican to Democratic, with none doing the reverse. But the change could also be due to 10 percent switching from Democrat to Republican, offset partially by 8 percent moving against the grain from Democrat to Republican. The key is that the Democratic gain would need to be two percentage points higher than the Republican gain in order to add up to a net 2 percent.[1]

Given the strong stability of the aggregate vote division, one might expect that the most plausible scenario at the individual level would be a degree of turnover at the individual level near the low end of what is theoretically possible rather than a continual churning of voter preferences back and forth. As we will see, this expectation is largely correct.

7.1.1 Vote Shifts across Elections

A useful starting point for understanding the stability of voter preferences within campaigns is to ask, How stable are presidential vote choices between elections—that is, from one election to the next? Over the fifteen elections of our study, the average absolute change in the two-party vote for president (compared to four years before) is 6.7 percentage points. In electoral politics, this is a large amount of change. So how much do individual voters change from one election to the next to account for the observed electoral change?

The American National Election Studies (ANES) has conducted four

Table 7.1 Reported vote choice by major party voters in successive elections in four ANES panels

		1956		
		Democrat (Stevenson)	Republican (Eisenhower)	Total
1960	Democrat (Kennedy)	33	17	50
	Republican (Nixon)	6	44	50
	Total	39	61	100
		1972		
		Democrat (McGovern)	Republican (Nixon)	Total
1976	Democrat (Carter)	26	21	47
	Republican (Ford)	3	49	53
	Total	29	70	100
		1992		
		Democrat (Clinton)	Republican (Bush)	Total
1996	Democrat (Clinton)	50	8	58
	Republican (Dole)	3	39	42
	Total	53	47	100
		2000		
		Democrat (Gore)	Republican (Bush)	Total
2004	Democrat (Kerry)	41	4	45
	Republican (Bush)	7	49	54
	Total	48	52	100

Source: Data are from ANES panel data sets.
Note: Panel percentages do not necessarily represent those of the voting population. Data are weighted where appropriate.

separate panel studies in which the same voters were asked their presidential vote following two successive elections. These panels were over the periods 1956–60, 1973–76, 1992–96, and 2000–2004. Table 7.1 displays the 2 × 2 turnover tables for these elections—that is, the Republican or Democratic vote choices in the second election as a function of the Republican or Democratic choices in the first election.[2]

In the two most recent panels (1992–96 and 2000–2004), the net vote division changed little between the first and second elections, either in the official verdict or among the ANES panel. Table 7.1 shows that this was also true at the individual level. From the first Clinton victory to the next (1992 and 1996) and from the first G. W. Bush victory to the next (2000 and 2004), about nine out of ten voters who cast a major-party ballot both times voted for the same party's presidential candidate both times.

The two earlier panels each involved a larger electoral shift—from Nixon's landslide in 1972 to Carter's victory over Ford in 1976 and from Eisenhower's landslide victory to Democrat John Kennedy's close victory over Nixon in 1960. Even in these examples of major electoral change, only a few individuals (among those voting both times) created the difference. The 1972-to-1976 change among the ANES panelists who voted in both elections was an 18-point Democratic gain, split as 21 percent Nixon voters switching to Carter and a mere 3 percent switching against the grain from McGovern to Ford. The 1956-to-1960 shift was 11 points, with 17 percent shifting from Eisenhower to Kennedy. A larger than usual 6 percent shifted against the grain from Stevenson to Nixon, perhaps in a rejection of Kennedy's Catholicism.

These examples ignore other aspects of electoral change. Consider, for example, panelists who report voting for a major-party candidate in one election but abstaining or casting a minor party ballot in the other. In the ANES panels, these respondents typically split their major-party votes about the same as those who cast major-party vote both times. Another source of change is by voters not in the panel: the differential between voters exiting the electorate in the first election and newly eligible voters in the second election. For example, one informed estimate of Obama's victory in 2008 is that it could not have been done without the newly enfranchised young voters and the turnout surge among African Americans (Ansolabehere and Stewart 2009). In other words, among established voters who had voted in 2004, Obama probably would have lost. For all the turmoil and change between 2004 and 2008, including the collapse of both Bush's popularity and the economy, very few voters changed their mind. The election of 2008 was decided by an infusion of fresh voters into the electorate.

The small amount of turnover of individual votes from one election to the next provides something of a ceiling regarding how much change we might find during a campaign. As we have seen, in the absence of a strong net swing of the vote, typically only about 10 percent will shift the party of their presidential vote. Common sense suggests even less shifting occurs within the context of a single presidential campaign. That is what we find.

7.1.2 Campaign Vote Intentions and Election Day Votes

In each presidential year since 1952, the American National Election Studies conducts both a pre- and a post-election interview for its panel of respondents. This makes it possible to assess the degree of turnover of choice from the campaign season to Election Day. Because pre-election interviews are scattered across the final 60 or so of the campaign, the date of the initial interview provides further leverage. We can assess not only the degree to which the respondent's vote departs from the respondent's stance during the campaign, but also the degree to which the change is a function of the date in the campaign timeline.[3]

We measure consistency of pre-election intention and post-election choice as follows. The cases consist of respondents who both expressed a major-party preference with their pre-election vote intention and then post-election said that they had cast a major-party vote on Election Day. Among these respondents, we simply counted the percentage of the cases in which their Election Day vote was for the same party/candidate as their pre-election vote intention expressed in September or October.

The answer is that 95 percent of ANES respondents maintained their pre-election position on Election Day. For caution, we should consider that it is possible that the panel interview format encourages an artificial degree of consistency. First, the respondents who continue in a panel might be somewhat more politically attentive—and therefore perhaps more consistent in their choice—than citizens at large. Second, and perhaps more importantly, the initial pre-election interview—in the home, lasting more than an hour—could sensitize people to defend their initial choice or see it as socially desirable to be consistent. Evidence exists, for instance, that ANES panel participation encourages respondents to vote at a higher than average rate (Burden 2003). Still, even if slightly inflated, the finding that 1 in 20 voters who express an intention in the pre-election ANES survey changes his or her choice in November is a sign that the vast majority of voters maintain the same vote choice over the campaign.

This result affirms that the small changes in the aggregate vote described in earlier chapters are a function of rare shifts by individual voters rather than a continual churning of preferences in response to campaign events. We next investigate the types of voters who shift their candidate preference from the campaign to Election Day.

Figure 7.1 documents the degree of shifting, campaign to Election Day, by year and by the voter's initial (campaign season) candidate preference.

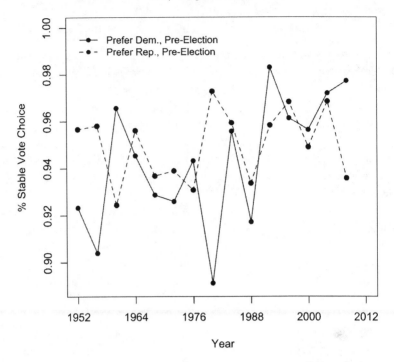

Figure 7.1. Stability of vote choice from pre-election interview to Election Day, by initial party choice, 1952–2008. *Source*: American National Election Studies.

A slight trend can be discerned in that choices have been getting more stable over the years. Thus, we have a paradox of sorts. Voters have become increasingly exposed to presidential campaigns on broadcast and cable television, and now the Internet. Yet at the same time the effectiveness of campaigns in terms of changing voters' minds seems to be on the decline. Although this finding is surprising given the greater access to campaign information, it is precisely what we would expect given increasing party structuring of the vote (Bartels 2000).

Also of interest is the possibility of asymmetry in the degree to which initial Democrats and initial Republicans (in terms of vote intention) stick with their choice on Election Day. Whether Republican conversions or Democratic conversions are more prominent varies from year to year with no clear pattern. The strongest party difference is for 1980, when ANES respondents (like the nation) shifted from Carter to Reagan as the campaign progressed. The 2008 election provides a lesser instance, where the conversion rates favored Obama over McCain.

7.1.3 The Timeline of Vote-Shifting

Further inference about vote choice stability can be learned from the degree to which rates of conversion vary with the time differential from the campaign interview to Election Day. Figure 7.2 presents the ANES respondents' stability as a function of date of initial interview, pooling over all fifteen election years. The dashed line represents the observed daily observations. The daily observations show an erratic pattern if observed "day to day." The curved line in the graph represents the smoothed (lowess) curve designed to provide the best fit to the data.[4] The curve shows a steady increase in pre-election to vote stability, rising from .93 at 60 days before the election to .97 on Election Day.

Thus, as one would expect, stability rises as Election Day approaches. The shift is within a very small range, however. When summed over many

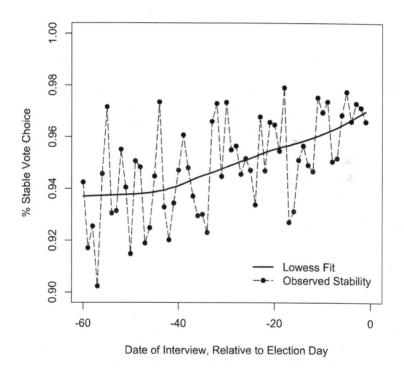

Date of Interview, Relative to Election Day

Figure 7.2. Stability of vote choice from pre-election interview to Election Day, by date of interview, pooling observations, 1952–2008.
Source: American National Election Studies.

elections, the data suggest that about 3 of 100 who hold a preference the day before the election switch on Election Day. The switch over the final 60 days is little over twice as high, about 7 in 100. A reasonable—simple but rough—inference is that from date ED-60 to date ED-1, only about 4 percent of voters switch their preferences. In other words, the data suggest about as much individual-level volatility over the fall campaign as on Election Day itself.[5]

7.1.4 Information and Vote Stability

If one looks to predict vote switching, the level of political knowledge is at the forefront. As is well known, informed voters tend to be resistant to campaign information because their knowledge leads them to form firm choices. It is the least informed who are more likely to switch during campaigns or from one election to the next (Converse 1962; Zaller 1992, 2004).

Figure 7.4 examines stability of vote choice as a function of both time and information level, keeping in mind that ANES data are available only for, at most, the last 60 days of the campaign. Information or knowledge level is measured using John Zaller's composite index of political knowledge for the years 1952–2004.[6] The index is standardized so that the mean is approximately 0 and the standard deviation is about 1.0 for each election year. Here, we divide the index into five categories from highest to lowest as follows, in terms of standard deviation units (SDUs):

5 = +1.5 SDUs or higher;
4 = +.5 to 1.5 SDUs;
3 = −0.5 to +0.5 SDUs;
2 = −1.5 to −0.5 SDUs;
1 = less than −1.5 SDUs.

For the most part, figure 7.3 shows precisely the pattern expected by theory. When measured shortly before the election, all information groups show high degrees of stability in the .97 range and are statistically indistinguishable. The most-informed groups, however, are consistent across the 60 days of the timeline, while the least-informed show a fairly steep lowess curve. Election Day votes by informed respondents are consistent with their choice 60 days earlier about 94 percent of the time. Informed voters have largely made up their mind before the fall campaign. But the

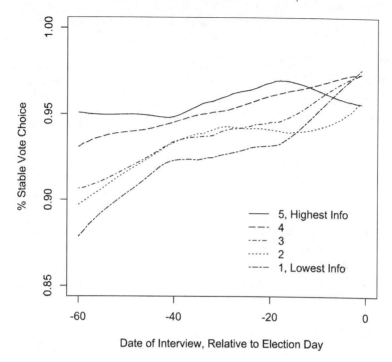

Figure 7.3. Stability of vote choice from pre-election interview to Election Day, by date of pre-election interview and Zaller's index of political knowledge level (lowess fit), pooling ANES observations, 1952–2004.

least-informed fifth of the electorate's votes are consistent with their early campaign preference only about 86 percent of the time.

Overall, the impact of information is sufficiently strong to compete with the date of interview as a predictor of the stability of the vote choice. When both linear date and the original Zaller information index are included as independent variables in a probit equation predicting stability or change, they are both highly significant ($z = 4.9$ and 4.7, respectively). A voter's level of information is about as good a predictor of whether she will defect from her pre-election choice as the date of the pre-election choice.[7]

The results of figure 7.3 serve to reinforce the conventional view that electoral change during the campaign arises mainly from the least sophisticated voters. Informed voters, particularly those in the two top information categories, were quite resistant to change. Among the relatively informed, only about 1 in 20 voters switches their candidate preference over the fall campaign. The less informed, while still highly stable, provided the most change. About 1 in 7 among the least informed voters will switch from the campaign interview to the vote. It is these voters to whom campaign appeals are most successful.

7.2 The Crystallization of Preferences over the Campaign

To a growing number of scholars, the primary function of election campaigns is to deliver the so-called fundamentals of the election. Recall from chapter 1 that we distinguish between external and internal fundamentals. Chapter 6 explored the external fundamentals—the political and economic conditions that structure candidate appraisals. These external fundamentals not only include the degree of economic prosperity but other aspects of performance and policy as well, including the policies and policy proposals of presidents and presidential candidates. Here we consider the "internal" fundamentals, whereby the campaign activates the political predispositions of voters.

As discussed in chapter 1, the literature on campaign effects finds considerable support for the campaign as causing voters to consult their predispositions. Finkel (1993) shows that much of the change in presidential vote preference during the 1980 campaign was due to "activation" of political predispositions, with voters bringing their candidate preferences in line with their *preexisting* partisan and racial identities. Relatedly, Gelman and King's (1993) detailed analysis of 1988 polls shows that the effects of various demographic variables on presidential vote preferences increased over the campaign. A similar study of Pew polls during the 2008 campaign found partisan and demographic factors increasing in importance (Erikson, Panagopoulos, and Wlezien 2010). In short, campaigns appear to "enlighten" voters about which candidate(s) best represent their interests.

Over the campaign, voter preferences crystallize. Early on, when most voters are not thinking of presidential politics, these preferences are largely unformed. When interviewed, some will say they are undecided. They also may express weak preferences. Some may flirt with candidates from the other party. As the campaign unfolds, voters increasingly support the candidate of their preferred party. Voters' preferences also increasingly reflect their true "interests" as reflected in their demographic characteristics. This crystallization may be driven by a number of mechanisms. Following Gelman and King (1993), campaigns help voters to learn which candidate best represent their interests, and typically this leads them back to their partisan attachments. Finkel (1993) argues that voters learn that the candidates really are partisans, representing Democratic and Republican positions and interests. Alvarez (1997) maintains that uncertainty about candidates' issue positions is reduced as campaigns unfold. Yet another possibility is that campaigns lead voters to perceive events using their partisan screens, leading them to see candidates of their party more favorably (and increase the intensity of their support) as the campaign unfolds. The latter mechanism is implied by *The American Voter* (Campbell et al. 1960) and subsequent work showing the effects of partisan preference on perceptions (e.g., Wlezien, Franklin, and Twiggs 1997; Bartels 2002; Shapiro and Bloch-Elkon 2008).

The general expectation from all of this research is that voters' preferences gravitate toward their partisan predispositions over the course of presidential election campaigns. We want to see whether this is true and, if so, the extent to which it is true. To do so, we analyze individual voters for each of the fifteen elections during 1952–2008, using Gallup poll data sets at our four key points of the campaign: mid-April, pre-conventions, post-conventions, and as close as possible to Election Day. Thus, our data consist of 60 polls, in a 15-year by 4-time-point grid.

7.2.1 Campaign Evolution and the Importance of Party Identification

We begin by testing for a growing role of party identification over the fifteen campaign cycles. Our first step is to estimate 60 probit equations to obtain 60 coefficients predicting the vote from party identification. For each equation, party identification is measured as a three-category variable: $-1 =$ Republican, $0 =$ Independent, and $+1 =$ Democrat. The coefficients represent the effect of party identification on the latent unmeasured variable that determines vote choice, which we can think of as a relative preference to vote Democratic versus Republican. Respondents above the unobserved threshold vote Democratic. Those below vote Republican.

Because the dependent variable is latent (unobserved) in a probit equation, its units must be normed by some convention for the coefficients to make sense. The convention is that the standard deviation (and variance) of the unexplained portion of the latent dependent variable equals 1.0. This seemingly arcane bit of statistical convention is important to keep in mind. With our data, the unobserved variance represents the portion of the unobserved dependent variable—the relative utility for the Democratic candidate's election versus that for the election of the Republican—that cannot be accounted for by our observed variable, respondent party identification. In chapter 3 we hypothesized that the variance in the relative utility for the candidates will grow during the campaign. Thus, the test for an intensified partisan effect is whether the variance induced by party identification grows faster than the variance from other sources.

Table 7.2 shows that the impact of party identification on individual vote choice does grow over the campaign timeline. The first row contains the probit coefficients from four time-specific equations that predict respondents' vote intentions from their party identification plus year dummy variables to control for year effects. The second row contains, for each time point, the average of the fifteen party identification coefficients predicting the vote from partisanship for the specific Gallup data set. In each case the coefficients grow over the campaign. As the campaign evolves, party identification increasingly accounts for voters' relative attraction to the Democratic and Republican candidates compared to other factors that motivate their vote.

Figure 7.4 shows this pattern directly, as partisan "defections" over the campaign timeline. For both Democrats and Republicans, it depicts the percentage (among major-party voters) of party identifiers who defect by voting for the other major party. The numbers are averages for the 15 elections, weighting each election equally. In April of the election year, about 20 percent of Democrats and 15 percent of Republicans tell Gallup that they intend to defect. By the final poll, each defection rate drops by about a fourth from its level in April.

The substantive implication is that over the presidential election campaign, voters increasingly consult their partisan dispositions in deciding their candidate likes and dislikes—and ultimately their presidential vote. Candidates who find themselves as underdogs in the early polling can count on many of their disaffected partisans to eventually drift back "home." Meanwhile, candidates enjoying a large lead will find their supporters becoming even more enthusiastic. For polling trends over the cam-

Table 7.2 Probit coefficients predicting the vote from party identification at four campaign time points

Coefficient source	April	Before conventions	After conventions	Final poll
Pooled equation, 15 years	0.98	1.07	1.22	1.28
Mean of 15 yearly equations	1.11	1.16	1.18	1.30

Source: Data are from Gallup polls via iPoll.
Note: The pooled equations include year dummies. From the year-specific equations, the coefficient grew in 31 of the 45 time point-to-time point comparisons. The coefficient shrunk in 12 instances, with 2 virtual ties. Each data set contains over 1,000 voting respondents.

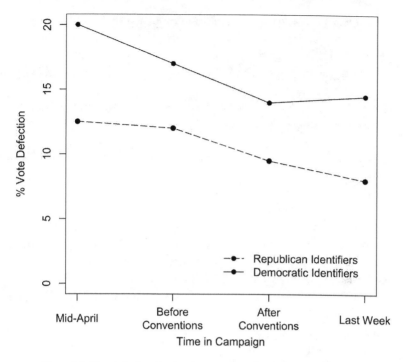

Figure 7.4. Vote defections by time in campaign. Times are mid-April, before conventions, after conventions, and final days of campaign. Observations are averaged from Gallup polls over fifteen elections, 1952–2008.

paign, the former dynamic is of greater consequence than the latter since it can cause the greater electoral movement. That is, there are more disaffected partisans to return home on the losing side than the winning side. This dynamic may not be sufficient to upend the outcome of the impending election, but it can help to make the contest closer, as we spelled out in chapter 3.

7.2.2 Campaign Evolution and the Importance of Demographic Fundamentals

The previous discussion is subject to an obvious critique: if party identification becomes more closely tied to the vote over the campaign, can we be sure of the causal story? The results in table 7.2 could be symptomatic of voters increasing their excitement over their favored candidate to the point of claiming to identify with their favorite candidate's party, as was raised earlier. It is plausible that this reverse causation is a part of the causal story, but probably not the main part. Consider that party identification is stable, like vote choice, over time. Also consider from chapter 6 that, across elections, the national division of party identification is not strongly correlated with the presidential vote.

As a useful crosscheck, however, we can look at other indicators of the "internal" fundamentals by exploring the impact of demographic factors over the campaign. Even collectively, demographic variables like race, economic status, and religion do not have the predictive power of party identification. They have, however, the advantage of being virtually constant for individual voters over the campaign, and thus immune to reverse causality. It cannot be argued that voters' group characteristics are affected by the respondent's vote choice. If we find that demographics increasingly predict the vote over time, the causal interpretation can only be that voters increasingly incorporate interests emanating from their group characteristics into their voting decisions as the campaign progresses.

We perform a demographic analysis in very similar fashion to Gelman and King's (1993) presentation. Whereas Gelman and King examined a considerable density of polls from 1988, we examine four polls in each of fifteen elections. All of the sixty data sets in our repertoire contain a sufficient number of demographic variables to construct a probit equation predicting vote choice from demographics. The demographic variables included in the data sets vary across years and to some extent within years as well. To test specifically for a growth in the importance of demographics over the campaign, we include for each year those relevant demographics that are in all four of our Gallup surveys for that year. This means that for some years the demographic equations will predict better than for other years as an artifact of the number of relevant variables included in the equations. Our interest, however, is not in how much of the variance we can explain by demographics, but rather in how much the explanation grows from April to November in the specific elections.

Instead of showing the details of these sixty equations, we summarize each equation's predictive power by use of the McKelvey and Zavoina (1975) "pseudo R-squared." The pseudo R-squared is the estimate of the degree to which the demographic equation statistically explains the unobserved, latent, "propensity to vote Democratic." This estimate is accomplished by first computing the variance of the predictions from the equation. Since the unexplained variance is set to 1.00, the proportion of the variance explained is the equation-induced variance divided by 1 plus the equation-induced variance.

Table 7.3 Pseudo-R^2 from probit equations predicting the two-party vote from demographic variables at four campaign time points in 15 presidential elections, 1952–2008

Election year	Mid-April	Before first convention	After second convention	Final pre-election poll	Variables
1952	.09	.08	.06	.11	I
1956	.06	.04	.09	.07	A,U
1960	.20	.20	.20	.25	A,C,U
1964	.17	.19	.27	.32	A,C,I,R
1968	.22	.22	.23	.25	A,C,I,R.U
1972	.16	.21	.33	.25	A,C,I,R,S,U
1976	.10	.15	.14	.18	A,C,I,R,U
1980	.13	.19	.19	.23	A,C,I.R,S,U
1984	.38	.30	.25	.34	A,C,H,I,R,S,U
1988	.06	.19	.17	.19	A,H,
1992	.10	.18	.18	.17	A,H,I
1996	.23	.24	.28	.25	A,H,I,S
2000	.21	.21	.21	.27	A,H,I,S
2004	.20	.26	.19	.28	A,H,I,S
2008	.29	.37	.52	.43	A,H,I,S,T
Mean	.17	.20	.22	.24	

Source: Gallup Polls via iPoll.
Note: The probit equations predict the two-party vote from a series of dummy variables. All equations include dummies for southern white, not high school graduate, college graduate, woman, and African American. Other dummies are included for some but not other years: A = age (under 30, over 64); C = city; H = Hispanic; I = income (top third, bottom third); R = religion (Catholic, Jewish, other); S = single; T = church attendance; U = union household. Dummies are included for the year only if they are present in all four surveys.

Table 7.3 presents the findings. Not too much should be made of the differences across years, since the variables differ considerably from year to year, as discussed. The pattern of interest is the over-time trend within each campaign. The evidence is clear: in every election year, the explained variance increases. On average, the proportion of the explained variance from demographics increases by almost 25 percent from April to November.[8] If we keep in mind that the explained variance from a probit equation is affected by the unobserved sources of variance in the latent dependent variable, the growing importance of demographics over the campaign may actually be underestimated. This is because the variation in individual assessments of relative candidate attractiveness (utility) presumably grows over the campaign, which increases the unexplained variance.

The result is that voters' preferences are more predictable as the campaign goes on. Early in the campaign year, survey respondents indicate their candidate preference by what is in the news plus their political predispositions. As the campaign progresses, their political predispositions take on greater force. Among the specific variables, the growth in impact tends to be in variables strongly tied to partisanship. In particular, blacks, Hispanics, and Jews appear to become more Democratic over the campaign. So do women (relative to men) from about 1980, when the gender gap first came into serious play. On the other hand, the rich-versus-poor split does not expand much over the campaign.

It is instructive that in those instances in which a candidate's demographic characteristics affected the campaign dynamic, voters who shared the candidate's unique demographic feature respond positively from the outset of the campaign. In our Gallup poll data from 1960, Catholic John Kennedy's support from Catholics was as strong in April as in November. In 1976, Georgia's Jimmy Carter drew consistent support from southern whites from April to November. And already by April 2008, African Americans supported Barak Obama over John McCain to an overwhelming degree.[9]

7.3 Voters from the Campaign to Election Day

We have seen that the internal fundamentals of the election—those forces that guide voters toward their personal predispositions—increasingly influence vote choices as the campaign progresses. But what about the leap from the late campaign to Election Day? Section 7.1 showed that the candidate preferences (of ANES respondents) are very stable from early in the fall campaign to Election Day. But what compelled 5 percent of the respondents to switch their candidate preference between the early fall and Election Day? In the ANES panel, 16 percent expressed a pre-election intent to vote for a major-party candidate but then failed to do so. Why did they stay home? Still another 12 percent reported lacking a preference for a major-party vote choice pre-election but then proceeded to vote Democratic or Republican on Election Day. Why did they show up on Election Day?

Section 7.2 showed that vote choices become increasingly consistent with voters' demographics and partisanship as the campaign progresses. This we see as voters responding to the lure of their internal fundamentals. We might think that this process advances further on Election Day, as voters "come home" to their basic partisan and demographic dispositions. Our analysis of the ANES panel, however, suggests that this is not the case. Panelists who expressed a vote intention during the campaign did not continue to evolve toward their internal fundamentals on Election Day. If anything, the "dropouts," whose preferences are recorded during the campaign but who do not vote, appear more responsive to the internal fundamentals than the "walk-ins," who make a late decision to vote.

ANES measures party identifications during the pre-election interview. If the influence of partisanship surges between the campaign and Election Day, we would expect to see party identification correlate more with actual vote decisions than with pre-election preferences, but by any test, the answer is no. In fact, in 9 of the 15 elections, the party identification probit coefficient is greater for pre-election vote intentions than for vote choice.

An obvious interpretation is that the influence of partisanship decays somewhat from late in the campaign until Election Day. It also is possible, however, that the influence of party actually grows, but the evidence gets distorted as an artifact of its measurement during the pre-election interview. That is, the vote–partisanship correlation could be dampened because Election Day vote choice and party identification are measured at different times.

Demographics seemingly are unaffected by measurement timing, and the late-campaign growth of its influence on voters deserves a closer look. For each election, we estimated a probit equation predicting September-October pre-election vote intentions and another predicting the vote decision, from an identical large set of demographic dummy variables. In contrast with our earlier analysis of vote intentions at different points in the election year, the same variables are in all of the equations, except for a Hispanic dummy that starts in 1984 when ANES began to ask respondents about a possible Hispanic heritage. The samples for each year are limited to those panelists who expressed both a pre-election vote intention and a vote decision for a major-party candidate. The variables and their coefficients predicting the vote are shown in figure 7.5. The variables include age, region, income, race, religion, education, and gender.

Figure 7.6 displays the pseudo R-squareds for the equations predicting the vote and also those predicting vote intentions. Clearly, the explained variance from demographics grew over the half-century of analysis. The important fact on display here, however, is the comparison of the pseudo R-squareds in each year, which demonstrate the explanatory power of demographics predicting pre-election vote intentions and Election Day vote choices. Unlike what we find for vote intentions over the campaign year using Gallup polls at different stages of the timeline, here we find no systematic growth in the explanatory power of demographics going from pre-election vote intentions to vote choice in the ANES panels. Demographic variables predict the vote no better than they predict pre-election vote intentions. The results imply that the increasing crystallization of preferences based on demographic fundamentals does not persist to the very end of the cycle. Indeed, the structuring of preferences is essentially complete by

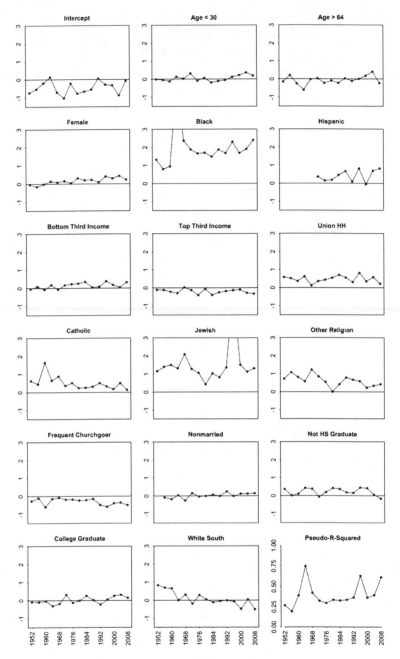

Figure 7.5. Effects of demographic variables on vote choice among ANES respondents, 1952–2008. Values are probit coefficients.

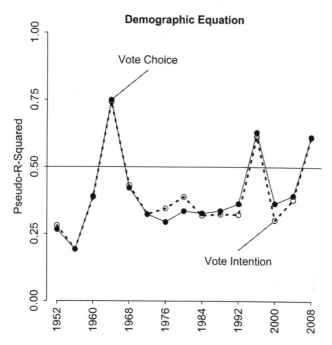

Figure 7.6. Comparison of pseudo R-squared predicting pre-election vote intentions and post-election vote choice. Equations are based on ANES respondents who offered a vote intention in the pre-election panel wave and reported a vote choice in the post-election panel wave.

the time of the formal campaign in the fall, when ANES respondents are first interviewed.[10]

7.4 "Variance Compression": A Further Look

Previous chapters have raised the puzzle of variance compression, whereby the variance of aggregate vote intentions—and then the vote division itself—shows a decrease over the campaign timeline. Why, we ask, does the partisan division of vote intentions tighten over the campaign timeline? And why is the Election Day verdict generally by a slimmer margin than found in even the final polls of the campaign? The analysis of individual-level data from the Gallup polls and the ANES pre- to post-election panels helps to explain. We consider first the compression of vote intentions from April to November by analyzing individual respondents in the sixty Gallup polls. Then we turn again to the fifteen ANES pre- to post-election panels to understand the compression of the vote variance on Election Day.

7.4.1 Variance Compression over the Campaign Timeline

Like trial-heat data generally (see chap. 2), the set of 60 Gallup surveys shows a decline in the aggregate yearly variance of vote intentions. An analysis of the individual data from these surveys reveals why this is so. Table 7.2 (in the first row) showed that, across the 15 elections, the impact of party identification (relative to the unobserved error term) increased over the four points in the timeline. This finding was based on equations that included dummy variables for year effects. These year effects are relevant because they incorporate the external fundamentals of the campaign. As vote intentions became more driven by internal partisanship, the impact of external campaign-specific forces also grew during two of the three comparison periods. The demonstration follows in table 7.4.

For reference, the first row of table 7.4 shows the cross-sectional variances of aggregate vote intentions (across years) among the Gallup respondents at the four points in the timeline. There are no surprises. Just as for our global poll of polls (chap. 2), the variance of the vote for our selected Gallup samples declines, especially over the convention season. The second row of table 7.4 shows the variances of year effects from probit equations predicting the vote from year dummy variables alone. Again, we see the variance decline over time, especially from before to after the conventions. Pre-convention, the election year can account for almost 10 percent of the variance in the propensity to vote Democratic. Post-convention, this proportion is cut virtually in half.

The third row of table 7.4 shows the variances of the dummy year variables, now controlling for individual-level party identification. The variances in row 3 represent year effects relative to within-year sources of individual variation other than partisanship. We can think of this year-specific variance as the electorate's *aggregate* relative utility for (liking of) the Democratic candidate versus the Republican candidate, independent of partisanship, relative to the within-year variance of individual voters' relative utility.

Recall that probit is normed so that the unexplained variance always equals a constant, 1.0. Yet we presume that, if we could measure it, this unobserved variance of individual-level relative utility (liking) for the candidates would increase over the campaign timeline due to learning. This follows from our discussion in chapter 3. It also follows from that discussion that we would expect the aggregate variance of net campaign effects to grow at about the same rate over the campaign as the growth of individual-level unobserved variance. With the unobserved variance calibrated in constant

Table 7.4 Variances of aggregate vote intentions over the campaign timeline

	Mid-April	Before first convention	After second convention	Final pre-election poll
Democratic vote	124.2	122.9	84.2	80.5
Year effects (probit)	0.097	0.087	0.055	0.054
Year effects, controlling for party ID (probit)	0.135	0.135	0.091	0.108
Party ID effects	0.675	0.806	1.090	1.115

Source: Data are from Gallup polls.

Note: All variances are calibrated as the percentage of the variance in the latent variable, the propensity to vote Democratic, as a proportion of the unexplained variance. Variances of year effects are normed to weigh each year equally, independent of year sample size in the Gallup meta-survey.

units in probit, the expectation is that the aggregate variance (year effects) would keep pace by also staying constant over the timeline.

We see this in two of the three periods of change. Relative to the individual-level variance, the external variance from year effects stays constant April to pre-conventions and even grows slightly post-conventions to election eve. *This is indirect evidence that external campaign effects on vote intentions actually increase under normal campaign circumstances even though the observed variance of the vote declines.*[11]

The convention season provides a strong exception. During that crucial interval, even with partisanship-adjusted year dummies, the year-effect variance declines. This implies that the variance of individual-level relative utility (affect) for the candidates grows at a faster rate from the conventions than does the net change in the net utility at the national level. In effect, individual voters' impressions of the candidates must be evolving at a faster rate than the net aggregate verdict. The information from the conventions induces considerable churning of the vote in both partisan directions, perhaps even more than the considerable amount of aggregate change would suggest.

Finally, we observe the fourth row of table 7.4. Here, we see that, with year effects controlled, party identification effects increase over the time line and in fact more than double in size. This is crucial. As we saw in the previous section, voting becomes more determined by partisanship as the campaign progresses. In fact, relative to the unobserved individual-level variation in net candidate attraction (the unobserved residual), partisanship's variance more than doubles from April to November.

Let us put the parts together to offer an interpretation of the declining variance of vote intentions over the campaign timeline. Setting aside convention effects for special treatment, we observe that before and after the conventions, the aggregate cross-election variance of net relative candidate attractiveness keeps pace with the within-election variance of relative candidate attraction. Meanwhile, the effect of partisanship grows at a much faster pace than relative candidate attraction. The growth of partisan effects (observed as keeping pace with residual individual level effects) means that over the campaign, partisan voters "come home" to their party after a possible initial attraction to the opposition. Put simply, the vote margin keeps getting closer because party identification pushes the vote toward the center (e.g., a normal vote based on the division of partisanship) faster than candidate evaluations push the vote away.[12]

7.4.2 Variance Compression, Campaign to Election Day

The pre- to post-election panels in the American National Election Studies offer a unique opportunity to test for the sources of the compression of the aggregate vote division between the fall campaign and the final vote. With ANES data, aggregate pre-election vote intentions and the aggregate vote division show variances of 10.05 and 6.86, respectively. The pre-election variance is similar to that reported for late surveys in chapter 2. The aggregate reported vote is similar to that for the actual vote. Thus, the panel shows the usual Election Day compression of the aggregate vote, with the variance dropping by about one-third. So let us use the leverage of panel data to decipher why the vote division (on Election Day or in post-election polls) tends to be closer than the division of vote intentions among respondents, pre-election.

The answer is not an increase in the role of partisanship between the pre-election poll and Election Day. The discussion in section 7.3 would seem to dispel that plausible idea. (Party identification measured during the campaign predicts vote decisions no better than it predicts vote intentions.) Instead, we can explain most (but not all) of the variance compression from the contrasting behavior among ANES respondents who are dropouts, who offer vote intentions but then do not vote, versus walk-ins, who initially abstain but do vote. The contrasting behavior of these two groups—the no-shows and the unexpected participants—is shown in figure 7.7.[13]

The vote intentions of the seemingly likely voters who do not follow through tend to favor the short-term forces of the day. They favor the eventual winner and then do not show up on Election Day. Their inclusion

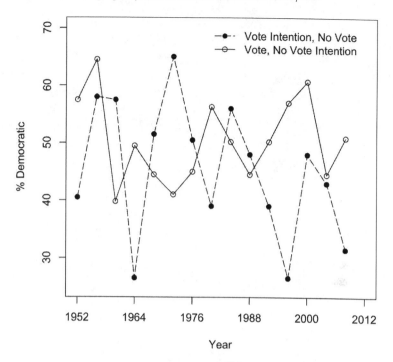

Figure 7.7. Campaign vote intentions by nonvoters and votes by those without
pre-election vote intentions, 1952–2008. Among ANES respondents
who were successfully interviewed post-election.

in polls serves to inflate the variance of aggregate vote intentions across
elections. The variance of vote intentions for dropouts is 13.69, compared
to 9.88 for eventual votes. This evidence suggests that when eventual dropouts are interviewed pre-election, their responses may be influenced more
by short-term forces than those of actual voters. Consider in contrast the
smaller sets of respondents who (a) either do not intend to vote or have
not decided on a major-party candidate but who (b) do vote for the Democrat or Republican on Election Day. These late-deciding walk-ins tend to
divide close to 50–50 on Election Day, thus deflating the variance of the aggregate vote. The variance of their aggregate vote decisions is a mere 5.68,
less than half that for the vote intentions of the dropouts.

We can see the net result by comparing the aggregate variance of vote
intentions and the Election Day vote for only those respondents who both
expressed a pre-election vote intention and voted. When measured for these
committed respondents, the aggregate variance is virtually constant from

pre-election to Election Day. For this set of voters, the variance of aggregate vote intentions is 9.88, whereas the variance of the aggregate Election Day vote is 8.84. Although there is still daylight between these two figures, we see that for committed voters, the variances of the pre-election vote intentions and the final vote are similar. Among this set of voters, there is little variance compression. The removal of dropouts and walk-ins reduces the variance gap between pre-election vote intentions and Election Day results by about two-thirds. The contrast between the no-shows and the unexpected voters is responsible for the bulk of the variance differential.

Even though pollsters take great pains to restrict their pre-election polls to likely voters, many slip through their screen. The good news (for pollsters) is that these erroneously counted nonvoters generally do not have preferences opposite the partisan tendency of the actual electorate. The bad news is that their support for winning candidates appears to be exaggerated. This results in some confounding of both the pollster's analysis and our attempt here to understand the electoral verdict.

7.5 Conclusions

Unlike preceding chapters, this chapter has focused on individual voters in national trial-heat surveys. We have learned that presidential vote choices are quite stable between elections and during presidential campaigns, and that the stability increases as the campaign unfolds. Over the campaign, vote choices are increasingly predictable from the internal fundamentals of partisanship and group identities. It is a general pattern, found over fifteen presidential election campaigns. As voters return to their partisan roots during a presidential campaign, the aggregate division of vote intentions gravitates toward its normal level. And on Election Day, the verdict closes further, as the short-term forces of the campaign attract many survey respondents who ultimately do not vote.

The analyses in this chapter take us a long way toward explaining a puzzle that has guided our work. Why does the cross-sectional variance of vote intentions decline over time? The pattern mostly reflects the internal fundamentals: voters with different partisan dispositions return to their partisan roots. As a result, as the campaign progresses over the timeline, voters behave less like Independents and more like committed partisans. With a verdict based increasingly on partisan dispositions, the aggregate result looks more like a partisan vote as Election Day approaches. The very late decline in variance reflects another factor, however. We see that many eventual nonvoters say they intend to vote in pre-election surveys, and these dropouts tend to vote for the winner. This expands the variance of pre-election aggregate vote intentions beyond what results on Election Day. Meanwhile, another group of voters decides to vote at the last minute. These walk-ins, as late deciders, tend to vote 50–50, thus serving to compress the variance of the aggregate Election Day vote.

EIGHT

The Evolution of Electoral Choice over the Campaign Timeline

In the previous chapters, we have examined the progression of voter preferences over the timeline of presidential elections. We have focused primarily on national trial-heat polls from April to November, for the last fifteen elections. In this chapter, we summarize what we have learned in general and consider what it tells us about the predictability of the different presidential elections we have examined.

8.1 The Presidential Election Timeline: A Summary

Our results at times seem to offer contradictions. Aggregate vote intentions seem to be stable over the campaign. Yet they obviously change, if mostly glacially, from April to November. Early polls from April appear to incorporate a considerable amount of extraneous information that does not survive to impact the election. Yet early polls do contain information that matters in November. Voters in early polls do not seem to take the economy into account very much. But by November, the economy shapes the result. In short, if we consider whether the campaign events from April to November are crucial or irrelevant to shaping the election, the answer is somewhere in between the two extremes.

8.1.1 Vote Intentions over the Campaign as a Time Series

Throughout this book we have structured the discussion in terms of modeling the campaign as a time series. We ask whether specific campaigns have their unique equilibria. The answer is a decisive yes. Yet, importantly, these equilibria often move, if slowly, over the campaign. Results from any one poll will have noise from sampling error, so we can never track the vote with total precision. Yet even if we could view it, the precise record of vote intentions would include short-term wobbles around the equilibrium of the moment. Every poll should be viewed within the context of past readings for the best guess regarding how much observed change is due to sampling error and what is real. And the real part can be a short-term blip or a change in the long-run equilibrium. Even if most true change is of the short-term variety, it is the small but real change that in the long-run is of electoral importance. Events may produce short-term bounces. But they may also leave a residue in the form of small long-term bumps. Except for the period immediately before the election, only the bumps last to Election Day.

8.1.2 The Pace of Change

We have also discovered some facts about the *pace* of change over the campaign timeline. As a very general rule, both long-term and short-term sources of change decrease as the campaign progresses. During the final 60 days of the campaign—when candidates have been chosen and the formal campaigning begun—very little change occurs. Yet even modest short-term shifts matter if they occur close to Election Day.

Three periods stand out as the most important of the campaign timeline, as having the greatest impact on voter choice—the beginning of the election year, the convention season, and the final days of the campaign. Consider first the very outset of the election year, 200 to 300 days before Election Day. With the nomination process under way, this period is often the voters' initial introduction to the eventual candidates. As voters gain what are often their first impressions of the candidates, preferences begin to take shape and eventually harden.

At convention time, the national vote division in the polls often gets considerably upended, as if the electorate is reshuffling. As the conventions take place, voters are especially attentive. In the days dominated by broadcast networks and print media, citizens can hardly avoid news of the conventions, and the shows the parties put on. It is easy to imagine that many voters shift as a result of the conventions, and the evidence indicates that they do. (This evidently is true even in recent elections with a growing cable and satellite television viewership and a declining print media.) The vote margin coming out of the conventions is different than that going in. And if we measure the consequences a few weeks after the dust of the final convention settles, the result is a decisive bump in the polls for whoever had the best convention—not a fading bounce.

The final days of the campaign present another period that concentrates political minds. Most voters have made up their minds long before the last minutes. But the small minority that has not yet decided can upset the best electoral predictions. Moreover, as we have seen, the gap between the final polls and the actual vote is also determined by composition effects—that is, likely voters and actual voters are not necessarily the same. Likely voters who do not vote are influenced by the events of the campaign in terms of the vote intentions they offer in surveys. Meanwhile, last-minute deciders who had not impacted pre-election surveys tend to split close to 50–50, helping to make elections appear closer.

8.1.3 The Campaign Fundamentals

When we speak of the equilibrium value of vote intentions, we are, in effect, speaking of the fundamentals of the campaign as they evolve. And what are these fundamentals that generate the long-lasting evolution of voter preferences over the campaign? In short, what drives the moving equilibrium?

The economy is an important factor. As the campaign progresses, perceptions of the degree of economic growth tend to push the arrow of change toward or against the incumbent presidential party. Measured by the objective economy or by subjective evaluations by the electorate, the economy helps to drive the moving equilibrium.

The equilibrium is a function of other factors as well. Some are captured by simply measuring the sitting president's approval level, which is a good summary indicator of presidential performance. In terms of tangible influences, the relative closeness of the two candidates on ideology or policy issues matters. We measure ideological closeness by separately measuring public opinion and the candidates' positions. From public opinion polls on issues (estimated via Stimson's mood), we know that the more liberal the electorate, the more it votes Democratic. But variability in the parties' ideological stances matter too. As either party platform moderates relative to its ideological base (as measured by Budge et al.'s scoring), it gains votes. This is exactly what theories (e.g., Downs 1957) predict will happen with a rational, issue-oriented electorate. Besides proximity, party identification plays a role—for a presidential candidate, it is good to be associated with a popular party.

The different fundamentals come into focus at different times. The economy begins to influence electoral preferences early in the election year, though its impact continues to grow over the campaign. Political factors matter later, around the time of the conventions. At the beginning of the fall general election campaign, vote intentions reveal the ultimate Election Day outcome. Preferences change only slightly thereafter, and mostly due to the growing impact of voters' internal fundamentals. To a large extent, then, the effects of campaigns are fairly predictable. Over the campaign timeline, voters take stock of economic conditions and the political choice before them and form "enlightened" electoral preferences (Gelman and King 1993). How this happens—whether the result of priming or learning, whether activated by the behavior of the candidates' campaigns or the "need to decide" as the election draws nearer—is unclear. What is clear is that certain knowable things matter on Election Day, and they actually are at least partly knowable in advance, even toward the beginning of the election year. They are not perfectly known at that point in time, however, as the fundamentals do change over the course of the election year.

We know we cannot measure all the fundamentals of presidential campaigns from observable variables. Some elections seem heavily influenced by important one-time events. Others may be influenced by forces that are simply intangible. To understand Republican Nixon's victory over Democrat Humphrey in 1968, it is necessary to move beyond statistical analysis to take into account President Johnson's unpopular Vietnam War. To account for Democrat Jimmy Carter's victory over Republican Gerald Ford in 1976, one must refer to the recent history of the Watergate scandal.

A possible example of intangibles at work is the 2000 election. By all statistical forecasts, Democrat Al Gore should have defeated Republican George W. Bush. Although Gore actually won the popular vote by a narrow margin, the truth is that Bush did considerably better than suggested by all predictive models based on the economy and presidential performance. Was this due to the aftermath of President Clinton's affair with Monica Lewinsky? Was it just a bad job of campaigning by Gore (or a great campaign by Bush)? Some (e.g., Vavreck 2009) cite Gore's failure to take proper credit for a good economy (and also Bush's successful "insurgent" campaign). Others (e.g., Fiorina, Abrams, and Pope 2003) say Gore's problem was a leftward shift instead of adopting a more centrist position. Or maybe Bush won because the economy really was not as prosperous as it was thought to be (Bartels and Zaller 2001). We still cannot say for sure.

8.2 Predicting Specific Elections

Back in chapter 2, we displayed poll results for our fifteen election campaigns, day by day, from April to November. In this section, we again present poll results over the fifteen campaigns, but this time with an eye for what the polls at any moment signify for the final outcome. In other words, we present the daily readings of the probable Democratic versus Republican win, conditional on the latest trial-heat polls. In effect, as if we could go back in time, we depict what informed observers of the contemporary polls might have or should have predicted about the November election. We ask: What would observers back in time have expected about the outcome if they had the statistical knowledge about how polls relate to the final vote that we present in this book? We also take a further step. We ask: How would these knowledgeable observers change their expectations if they knew further information about the likely outcome from the knowable fundamentals, apart from trial-heat polls? Here we present day-to-day election predictions based on the combination of polls, economic growth, and presidential approval.[1]

This exercise is motivated by several objectives. One is to visualize in a few glances how predictable (or not) elections are when seen from advance information. Another is to visualize the gap between the strictly poll-based prediction and the secondary prediction that includes the fundamentals. A third motivation is to show the relevance of campaigns. At any one point in the campaign timeline, we gain a probabilistic prediction of the winner. The difference between the probability distribution on a given date (e.g., 60–40 that the Republican would win) and the final outcome (either a Republican or Democratic win) is one measure of the effect of the campaign yet to be conducted. There is a final, fourth motivation. Our analysis can reveal that some elections are harder to predict from a set of defined, tangible variables than others. As we will see, the prediction game involves a large set of prediction successes, plus a smaller set of prediction failures. The daily forecasts are shown in figures 8.1–8.3, ahead. The details of their construction follow directly.

8.2.1 Predictions Based on Trial-Heat Polls

For 200 days across 15 campaigns (3,000 observations), we observe the pooled polls reported over the previous seven days. (To identify polls observable on each date, we code the date as two days later than the midpoint of the polling period.) In many instances, of course, there are no polls over this seven-day window. In these instances, we report the vote intentions from the most recent poll, whenever that occurred. For every date (measured as the number of days before the election), we regress the final Democratic versus Republican vote on the seven-day poll results. The predictions from these 200 equations provide the vote projections. Then we use the degree of fit to estimate the probable outcome based on polls observed for that date.

As in chapter 5, the generic vote projection equation is

(8.1) $VOTE_j = a_T + b_T V_{jT} + e_{jT}$

where $VOTE_j$ = the actual Democratic percentage of the two-party vote in year j, and V_{jT} = the corresponding trial-heat poll division in year j on day T of the campaign. As per our usual procedure, and for interpretive convenience, the vote division is measured as deviations from a tied 50–50 vote.

If α were zero and β were unity, the projection $\hat{V}$ would be identical to the raw two-party vote division of the polls. But, as we have seen, early leads fade. The daily β estimates are thus all below 1.0. The vote projection equations can be used not only to obtain an expectation of the vote but also the variance around that expectation. The estimated variance in the error term, or σ_T^2, is used to estimate the probable outcome. Knowing σ_T^2, we estimate the cumulative normal density Φ_{YT} at zero (50–50 split), that is, the probability of a Democratic victory in year Y based on the polls at time T.[2] For the actual daily probabilities, we show the estimate at the time of the most recent poll. This way, every time there is a new poll reported, the probability can shift. For dates without a poll, the probability does not move since the informed voter at the time would possess no new polling information.

Construction of the fundamentals-based forecasts is different. Here, since the fundamentals affect the incumbent presidential party, we model the presidential party vote rather than the Democratic vote. Then we convert the incumbent party vote to a prediction for the Democratic candidate.[3] Independent variables for the daily equations include the trial-heat polls (with the two-day lag as above), presidential approval, and the measure of Economic Growth, that is, per capita income growth, from chapter 6. Since the latter two measures are interpolated, they are admittedly imprecise for daily readings, though we do not attempt to lag them. In effect, we assume a forecast based on what an observer at the time might have "felt" about the political and economic environment rather than what he or she might have read or heard in terms of news reports about measures of the president's popularity or the economy. Thus, while the movement of the trial heat–based prediction is discrete, changing only with a new poll or polls, the movement of the fundamentals prediction is continuous, shifting with each daily imputation of the model's inputs.

The choice of variables for the fundamentals is parsimonious. There is no measure of macropartisanship, mood, or party platform ideology. As shown in chapter 6, these variables tend to be incorporated into the president's approval rating. The president's approval level is a proxy for these omitted variables, plus other factors in the political environment that matter but cannot be directly observed. Even so, it is not a perfect proxy, and so this analysis provides a conservative estimate of what we might have predicted based on the knowable fundamentals.

8.2.2 Electoral Expectations over the Campaign Timeline

We follow the running forecasts of the vote over the campaign timelines of the fifteen elections. These elections are presented in three separate figures for three types of elections, each representing a unique political environment. Figure 8.1 shows a set of six contests without the sitting president on the ballot, a circumstance that usually results in a close election. Figure 8.2 follows the outcome over the campaign timeline for four elections in which the incumbent ran for reelection, but under some degree of political distress. Figure 8.3 shows the remaining set of five elections, in which the sitting president won reelection handily.

Figure 8.1 shows the data for the six contests in which the sitting president did not run. Only in 1952 did the outcome seem certain throughout the campaign. In that year the electorate was ready to elect Republican Dwight Eisenhower after twenty years of Democratic presidents. In the other five cases, on the basis of the polls alone, the outcome was volatile, with each candidate favored at some point in the timeline. The predictions incorporating the fundamentals showed more stability and certainty.

Figure 8.2 shows the data for the four campaigns in which the sitting president sought reelection in an uncertain environment. Three instances were presidential losses (Ford in 1976; Carter in 1980; Bush I in 1992). Of the four, only in 2004 did the president succeed (Bush II over Kerry).

Figure 8.3 presents the final five examples. These are less interesting as they represent sitting presidents who basically coasted to reelection. In these five contests, the signs pointed to reelection throughout. The result should not have surprised.

Of the fifteen elections, nine showed variability in the likely outcome over the campaign. (The election of 1976 arguably is a close call.) Thus about half the time, the contest has meaning through much of the campaign and should not be treated as a foregone conclusion. First we look at the five instances of closely contested elections without the president running for reelection.

The 1960 contest (Kennedy versus Nixon) was close throughout. Ken-

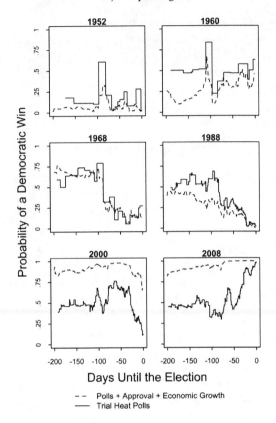

Days Until the Election

– – Polls + Approval + Economic Growth
—— Trial Heat Polls

Figure 8.1. Probable outcomes over the campaign timeline in six elections in which the incumbent president did
not seek reelection. Trial-heat poll probabilities are from
regression equations predicting the vote from the polls
over the recent seven days. The "polls + approval
+ economic growth" predictions are from equations
adding interpolated presidential approval and income
growth. See the text for further details.

nedy led in the polls more often than not, and the poll-based predictions
generally show him in a slight lead. Eight years later the 1968 contest
showed Democrat Humphrey slightly favored in matchups with Nixon
until the dissension-filled Democratic convention. Nixon's lead in the fall
looked safe, with a slight upturn of doubt toward the end.

The 1988 contest was one in which the polls and the fundamentals
started off at odds. On the basis of the trial-heat polls alone, it looked as
though Democrat Dukakis was likely to defeat George H. W. Bush. By the
end of the convention season, however, the polls turned toward Bush. Vot-

ers gravitated toward the fundamentals, which had Bush the winner all along.

The 2000 contest was one in which the polls and the fundamentals were at odds for much of the campaign. Republican Bush led Democrat Gore in the polls for most of the campaign, even though the fundamentals seemed to favor Gore. As discussed earlier, the 2000 election is a case in which the observable fundamentals suggested a stronger showing for Gore. In fact, Gore did surge at the end and, in fact, win the popular vote, while losing the contested Electoral College outcome.

The most recent nonincumbent race, of course, is 2008. Figure 8.1 shows

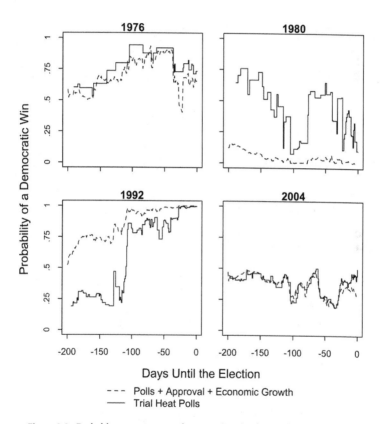

Figure 8.2. Probable outcomes over the campaign timeline in four elections in which the incumbent president faced a strong reelection challenge. Trial-heat poll probabilities are from regression equations predicting the vote from the polls over the recent seven days. The "polls + approval + economic growth" predictions are from equations adding interpolated presidential approval and income growth. See the text for further details.

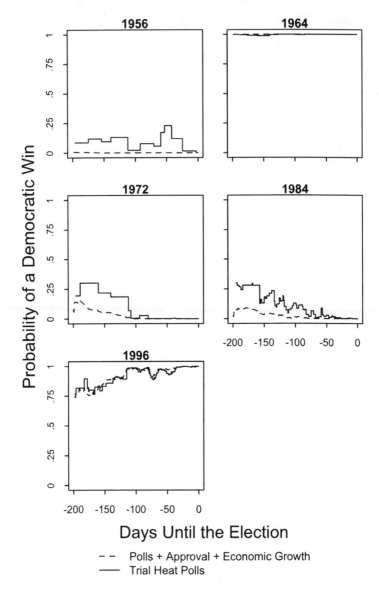

Figure 8.3 Probable outcomes over the campaign timeline in five elections in which the incumbent president coasted to reelection. Trial-heat poll probabilities are from regression equations predicting the vote from the polls over the recent seven days. The "polls + approval + economic growth" predictions are from equations adding interpolated presidential approval and income growth. See the text for further details.

that, on the basis of the polls alone, Obama was only the slight favorite for much of the year and became the underdog briefly after the conventions. But he became the likely choice after the Republican convention, and once the economy went into freefall in September. Importantly, the signal of the fundamentals was that this was an election for the Democrats to win all along.

Of the five close contests with a sitting president, the least close was 1976, where President Gerald Ford was a continual underdog, with a continuously low probability of reelection according to the polls. As measured, the fundamentals were not that unfavorable. Here is an instance in which the trial-heat poll predictions were more accurate than the fundamentals' predictions (although Ford's chances improved slightly toward the end). One big issue lurking in 1976 was Nixon's Watergate scandal and Ford's pardon of Nixon. Perhaps Jimmy Carter, the Democrat, was elected with the help of the unmeasured fundamental effect of the Watergate scandal.

In 1980, Carter's reelection prospects against Reagan moved up and down with the polls, as shown in figure 8.2. The fundamentals this time worked very much against Carter, due to the poor economy and his unpopularity. This is a case in which the polls gravitated toward the fundamentals.

In 1992, it was G. H. W. Bush's turn to be defeated by poor fundamentals. The early polls suggested he would probably defeat the unknown Bill Clinton in a matchup. But this changed following the conventions as the poll prediction turned in the direction of the fundamentals, which had Bush losing all along.

The 2004 election is our final example, and in this instance the embattled president escaped unscathed. Noteworthy about 2004 is that although the polls were close, they tended to place President Bush as the favorite, if not by as much as the fundamentals until late in the campaign. Staying close was not enough for Kerry to have much chance, as vote intentions usually move too slowly for that to happen.[4]

8.2.3 Election Predictability and the Role of Campaigns

One lesson from figures 8.1–8.3 is that, since the probability of a Democratic versus a Republican president often undergoes meaningful changes over a campaign, the campaigns must matter. For any point on the timeline, the gap between the probability of a Democratic win and the actuality (0 or 100 percent) stands out as the effect of the remaining campaign period. In general, although the likely verdict can change, it changes less than commonly believed.

One way we know this is because the poll-based prediction tends to be more certain than the beliefs of investors who gamble on election outcomes. Presumably, the most informed and unbiased views are those of the gamblers who bet on elections to make money.[5] Most election markets, both today and in the past, are winner-take-all, in which investors wager on the winner, given the candidates' odds of victory.[6] The important thing is that the price of a candidate registers the probability that he will win. We thus can directly compare these prices and the probabilities associated with our poll-based predictions as well as those including the fundamentals.

Interestingly, in recent elections, for which we have data from electronic election stock markets, prices have persistently overvalued underdog candidates (see Erikson and Wlezien 2008a).[7] This is as if wagerers believe that electoral preferences are more volatile than they are in reality and overestimate the likelihood that the candidate who is behind can pull it out between the moment of the wager and Election Day. Assuming that market prices reflect informed opinion, the underdog bias carries an important implication: *The campaign dynamics we have described in this book are less fluid than informed observers believe.*

We can consider examples of election markets from recent elections, starting with IEM's pioneering winner-take-all model for 1992. That election was seen as problematic for Clinton, but the Iowa Electronic Market price gave Bush a far greater chance of winning than our poll analysis would have it. Similarly, Clinton's near certain victory in 1996 according to the polls was not mirrored in the market prices, which gave Republican Dole an appreciable (25 percent) chance of victory even into the fall campaign, in clear defiance of the polls .

The 2000 and 2004 elections are not a good venue for comparing poll predictions and market predictions because these contests were reasonably close throughout. The 2008 election, however, provides a useful example. Throughout the 2008 campaign, both the Iowa Election Market and the Intrade commercial election markets gave McCain a greater chance than the polls implied he deserved. The difference between the two opened up as the campaign entered the summer. At that point in time the markets gave McCain a 40 percent chance of winning and the polls predicted only a 25 percent chance (see fig. 8.1 above). The market price did move sharply toward Obama throughout the fall, but gave McCain a 20 percent chance on average over the last month of the campaign, when the polls indicated little more than 5 percent. Again, this suggests that informed opinion (as reflected in market prices) overestimates the volatility of campaigns.

These examples reveal that poll predictions are more certain and accurate than market predictions. It is often said, however, that markets prices are the more accurate predictor because they incorporate information not in the polls (Kou and Sobel 2004; Wolfers and Zitzewitz 2004; Arrow et al. 2008; Berg et al. 2008; Berg, Nelson, and Rietz 2008). In theory, market investors should be able to improve on the poll prediction by taking into account the fundamentals. Where the polls prediction and the fundamentals prediction diverge, the poll prediction and the outcome generally move in the direction of the fundamentals prediction. This fact should help investors profit and provide a gauge of the election that improves on the polls.

Surprisingly, this has not happened. Both in 1992 and 2008, the fundamentals favored the winning Democratic candidate even more than the poll-based prediction at the same time. Yet the markets remained more cautious about the outcome than either. This is further evidence that the role of campaign events on outcomes may be less than observers think. Election outcomes generally become discernable from the polls. And a consideration of the fundamentals provides further clarity.

At the same time, we observe that the forecasts from polls and from the fundamentals sometimes change over the campaign. Campaigns matter, as they bring the fundamentals to the voters, and the vote outcome is a slow evolution over the course of the campaign. And, while elections are generally predictable, the results are not fully knowable in advance.

8.3 Presidential Campaigns over the Timeline

Presidential election campaigns matter, and they matter in predictable ways. Voters' intentions evolve over the course of the election year. At the beginning of the year, they are largely unformed. As the campaign unfolds, preferences come into focus. This happens in patterned ways from the very beginning of the nomination process and continuing through Election Day itself. Major events, such as the party conventions, are important, but so are the many other smaller inputs over the election cycle. Indeed, what most defines the evolution of voter intentions is its incremental quality— candidate preferences typically change very slowly, and this is especially true during the intense general election campaign of the fall.

The effects of presidential campaigns are not random. The outcome tends to reflect certain "external" fundamentals, including the economy and other aspects of presidential performance. It also reflects "internal" fundamentals, such as voters' partisan dispositions. The campaign (gradually) brings these things to the voters. The Election Day vote is not perfectly predictable, however. Sometimes those fundamentals don't come to matter. Plus, other fundamental variables influence voter preferences, and their effects become clear in the polls over time.

The fundamentals represent only the effects of the campaign that are long lasting and persist until Election Day. Some events impact vote intentions in the short term and do not leave a permanent trace. These short-term effects are of consequence only if they occur at the end of the campaign, and matter for the result only when the fundamentals largely balance out. While rare, late events sometimes matter, as in the 1960 and 2000 election campaigns. In these years, anything could have swung the result. In other years, the final result is clear in the polls throughout the general election campaign. It is the "long" campaign that plays out over the year that typically matters most of all.

APPENDIX

Table A.1 Vote intention data by year and week of the campaign

Week of campaign	Election year														
	'52	'56	'60	'64	'68	'72	'76	'80	'84	'88	'92	'96	'00	'04	'08
ED-29	x	x	—	—	—	x	—	—	x	x	x	x	—	x	x
ED-28	—	—	x	x	x	x	x	x	x	x	x	—	x	x	x
ED-27	—	—	—	—	x	—	x	x	x	x	x	x	x	x	x
ED-26	x	x	—	x	—	—	—	—	—	x	x	x	x	x	x
ED-25	—	—	x	x	x	x	x	x	—	—	x	x	—	x	x
ED-24	—	x	—	—	x	x	x	—	—	—	x	x	x	x	x
ED-23	x	x	—	x	—	—	—	x	x	x	x	x	x	x	x
ED-22	—	—	x	x	x	—	—	x	x	x	x	x	x	x	x
ED-21	x	x	—	x	x	x	x	x	x	x	x	—	x	x	x
ED-20	x	—	—	—	—	—	x	x	x	x	x	x	x	x	x
ED-19	—	—	x	x	x	—	—	x	x	x	x	x	x	x	x
ED-18	—	x	—	x	—	—	—	x	x	x	x	x	x	x	x
ED-17	x	x	—	x	x	x	x	x	x	x	x	x	x	x	x
ED-16	x	—	x	x	x	x	—	x	x	x	x	x	x	x	x
ED-15	x	x	—	x	x	—	x	x	x	—	x	x	x	x	x
ED-14	—	—	x	x	—	x	—	x	x	x	x	x	x	x	x
ED-13	—	x	—	x	x	x	x	x	x	x	x	x	x	x	x
ED-12	x	—	x	x	—	—	—	x	x	x	x	x	x	x	x
ED-11	—	x	—	x	x	x	x	x	x	x	x	x	x	x	x
ED-10	—	x	—	x	x	—	x	x	x	x	x	x	x	x	x
ED-9	x	x	x	x	—	x	—	x	x	x	x	x	x	x	x
ED-8	x	x	—	—	x	x	x	x	x	x	x	x	x	x	x
ED-7	—	x	x	x	x	x	—	x	x	x	x	x	x	x	x
ED-6	x	—	x	x	x	x	x	x	x	x	x	x	x	x	x
ED-5	x	—	—	—	x	x	—	x	x	x	x	x	x	x	x
ED-4	x	x	x	x	—	x	x	x	x	x	x	x	x	x	x
ED-3	x	—	—	—	x	x	x	x	x	x	x	x	x	x	x
ED-2	—	—	x	—	x	x	x	x	x	x	x	x	x	—	x
ED-1	x	x	x	x	—	x	x	x	x	x	x	x	—	x	x

Note: x = the presence of at least one trial-heat poll for the week. Where there are no polls indicated for week ED-29, at least one trial-heat poll exists for week ED-30 or earlier.

CHAPTER ONE

1. The 2000 April polls were technically correct in identifying Bush as the winner but wrong in projecting Bush as the popular vote winner.

2. The role of short-term forces in the United States actually may have decreased with the apparent rise in party identification (see Kayser and Wlezien 2011).

3. An alternative way of defining the fundamentals is to say that they are whatever motivates voters on Election Day. Various factors caused the final vote, and, tautologically, that collection of variables represents the fundamentals. Thus, if the outcome differs from early trial-heat polls, *by definition* the campaign brings home the fundamentals to the voters.

4. At some risk of extending an analogy too far, we can point to this discussion's similarities to fundamentals in the analysis of stock prices. Economic fundamentalists see stocks as having a "fundamental" price, based on some measure of their long-term value. This value might not be reached in the short run, however. Another view is that stock prices follow a random walk—price changes respond to market forces, but their direction cannot be forecast from their initial values. We can reconcile these views if the fundamentals themselves move as a "random walk." Then investors seek profit by identifying short-term departures from the (moving) fundamentals. The same logic applies to election prediction markets, where investors in effect bet on election outcomes. In theory, the investor can observe the polls and the fundamentals and seek to invest (bet on) candidates whose price falls below its fundamental value.

5. For more on how engagement with an upcoming election influences voter preferences, see Enns and Richman (2009).

6. A concept closely related to issue priming is "framing." Although it can be difficult to operationally separate priming and framing, the latter typically is used to refer to how an issue is presented, not just whether we think about it per se (Druckman 2001). Like priming, framing can influence electoral preferences, though research indicates that there are real limits on framing effects (Druckman 2001, 2004).

7. As Lenz (2009) argues, not all claims for priming effects are valid. One example that Lenz addresses is privatization of Social Security, brought to voter attention by the first presidential debate in 2000. As the differences between Bush and Gore on this issue became salient to voters, voters' candidate choices become more aligned

with their policy preferences. Was this priming? Lenz's analysis shows the answer is no. Voters switched their positions on Social Security privatization to fit their vote choice much more than the other way around. The increased clarity of candidate positions on Social Security caused few votes to change.

8. Studies of political attitudes reveal a disjuncture between people's stable long-term "latent" attitudes and their short-term attitudinal reaction to political news as it occurs. As the term implies, people change their long-term component only slowly. A political conservative today, for instance, will probably be a conservative the following year. Yet in the short term, when people express their attitudes in surveys, the response can vary considerably. One interpretation is that when people shift their survey response between interviews, the change typically is the result of what Zaller (1992) calls their "top of the head" responses to whatever considerations occur to them at the moment. When voting decisions are modeled as a function of long-term dispositions on policy issues (ignoring short-term variation), voting decisions become far more predictable. The details are technical. See Ansolabehere, Rodden, and Snyder (2008). For earlier literature, see Converse (1964).

9. For one useful discussion, see Hill et al. (2011).

CHAPTER TWO

1. Of course, there were many earlier nonscientific "straw" polls, the most famous of which was the 1936 *Literary Digest* poll. For an analysis of how that poll failed, see Squire (1988). For a basic summary of the evolution of public opinion polling in the United States, see Herbst (1993). See also Erikson and Tedin (2011).

2. Internet and IVR polls are not included in our counts of polls by year mentioned above.

3. Multistage random sampling was particularly necessary for in-person interviews. In multistage random samples, the first stage is the selection of a limited number of geographic areas (e.g., counties) where the areas' chances of inclusion in the survey are proportional to their populations. Following intervening randomization steps, the final stage is the random selection of households within randomly determined small geographic areas and then the random selection of individuals within households.

4. Although some questionnaire effects can be consequential (McDermott and Frankovic 2003), they are beyond the scope of our analysis, as we lack adequate measures of the differences that appear to matter.

5. Most polling organizations rely on likely voter "screens" to isolate people who are most likely to vote. This is not easy to do, and it can create more problems than it solves, though some approaches—probability-based ones—are highly recommended. The problem is that increasing numbers of organizations use different likely voter screens, about which we still have only limited information. See Wlezien and Erikson (2001), Blumenthal (2005), and AAPOR (2009).

6. Although these decision rules may seem innocuous enough, they occasionally affect the tally, particularly in recent election years (Wlezien and Erikson 2001; Erikson, Panagopoulos, and Wlezien 2004). Particularly if they have a strict screen for inclusion among the "likely," likely voter samples sometimes distort the vote division due to short-term swings in which a candidate's partisans are the most enthusiastic about voting. Near the end of the campaign, however, likely voter samples are more accurate than registered-voter samples.

7. In other words, we take a weighted average of all polls by date, weighting each poll in proportion to the number who intend to vote either Republican or Democratic.

8. We refer here to variation in polls within a campaign from one period to the next. Later we treat variance of poll results between elections at specific points in the campaign timeline.

9. Seemingly the famous campaign of 1948 should have shown little change because Truman and Dewey were known quantities at the time. Pollsters of the day must have thought so, as they quit polling about two weeks before the election, missing Truman's late surge to victory.

10. Specifically, survey results can vary across houses due to differences in question wording, target populations, sample weights, data collection mode, interviewer training, and procedures for coping with refusals (see, e.g., Converse and Traugott 1986; Lau 1994; also see Crespi 1988). As a separate manner, design effects also can vary with the survey house, that is, if some houses poll more efficiently than others.

11. Simple random sampling implies that everyone has the exact same chance of being selected. Although modern scientific surveys are always based on random sampling, the sampling generally is not "simple." Pollsters often sample by first randomly selecting clusters of voters (counties, telephone exchanges, and even smaller units) to sample and then sample within those clusters. This mild departure from simple random sampling is one more reason why our estimates of the error variances may be too conservative. One current practice of survey organizations has the opposite effect—of tightening the actual sampling error. This is the practice of post-stratification weighting, which in recent years has become the pollsters' norm. With post-stratification, pollsters weight their respondents by known characteristics of the population. For example, if 10 percent of the targeted population is Latino, but only 8 percent of their sample is Latino, they may weight Latinos as 1.25 (instead of 1.0, and weighting non-Latinos by the ratio of .90/.92). Weighting dampens the random bouncing around of reported results from poll to poll. It is not clear, however, that weighting improves polls to the point that the error falls below that from simple random sampling, as its benefit is offset by the various sources of error noted in the text, particularly house effects.

12. The 1948 campaign, which is not included in our analysis, is another exception. If we estimate true variance of the 1948 polls, preferences were more volatile during the final 60 days than the 60 days preceding.

13. As measured by the mean rather than median variance, the differences in volatility across periods are even greater. The finding of greater volatility early in the campaign also survives further scrutiny. For example, suppose we divide the dates into six groups of 20 days, and then for each election measure the change in mean preferences from one period to another. Illustrative of the greater volatility during the summer period of the campaign, the median variances of 20-day change are over twice as high during dates 61–80, 81–100, and 101–120 than for the other periods.

14. The pattern of declining variances holds even excluding the distinctive 1964 case, when President Johnson's vote share in the polls throughout the campaign far exceeded Johnson's final vote percentage. This is quite visible in figure 2.4.

15. The estimation of the reliability of the daily readings is as follows. First, we estimate the average error variance per day from the *observed* cases, if any. Then we estimate the total variance from the interpolated data. The difference between the two is the estimate of the true variance. The true variance divided by the observed variance of

the *interpolated* data becomes the reliability estimate. These estimates do not take into account that the true value of the interpolated observation could in theory veer far from the straight-line interpolation, even if the interpolation were based on perfect data. The interpolated data, however, take on strength from the fact that they are based on the pooled variance estimate from polls at two nearby time points. If anything, the .98 estimate of the mean daily reliability may be too conservative.

16. We chose to ignore dates within two weeks of the conventions. The reason is to avoid contamination of the interpolated polls by incorporating poll readings from the convention period.

CHAPTER THREE

1. These are assumed to be independent and drawn from a normal distribution.

2. The true value of β cannot be greater than 1. That would be implausible on statistical grounds, as the variance would become explosive.

3. If β approaches but does not reach 1.0, the series is said to be "near integrated"; see DeBoef and Granato (1997) for a political science perspective on the issue. When β approaches 1.00, campaign shocks could move V_t far from its equilibrium value, thus mimicking a random walk.

4. Some will reject a random walk for a bounded variable, such as a vote division that is restricted to the space between 0 and 100 percent. To meet this objection, the vote division can readily be transformed into an unbounded variable by taking the log of the odds of the ratio of the vote for Party A over the vote for party B and then converting back to percentages. Doing this makes little difference, however, except when the vote variable approaches the bounds of zero or 1.0.

5. We can add even more complexity and allow the rate of decay (β) to vary across different types of shocks and individuals. Our series of polls might then represent the sum of an integrated series and a possible fractionally integrated series. In a fractionally integrated series, effects decay but much more slowly than a stationary series. See, for example, Box-Steffensmeier and Smith (1998), DeBoef (2000), and Lebo, Walker, and Clarke (2000).

6. See Wlezien (2000) for more on such combined time-series processes.

7. We are tempted to describe this process with the popular term "polarization," but that would not quite be right. The posited increasing spread of voter attitudes over the campaign would not necessarily be bipolar.

8. See Green, Palmquist, and Shickler (2004) for more on the importance (and exogeneity) of partisan dispositions.

9. Our model of the dynamics of voters' relative candidate evaluations bears a kinship to models of party identification as Bayesian updating (Achen 1992; Gerber and Green 1998; and Bartels 2002). These models can account, for instance, for why citizens are less likely to switch party preference as they age. This narrative is similar to our model's prediction that voters become more resistant to changing their candidate preference as the campaign evolves.

CHAPTER FOUR

1. For this illustration, where there is no reported poll for the first (29th) week, we include the most recent poll (in week 30 or earlier) as a substitute. This expands the "week" by a few days and avoids missing data.

2. Further calculations suggest that with this scenario, the unexplained variance from

week to week would be about 2 percent of the lagged observed variance, starting out at about 3 points and ending at about 1.5 points. The implicit model behind these calculations is an AR1 process with a constant autoregressive parameter and (to account for the declining cross-sectional variance of vote intentions) a declining variance of the weekly disturbances (shocks).

3. We cover 28 weeks where the vote division is the dependent variable and the lagged vote division from the week before is the independent variable. Thus, the vote division 29 weeks in advance (with a midpoint exactly 200 days in advance of the election) is the independent variable for the prediction 28 weeks in advance.

4. The measurement error correction is based on sampling theory, as if the surveys had the error expected with simple random sampling. See chapter 2. The error-adjusted equation (and others that follow) is calculated using STATA's eivreg program. The R-squared and RMSE are further adjusted to take into account the measurement error in the dependent variable.

5. Although tighter week-to-week fits in the later stages of the campaign could be the product of diminishing measurement error due to the greater polling in the final weeks, this does not seem to be a major factor. We discuss the attenuation of relationships due to measurement error in the text immediately below.

6. We have modeled the vote division in trial-heat polls as if it is an AR1 process—that is, as a function solely of its most recent lagged values—from the previous week. Now, for the pooled equations for the final eight weeks, suppose we add as a second independent variable the vote division two weeks earlier. For the OLS version of this equation, this lag-2 value is statistically significant. This result is expected, given the presence of sampling error in the lag-1 measure. Correcting for measurement error with the eivreg version of the equation, the lag-2 vote coefficient remains positive but is no longer significant. A positive (if no longer significant) coefficient is plausible, given the presence of both long-run and short-run influences on the vote division. See the discussion ahead.

7. For weeks when the lag-9 reading is missing (no polls), we incorporate the most recent poll prior to week lag-9.

8. The covariance between two weekly readings will vary with the lag length. However, these correlation values plateau by the time we get to eight weeks. This is a sign that short-term shocks do not last past the sixth week.

9. The persistence of the short-term influence is a function of β^m, where β = the decay parameter and m is the lag length (see sec. 3.3.2). The β^m term presumably declines toward zero by lag-9.

10. With weekly readings Tuesday through Monday and conventions opening for business on Monday, the pre-convention reading is set to surveys with the mid-date in the field being in the week beginning 13 days prior to the opening of the convention. This avoids any contamination of the pre-convention reading from any surveys in the field during the early convention period. For similar reasoning, the post-convention reading is based not on polls centered on dates beginning the Tuesday after the convention but rather the week following. This timing also avoids the early bounce from the second convention. To ensure no missing data for our fifteen election campaigns, in some years the pre-convention reading or the post-convention reading incorporates polls conducted a few days before the designated pre-election window or a few days beyond the designated post-convention window.

11. In two of the three comparisons, the TSLS estimate of the lagged-vote coefficient

exceeds that for OLS. The exception is the equation predicting the pre-convention polls from April polls. Here, the TSLS estimate is lower, but based on only the twelve available cases for which earlier polls were available as the instrument.

12. If the number of weeks between conventions is odd, the middle week is designated for our midconvention season reading. With an even number of weeks, we take a 7-day period straddling the two middle weeks. In some instances, our measure must incorporate readings that are slightly outside the designated week's window but are still well within the boundaries of the two conventions. For 1956, there is no mid-convention reading.

13. Here we must rely on OLS for answers as we do not have separate instruments for the vote division on the eve of the first convention and the convention-season shifts.

14. Http://blog.nielsen.com/nielsenwire/media_entertainment/top-ten-presidential-debates-1960-to-present/ (accessed September 20, 2011).

15. Specifically, we take a poll of polls with a survey midpoint from 7 to 13 days before the debate to 7 to 13 days after the debate. This rule helps to ensure that we do not incorporate interviews within the actual debate period.

CHAPTER FIVE

1. The table shows slightly higher R-squared for the Democratic vote equations, due to the slightly higher variance in the Democratic vote than in the incumbent party vote.

2. The N's, of course, are of the sums of reported Democratic and Republican voters pooled over all days of the final week, where the poll date is the midpoint of the survey period. For 1968, there is no available poll centered on a date in the final week, and so we substitute the last pre-election poll from that cycle, centered on the eighth day before the election.

3. If, instead of using the post-conventions vote division as the instrument, we use the lagged vote from eight weeks earlier as the instrument, we get the same result. Using the post-conventions vote division ensures an estimate based on all fifteen elections.

4. Recall from chapter 4 that the TSLS estimates are designed to estimate only the long-term and not any short-term component of electoral preferences. The idea is that OLS coefficients are depressed as estimates of the long-term component. If the TSLS coefficient and the OLS component are similar, this is a sign of little "contamination" from short-term influences. Applied to the prediction of the vote from the final week's polls, however, this becomes an ambiguous test. Consider that the short duration from polls to Election Day does not allow much time for short-term effects to fade.

5. For instance, we measured vote preferences as the gap between the Democratic and Republican candidate percentages of the entire sample, including undecideds and those who prefer third (and fourth) candidates. We then used these measures to predict the gap between the actual vote for the Democratic and Republican candidates, measured as the difference between their percentages of the total vote. Although the resulting coefficients all are slightly larger than those in table 5.1, they nevertheless remain well below 1.00. For instance, the OLS estimate rises from 0.74 (table 5.1) to 0.78. Adjusting for reliability, omitting 1964, using the incumbent party vote *plus* measuring the independent and dependent variables in terms of the incum-

bent party minus challenger party percentage of all respondents or votes manages to push the coefficient for vote intentions in the final weeks' polls up to 0.92.

6. Specifically, given poll readings on days $t - x$ and $t + y$, the estimate for a particular day t is generated as follows:

$$\hat{V}_t = \frac{yV_{t-x} + xV_{t+y}}{x + y}.$$

7. The reader will recall that we did not use interpolated poll results for the analysis of chapter 4 because that would often mean predicting one interpolated poll from another, perhaps even derived from the identical polls on surrounding dates. Here, the interpolated poll data are measured for only the predictor variable but not, of course, for election results.

8. To be clear, this number and the others that follow represent absolute differences.

9. Even this difference is inflated because the final pre-election polls often end a few days in advance of the election and we simply carry forward the results. Recall from our earlier discussion in section 5.1 that the final poll percentage predictably inflates the lead.

10. It also comports with previous research (Campbell and Wink 1990; Wlezien and Erikson 2002; Campbell 2008a).

11. The a_T intercepts are themselves a matter of some interest. In the equations, both the final vote and the poll vote division are measured as deviations from 50 percent. By subtracting 50 points, we set up the intercept as a natural indicator of possible bias. Although not significantly different from zero, this slope is persistently but trivially negative across the timeline. When the polls predict a close 50–50 split, the result is slightly less than a 50–50 split.

12. Although the short-term and long-term shocks would quite plausibly be highly correlated, the cross-sectional correlation between the two components would be negligible. Past shocks generate the permanent series but have minimal contribution to the short-term series.

13. The .25 discounting at the end does not affect our theoretical analysis that follows. We can simply stretch the metric of the actual vote by one-third. Alternatively we can shrink the poll metric by 25 percent.

14. The assumed autoregressive term of the short-term component is smaller for the model of panel D than for the model of panel A.

15. The variance of V_{yt}^s is exaggerated in the panel D above its real-world likelihood, in order to illustrate the late curvature in slope.

16. In the accounts of this section, the explained variance is based on the *adjusted* R-squared, where the R-squared is adjusted for the modest degrees of freedom with an N of only 11 or 15 cases. The raw (unsquared and unadjusted) correlation coefficients will be much higher. For instance, the correlation between polls at ED-300 and the vote is a seemingly high +.37.

17. For this chapter we measure the vote division at an eight-week lag in terms of daily polls at precisely eight weeks earlier. We measure this instrument not from the daily interpolation but rather as the results of the most recent available daily poll as of eight weeks earlier. This is to ensure that the lagged polls and the current (interpolated) polls do not share a common source in terms of observed polls during the eight-week interval.

18. The series does not extend earlier than ED-160 because it is the earliest date for

which we have poll preferences from eight weeks prior and so can obtain a TSLS estimate for all fifteen elections based on polls six weeks earlier.

19. Statistically, the convention breaks are highly significant as indicated by a regression discontinuity test. First we create a new time variable measuring days before the conventions and days after the conventions. For days after the conventions, we add 29 days to represent the average number of days between conventions. Then we regress the coefficient (adjusted R-squared or b) on the actual days before or after the convention and a dummy variable scored 1 after the conventions and zero if before. The coefficient for the dummy variable is highly significant for both coefficients, and for all plausible choices as to which pre- or post-convention dates to include in the analysis.

20. The regression discontinuity test for the pre- versus post-convention season effect is highly significant. The procedure is analogous as for OLS coefficients, described in the previous footnote.

21. The same result looks very different from the perspective of the Democratic rather than in-party vote division. Measured as percentage Democratic, the vote division between conventions actually correlates slightly less with the final vote (.78 versus .79) than does the pre-convention vote division. The between-conventions percentage Democratic is temporarily scrambled up or down, depending on which party has its convention first. As percentage Democratic, the post-convention vote division correlates at .90 with the final Election Day division, indicative once again that the conventions provide some learning. See also the differences between the Democratic vote equations and the in-party vote equations in table 5.2—notably the differences in the intercepts and R-squared when predicting the Election Day vote from between-conventions readings.

22. The post-convention correlation of the in-party vote is .87 for all fifteen elections, but .89 when the 1956 case (no between-conventions polls) is excluded.

23. The one bit of evidence for a bounce (in addition to bump) in the polls is that the in-party vote prediction from the between-conventions vote division shows a smaller slope in the TSLS version than the OLS version. The between-conventions reading is by necessity close in time to the end of the first convention, and may reflect an artificial boost from its convention. By two weeks after the second convention, the convention effects that are truly short term have largely evaporated.

CHAPTER SIX

1. The literature on economics and elections in the United States is vast; for a useful review, see Linn, Nagler, and Morales (2010). There is a large and growing comparative literature as well. For reviews, see Lewis-Beck and Stegmaier (2000) and Hellwig (2010).

2. With relatively few cases in terms of elections to predict, it is safest to choose one composite measure of the economy rather than several (see, e.g., Rosenstone 1983; Campbell and Garand 2000). It is plausible, however, to incorporate multiple measures if the time frame is extended back in history. For an example, see Fair (2002).

3. To create proper averages, we adjust weighted cumulative growth in each quarter by the sum of the weights used through that quarter, for example, for the third quarter of the election cycle (in the first year of a presidency), we divide by 2.44, which is the sum of weights (.64, .8, and 1.0) for the three quarters.

4. The discount rate is based on previous research (Hibbs 1987; Wlezien and Erikson 1996). In recent updates, Hibbs estimates the rate to be .9 instead of .8.

5. In rare instances when the survey measure was missing for a quarter in the early years of our analysis, we interpolated using the scores for surrounding quarters.

6. Months of the year differ in their number of days, and thus the midmonth date used to anchor the interpolation does as well. For months with 30 days, the observed monthly score is assigned to days 15 and 16. For months with 29 or 31 days, the observed monthly score is assigned only to the middle day, 15 or 16, respectively. Scores for other days of the month are then interpolated based on their temporal distance from the midmonth scores.

7. If we use the estimated daily Income Growth measure for the day before the election (incorporating information from quarter 16 of the election cycle), the correlation between Income Growth and the presidential party vote is a marginally smaller +.74.

8. Income Growth is not the only measure of economic conditions that tracks the vote. A (weighted) cumulative measure of leading economic indicators works just as well. And for early quarters (extending back to quarter 12 of the presidential cycle and before), this measure is far superior to Income Growth. The reason is that, as its name implies, the index of leading economic indicators takes into account information about the future economy. See Wlezien and Erikson (1996); Erikson and Wlezien (2008b).

9. For this illustration, the measure of vote intentions is not interpolated but observed from the weekly readings at ED-200—the week surrounding ED-200. The low (+.31) correlation with all fifteen cases plunges to virtual zero (+.02) when 1964 is excluded. The 1964 election stands out as a persistent outlier. Election analysts usually attribute President Johnson's success not just to the economy. (In 1964, the economy was in good shape but not good enough to support Johnson's ridiculously large 60-point lead in the early polls.) Key factors included the holdover support from the Kennedy assassination a few months before and the fact that Johnson's opponent, Senator Goldwater, was largely seen at the time as an extreme conservative (Converse, Clausen, and Miller 1965).

10. This does not necessarily mean that voters are more (altruistically) concerned for the national than (selfishly) for themselves. Self-interested voters realize that they are personally affected by national economic circumstances and the government has little to do with their personal economic fortunes.

11. Personal retrospections actually outperform business expectations as predictors of vote intentions through most of the last 200 days, but not at the end and on Election Day itself. Using personal expectations in place of business expectations makes little difference in the analyses that follow.

12. The day ED-80 with the peak correlation falls in the midst of most convention periods. It is unclear, however, that it is learning from the conventions that triggers the objective–subjective connection. Measured just before, after, or during (as days relative to the conventions), the objective–subjective correlation stays in the range of +.84. For more on the relationship between the measure of Business Retrospections and per capita income growth, see Erikson, MacKuen, and Stimson (2002), especially chapter 3.

13. As with Income Growth, we capitalize our specific measure of Economic Perceptions where it refers to the specific definition used in our measurement rather than a general concept. A close competitor to Business Retrospections in the correlation game is the generic Economic News Heard. The two measures perform similarly in the tests that follow. Economic News Heard, however, is available only for 1960 and beyond, yielding just thirteen cases.

14. The reader may expect that presidential approval is a stronger predictor of vote intentions when the incumbent president runs for reelection. Indeed, this is the case. However, the small number of elections—9 with incumbent presidents running, only 6 open races—precludes separating approval "effects" under the two conditions. Interestingly, the date when trial-heat polls predict vote intentions better than approval for the restricted set of elections with incumbent presidents running is day ED-111, 18 days earlier than when all 15 elections are included.

15. The statistical argument can be elaborated by the following exercise. First, day ED-200 approval is regressed on ED-200 economic perceptions. The predictions from this equation comprise the economy-induced component of presidential approval and in fact it accounts for 54 percent of the variance in approval at the time. The residuals from this equation comprise the non-economic portion of approval. Next, trial-heat vote intentions at ED-200 are regressed on the two components of presidential approval. The coefficients are 0.07 for the economic portion but 1.00 for the non-economic portion. Translation: the economy affects approval in April but does not translate into vote intentions at that time. Meanwhile, the non-economic residual component of approval can by itself account for half the variance in the April trial-heat polls.

16. Some might object that because macropartisanship can be "endogenous" to the vote (influenced by the vote as well as being the causal variable), it should not be in models of the vote. What is important for our analysis is that including the variable in the model allows us to control for the confounding variables that obscure the effect of ideological proximity (mood and platform ideology). When causes other than ideological proximity influence the vote, they induce changes in macropartisanship. Thus the control for macropartisanship allows a clearer observation of the effect of mood on the vote. Moreover, there is correlational evidence that parties are more likely to move (ideologically) toward the median voter at times when they are at the greatest disadvantage in terms of macropartisanship. See Erikson, MacKuen, and Stimson (2002).

17. We borrow heavily from James Stimson's compilation of macropartisanship data, collected from the Roper Center, and are grateful to him for making available the data.

18. The macropartisanship measure used here is denser than that from *The Macro Polity* in that the book relied solely on Gallup samples, whereas we use all survey houses that meet our criteria, as described in chapter 2.

19. The RMSE from predicting Election Day macropartisanship from macropartisanship at ED-200, however, is smaller than the RMSE from the comparable approval equation (3.23 versus 4.77). The largest shifts in macropartisanship over the campaign were a Republican gain in 1972 and a Democratic gain in 1992. One can infer that these shifts reflected major changes in the electorates' evaluations of party competence.

20. Stimson includes a quarterly measure of mood in addition to the annual (and biennial). We decided against using it because the quarterly series does not start until after the 1956 election, and it does not match well with the annual series for splicing the two together. It also shows a sufficient wobble that leads to suspicions of low reliability due to the inevitable thinness of relevant polls for some quarters.

21. We thank Michael D. McDonald for providing platform ideology scores updated through 2008. As scored by Budge et al., the ideological distance between parties

has not grown. This is in contrast to the widening ideological polarization observed when measurement is based on congressional roll call behavior (e.g., Poole and Rosenthal 2007).

22. Of course each party faces a limit to the value of moderation if it "jumps over" the other party, changing places on the ideological spectrum. Such an event has not been observed with US party platforms.

23. If mood and platform ideology were on the same scale (which they are not), mood minus the Democratic platform position represents proximity to the Democrats. Mood relative to Republican platform ideology represents relative proximity to the Republicans. Given that the Democratic platform is always to the left of the Republican platform—and assuming that the median or mean voter represented by mood is ideologically in between the two parties—we can derive the following expressions. The relative proximity of the two parties (treated as closeness to the Democrats minus closeness to the Republicans) equals (mood − Dem. platform score) − (Rep. platform score − mood). This simplifies to 2 × mood − Dem. platform liberalism − Rep. platform liberalism. This quantity is identical to 2 × (mood − platform mean liberalism). We do not measure these two variables on a common scale, of course, but instead treat them separately as the components of ideological proximity of the voters to the candidates.

24. According to Erikson, MacKuen, and Stimson (2002, chap. 7), the three variables account for 95 percent of the variance in the vote, 1952–1996. The lesser explained variance reported here is due in small part to the addition of three elections. More important, the measurement has changed from the earlier study. Stimson's mood is modified with every update, so that the most recent readings of mood's history are different from the readings for the same years at the writing of *The Macro Polity*. Also, here the readings of party identification include more than Gallup's. Further, our macropartisanship readings based on telephone surveys are not adjusted as they were in *The Macro Polity*. (Early Gallup phone surveys had an obvious Republican bias.)

25. We stress again that the relationship between the vote and party identification is causally ambiguous. Possibly they become more correlated over time because the vote influences macropartisanship, not the other way around. The key here is that the control for partisanship allows the role of issue proximity to be visible.

26. Inserting presidential approval in the equation predicting the vote would have an effect similar to inserting trial-heat polls through much of the election cycle (see fig. 6.6). We are not particularly interested here in estimating the contributions of the independent variables with trial-heat poll vote intentions and/or presidential approval held constant. Besides, given our limited degrees of freedom, such estimation cannot be performed with a high level of statistical confidence.

27. By the time Election Day approaches, one can enter the three political variables separately along with the prediction from cumulative income growth as a fourth. Each of the four variables is statistically significant with a *t*-value of 3 or greater.

CHAPTER SEVEN

1. We keep the story simple by ignoring change in and out of the "undecided" and "won't vote" categories.

2. Respondents are excluded if they lack a pre-election preference or do not vote or if they select a minor-party candidate. Thus the respondents in table 7.1 do not neces-

sarily reflect the electorate (or ANES sample) as a whole. Respondents who were interviewed pre-election but could not be interviewed post-election are also excluded
from the calculations.

3. The stability of vote choice in ANES panels has been the subject of surprisingly little
study. For one exception, see Miller and MacKuen (1979).

4. Fitting a lowess ("locally weighted scatterplot smoothing") curve to data is a standard way to graphically depict nonlinear relationships from scatterplots.

5. It may defy common sense that so much of the small amount of turnover occurs at
the very last minute. A real possibility is that most of the observed conversion on
Election Day from the day before is measurement error, due to coding mistakes and
other clerical errors. If so, the same amount of measurement error applies to the
measured stability at earlier days, and the net amount of true conversion is even
smaller than shown.

6. We thank John Zaller for sharing his data on voter informedness. For an application
of this index, see Zaller (2004). As of this writing, the final version of Zaller's index
for 2008 is unavailable.

7. If one also enters the interaction term as the product of date and knowledge, the
coefficient is not significant. The differences across information types that appear in
figure 7.3 are real, but they appear as interactions only because of the nature of the
dichotomous dependent variable, where for informed voters the degree of stability
approaches its 100 percent ceiling.

8. The coefficients for specific variables (e.g., southern white) sometimes change their
signs over the years. Within years, the coefficients do not change, except for the trivial exception where a variable is not close to being statistically significant.

9. For these comparisons, one should be wary of using probit coefficients because as
the overall variance explained expands, the individual coefficients do too. The best
way is to simply record the mean vote intention of groups over time. For instance,
the division in vote intentions between blacks and whites tends to grow over the
campaign. The division (among whites) between Catholics and Protestants in 1960
did not.

10. The data also reveal at least a hint that ANES respondents were more responsive
to the economy with their votes than with their pre-election vote intentions. Vote
switchers tended to be in the direction of the economic forces of the election. Walk-
ins, however, appear largely unresponsive to economic conditions.

11. For further discussion of why the utility variance should increase while the vote
division variance does not, see chapter 3.

12. A further bit of evidence comes from state-level polls of presidential preferences.
Consider the set of state-level polls for a given election over the campaign timeline.
A growing impact of partisanship will separate the states based on their differing
tendencies rather than bring them closer together. Meanwhile, the states presumably respond in a somewhat uniform way to campaign events, so that external fundamentals are fairly constant across states. The growing separation of states based
on growing partisan influence (internal fundamentals) should cause the cross-state
aggregate variance of state-level preferences to grow over the campaign timeline.
And this is what we find. State-level differences in vote intentions start out relatively
homogenous and then differ, presumably because partisanship becomes more salient to the voters.

13. While the figure is presented to display the differential variances of the two sets of

respondents, the vote intentions or vote choice for any particularly year should be read with considerable caution, due to small sample sizes.

CHAPTER EIGHT

1. Notice that this method for estimating the fundamentals provides a conservatives estimate, as we do not incorporate the variables from our political model, all of which cannot be measured throughout the election year. Party identification, ideological mood, and platform ideology all contribute to electoral explanation, as shown in chapter 6, especially after the party conventions. These variables are incorporated to some extent by presidential approval.

2. A more refined estimate would have the forecast error also include the estimated error in the b term. This would be the forecast error as $\varphi_T = \sqrt{\sigma_T^2 + Var(\beta_T)(V_{jT} - \bar{V}_T)}$. See Erikson and Wlezien (2008a). Here, we ignore the second term under the radical. Thus, we are pretending to be omniscient about the value of b. The implication is that our predictions present slightly greater certainty than would be warranted if we take into account the uncertainty of the equation parameters. Further, to make the exercise tractable, they are within-sample rather than out-of sample forecasts.

3. For instance, if the president is a Republican and the probability of a Republican win is estimated to be p, we convert to the probability of a Democratic win as $1 - p$.

4. Our analysis of the polls over the final thirty days of the 2004 campaign, a period when there were three presidential debates that by most accounts had Kerry winning, the movement of voter preferences was no greater than would be encountered if preferences remained constant while the polls were subject to sampling error. In other words, a test of statistical significance that takes into account the sampling error in the polls is not able to reject the null hypothesis that preferences did not move.

5. Legal betting on elections was once widespread in the United States (see Rohde and Strumpf 2004). By 1960, even Nevada had made election betting illegal, leaving reported betting markets in the hands of bookmakers in London, where it was (and is) legal. Meanwhile, since 1992, the Iowa Election Market has conducted "winner takes all" election markets—these have been declared legal as an educational tool for understanding how stock markets work. In recent elections, there are more prominent Internet-based election markets (e.g., Intrade) that originate outside the United States as commercial markets. Their prices on election outcomes are closely watched among US election observers.

6. In a winner-take-all market, one share of a candidate pays off one dollar if the candidate wins on Election Day and nothing if the candidate loses. For instance, a trader who bought one share of Obama for 50 cents and held it until Election Day received one dollar, for a 50-cent profit, fully 100 percent of the investment. Of course, bettors do not have to buy and hold, that is, they can sell at any time they can agree on a price with another buyer. In the less common vote share market, the Election Day payoff reflects the actual vote share, for example, 52.9 cents for Obama in 2008.

7. The more general tendency to overvalue underdogs is known as "long shot bias" (Wolfers and Zitzewitz 2004, 2008).

Abramowitz, Alan I. 1978. "The Impact of a Presidential Debate on Voter Rationality." *American Journal of Political Science* 22:680–90.

———. 2008. "Forecasting the 2008 Presidential Election with the Time-for-Change Model." *PS: Political Science and Politics* 41:691–95.

Achen, Christopher. 1992. "Social Psychology, Demographic Variables, and Linear Regression." *Political Behavior* 14:195–211.

Alvarez, R. Michael. 1997. *Information and Elections.* Ann Arbor: University of Michigan Press.

American Association for Public Opinion Research (AAPOR). 2009. *An Evaluation of the Methodology of the 2008 Pre-Election Primary Polls.* Http://www.aapor.org/uploads/AAPOR_Rept_FINAL-Rev-4-13-09.pdf.

Andersen, Robert, James Tilley, and Anthony F. Heath. 2005. "Political Knowledge and Enlightened Preferences: Party Choice through the Electoral Cycle." *British Journal of Political Science* 35:285–302.

Ansolabehere, Stephen. 2006. "Campaigns as Experiments." In *Capturing Campaign Effects*, edited by Henry E. Brady and Richard Johnston. Ann Arbor: University of Michigan Press.

Ansolabehere, Stephen, Jonathan Rodden, and James Snyder. 2008. "The Strength of Issues: Using Multiple Measures to Gauge Preference Stability, Ideological Constraint, and Issue Voting." American Political Science Review. 102:215–32.

Ansolabehere, Stephen, and Charles Stewart III. 2009. "Amazing Race: How Post-Racial was Obama's Victory?" *Boston Review*, January/February. Http://bostonreview.net/BR34.1/ansolabehere_stewart.php.

Arceneaux, Kevin. 2005. "Do Campaigns Help Voters Learn? A Cross-National Analysis." *British Journal of Political Science* 36:159–73.

Arrow, Kenneth J., Robert Forsythe, Michael Gorham, Robert Hahn, Robin Hanson, John O. Ledyard, Saul Levmore, Robert Litan, Paul Milgrom, Forrest D. Nelson, George R. Neumann, Marco Ottaviani, Thomas C. Schelling, Robert J. Shiller, Vernon L. Smith, Erik Snowberg, Cass R. Sunstein, Paul C. Tetlock, Philip E. Tetlock, Hal R. Varian, Justin Wolfers, and Eric Zitzewitz. 2008. "The Promise of Prediction Markets." *Science* 320:877–78.

Bartels, Larry. 1988. *Presidential Primaries and the Dynamics of Public Choice.* Princeton: Princeton University Press.

———. 2000. "Partisanship and Voting Behavior, 1952–1996." *American Journal of Political Science* 44:25–50.

———. 2002. "Beyond the Running Tally: Partisan Bias in Political Perceptions." *Political Behavior*. 24:117–30.

———. 2006. "Priming and Persuasion in Presidential Campaigns." In *Capturing Campaign Effects*, edited by Henry E. Brady and Richard Johnston. Ann Arbor: University of Michigan Press.

———. 2008. *Unequal Democracy*. New York: Russell Sage Foundation.

Bartels, Larry, and John Zaller. 2001. "Presidential Vote Models: A Recount." *PS: Political Science and Politics* 34:9–20.

Berelson, Bernard, Paul Lazarsfeld, and William McPhee. 1954. *Voting*. Chicago: University of Chicago Press.

Berg, Joyce, Robert Forsythe, Forrest Nelson, and Thomas Rietz. 2008. "Results from a Dozen Years of Election Futures Market Research." In *Handbook of Experimental Economic Results*, edited by Charles Plott and Vernon Smith. Elsevier: North Holland.

Berg, Joyce, Forrest Nelson, and Thomas Rietz. 2008. "Prediction Market Accuracy in the Long Run." *International Journal of Forecasting* 24:285–300.

Blumenthal, Mark. 2005. "Toward an Open-Source Methodology: What We Can Learn from the Blogosphere." *Public Opinion Quarterly* 69:655–69.

Box-Steffensmeier, Janet, and Renee Smith. 1998. "Investigating Political Dynamics using Fractional Integration Models." *American Journal of Political Science* 42:661–89.

Budge, Ian, Hans-Dieter Klingemann, Andrea Volkens, Judith Bara, and Erik Tannenbaum. 2001. *Mapping Policy Preferences: Estimates for Parties, Electors, and Governments, 1945–1998*. Oxford: Oxford University Press.

Budge, Ian, David Robertson, and Derek Hearl. 1987. *Ideology, Strategy and Party Change: Spatial Analyses of Post-War Election Programmes in 19 Democracies*. Cambridge: Cambridge University Press.

Burden, Barry. 2003. "Internal and External Effects on the Accuracy of NES Turnout." *Political Analysis* 11: 193–95.

Campbell, Angus, Philip E. Converse, Warren E. Miller, and Donald E. Stokes. 1960. *The American Voter*. New York: Wiley.

———. 1966. *Elections and the Political Order*. New York: Wiley.

Campbell, James E. 2008a. *The American Campaign: U.S. Presidential Campaigns and the National Vote*. 2nd ed. College Station: Texas A&M University Press.

———. 2008b. "The Trial-Heat Forecast of the 2008 Presidential Vote." *PS: Political Science and Politics* 41:697–701.

Campbell, James E., Lynne Cherry, and Kenneth A. Wink. 1992. "The Convention Bump." *American Politics Quarterly* 20:287–307.

Campbell, James E., and James C. Garand. 2000. *Before the Vote: Forecasting American National Elections*. Thousand Oaks, CA: Sage Publications.

Campbell, James E., and Kenneth A. Wink. 1990. "Trial-Heat Forecasts of the Presidential Vote." *American Politics Quarterly* 18:251–69.

Converse, Philip E. 1962. "Information Flow and the Stability of Partisan Attitudes." *Public Opinion Quarterly* 26:578–99.

———. 1964. "The Nature of Belief Systems in the Mass Public." In *Ideology and Discontent*, edited by David Apter. New York: Free Press.

Converse, Philip E., Aage R. Clausen, and Warren E. Miller. 1965. "Electoral Myth and Reality: The 1964 Election." *American Political Science Review* 59:321–36.

Converse, Phillip E., and Michael W. Traugott. 1986. "Assessing the Accuracy of Polls and Surveys." *Science* 234:1094–98.

Crespi, Irving. 1988. *Pre-Election Polling: Sources of Accuracy and Error*. New York: Russell Sage.

DeBoef, S. 2000. "Persistence and Aggregations of Survey Data over Time: From Microfoundations to Macropersistence." *Electoral Studies* 19 (March): 9–29.

DeBoef, Suzanna, and Jim Granato. 1997. "Near Integrated Data and the Analysis of Political Relationships." *American Journal of Political Analysis* 41 (April): 619–40.

Downs, Anthony. 1957. *An Economic Theory of Democracy*. New York: Harper and Row.

Druckman, James N. 2001. "On the Limits of Framing Effects: Who Can Frame?" *Journal of Politics* 63:1041–66.

———. 2004. "Political Preference Formation: Competition, Deliberation, and the (Ir)relevance of Framing Effects." *American Political Science Review* 98:671–86.

Enns, Peter, and Brian Richman. 2009. "Presidential Polls and the Fundamentals Reconsidered." Paper presented at the Annual Meeting of the American Political Science Association, Washington, DC.

Erikson, Robert S. 1989. "Economic Conditions and the Presidential Vote." *American Political Science Review* 83 (June): 567–73.

———. 2009. "The American Voter and the Economy, 2008." *PS: Political Science and Politics* 42:467–71.

Erikson, Robert S., Michael B. MacKuen, and James A. Stimson. 2002. *The Macro Polity*. Cambridge: Cambridge University Press.

Erikson, Robert S., Costas Panagopoulos, and Christopher Wlezien. 2004. "Likely (and Unlikely) Voters and the Assessment of Campaign Dynamics." *Public Opinion Quarterly* 68:588–601.

———. 2010. "The Crystallization of Voter Preferences during the 2008 Presidential Campaign." *Presidential Studies Quarterly* 40:482–96.

Erikson, Robert S., and Kent L. Tedin. 2011. *American Public Opinion*. New York: Longman.

Erikson, Robert S., and Christopher Wlezien. 1999. "Presidential Polls as a Time Series: The Case of 1996." *Public Opinion Quarterly* 63:163–77.

———. 2008a. "Are Political Markets Really Superior to Polls as Election Predictors?" *Public Opinion Quarterly* 72:190–215.

———. 2008b. "Leading Economic Indicators, the Polls and the Presidential Vote." *PS: Political Science and Politics* 41:703–7.

Fair, Ray C. 1978. "The Effect of Economic Events on Votes for President." *Review of Economics and Statistics* 60:159–73.

———. 2002. *Predicting Presidential Elections and Other Things*. Palo Alto: Stanford University Press.

Finkel, Steven F. 1993. "Reexamining the 'Minimal Effects' Model in Recent Presidential Elections." *Journal of Politics* 55:1–21.

Fiorina, P. Morris. 1981. *Retrospective Voting in American Elections*. New Haven: Yale University Press.

Fiorina, P. Morris, Samuel J. Abrams, and Jeremy C. Pope. 2003. "The 2000 Presidential Election: Can Retrospective Voting Be Saved?" *British Journal of Political Science* 48:723–41.

Fiorina, P. Morris, and Paul E. Peterson. 2002. *The New American Democracy*. New York: Longman.

Geer, John G. 1988. "The Effects of Presidential Debates on the Electorate's Preferences for Candidates." *American Politics Quarterly* 16:486–501.

———. 2006. *In Defense of Negativity: Attach Advertising in Presidential Campaigns.* Chicago: University of Chicago Press.

Gelman, Andrew, and Gary King. 1993. "Why Are American Presidential Election Polls so Variable When Votes Are so Predictable?" *British Journal of Political Science* 23: 409–51.

Gerber, Alan, James G. Gimpel, Donald P. Green, and Daron R. Shaw. 2011. "How Large and Long-lasting Are the Persuasion Effects of Televised Ad Campaigns." *American Political Science Review* 105:135–60.

Gerber, Alan, and Donald P. Green. 1998. "Rational Learning and Partisan Attitudes." *American Journal of Political Science* 42:794–818.

Granger, Clive. 1980. "Long Memory Relationships and the Aggregation of Dynamic Models." *Journal of Econometrics* 14:227–38.

Green, Donald, Bradley Palmquist, and Eric Schickler. 2004. *Partisan Hearts and Minds.* New Haven: Yale University Press.

Groves, Robert M. 1989. *Survey Errors and Survey Costs.* New York: Wiley.

Hellwig, Timothy. 2010. "Elections and the Economy." In *Comparing Democracies 3: Elections and Voting in Global Perspective,* edited by Lawrence LeDuc, Richard G. Niemi, and Pippa Norris. London: Sage.

Herbst, Susan. 1993. *Numbered Voices: How Opinion Polling Has Shaped American Politics.* Chicago: University of Chicago Press.

Hibbs, Douglas A., Jr. 1987. *The American Political Economy.* Cambridge: Harvard University Press.

Hill, Seth, James Lo, Lynn Vavreck, and John Zaller. 2011. "How Quickly We Forget: Late Campaign Advertising and Electoral Advantage." Manuscript.

Hillygus, D. Sunshine. 2010. "Campaign Effects on Vote Choice." In *The Oxford Handbook of American Elections and Political Behavior,* edited by Jan E. Leighley. Oxford: Oxford University Press.

Hillygus, D. Sunshine, and Todd G. Shields. 2008. *The Persuadable Voter: Wedge Issues in Presidential Election Campaigns.* Princeton: Princeton University Press.

Holbrook, Thomas. 1996. *Do Campaigns Matter?* Thousand Oaks, CA: Sage Publications.

———. 2010. "Forecasting U.S. Presidential Elections." In *The Oxford Handbook of American Elections and Political Behavior,* edited by Jan E. Leighley. Oxford: Oxford University Press.

Huber, Gregory, and Kevin Arceneaux. 2007. "Uncovering the Persuasive Effects of Presidential Advertising." *American Journal of Political Science* 51:957–77.

Iyengar, Shanto, and Donald Kinder. (1987) 2010. *News That Matters.* Reprint. Chicago: University of Chicago Press.

Johnston, Richard, Andre Blais, Henry E. Brady, and Jean Crete. 1992. *Letting the People Decide: Dynamics of a Canadian Election.* Kingston, Canada: McGill-Queen's Press.

Johnston, Richard, Michael G. Hagen, and Kathleen Hall Jamieson. 2004. *The 2000 Presidential Election and the Foundations of Party Politics.* Cambridge: Cambridge University Press.

Kahn, Kim Fridkin, and Edie N. Goldenberg. 1991. "Women Candidates in the News: An Examination of Gender Differences in U.S. Senate Campaign Coverage." *Public Opinion Quarterly* 55:180–99.

Kayser, Mark, and Christopher Wlezien. 2011. "Performance Pressure: Patterns of Partisanship and the Economic Vote." *European Journal of Political Research* 50:365–94.

Kiewiet, Roderick. 1983. *Macroeconomics and Micropolitics*. Chicago: University of Chicago Press.

Kou, S. G., and Michael E. Sobel. 2004. "Forecasting the Vote: A Theoretical Comparison of Election Markets and Public Opinion Polls." *Political Analysis* 12:277–95.

Krosnick, Jon A., and Donald R. Kinder. 1990. "Altering the Foundations of Support of the President through Priming." *American Political Science Review* 84:497–512.

Ladner, Matthew, and Christopher Wlezien. 2007. "Partisan Preferences, Electoral Prospects, and Economic Expectations." *Comparative Political Studies* 40:571–96.

Lanoue, David J. 1991. "The 'Turning Point': Viewers' Reactions to the Second 1988 Presidential Debate." *American Politics Quarterly* 19:80–95.

Lau, Richard R. 1994. "An Analysis of the Accuracy of 'Trial Heat' Polls during the 1992 Presidential Election." *Public Opinion Quarterly* 58:2–20.

Lau, Richard R., and David P. Redlawsk. 2006. *How Voters Decide*. New York: Cambridge University Press.

Lebo, Matthew J., Robert W. Walker, and Harold D. Clarke. 2000. "You Must Remember This: Dealing with Long Memory in Political Analyses." *Electoral Studies* 19:31–48.

Lenz, Gabriel. 2009. "Learning and Opinion Change, Not Priming." *American Journal of Political Science* 53:821–37.

Lewis-Beck, Michael S. 2005. "Election Forecasting: Principles and Practice." *British Journal of Politics and International Relations* 7:145–64.

Lewis-Beck, Michael S., and Tom W. Rice. 1992. *Forecasting Elections*. Washington, DC: Congressional Quarterly Press.

Lewis-Beck, Michael S., and Mary Stegmaier. 2000. "Economic Determinants of Election Outcomes." *Annual Review of Political Science* 3:183–219.

Linn, Suzanna, Jonathan Nagler, and Marco A. Morales. 2010. "Economics, Elections and Voting Behavior." In *The Oxford Handbook of American Elections and Political Behavior*, edited by Jan Leighley. Oxford: Oxford University Press.

Lodge, Milton, Marco Steenbergen, and Shawn Brau. 1995. "The Responsive Voter: Campaign Information and the Dynamics of Candidate Evaluation." *American Political Science Review* 89:309–26.

MacKuen, Michael. 1983. "Political Drama, Economic Conditions, and the Dynamics of Presidential Popularity." *American Journal of Political Science* 27:165–92.

MacKuen, Michael, Robert S. Erikson, and James A. Stimson. 1989. "Macropartisanship." *American Political Science Review* 83:1125–42.

———. 1992. "Peasants or Bankers? The American Electorate and the U.S. Economy." *American Political Science Review* 86:597–611.

McDermott, Monika, and Kathleen Frankovic. 2003. "Horserace Polling and Survey Method Effects: An Analysis of the 2000 Campaign." *Public Opinion Quarterly* 67: 244–64.

McDonald, Michael, Ian Budge, and Richard Hofferbert. 1999. "Party Mandate Theory and Time Series Analysis: A Theoretical and Methodological Response." *Electoral Studies* 18:587–96.

McKelvey, Richard D., and William Zavoina. 1975. "A Statistical Model for the Analysis of Ordinal Level Dependent Variables." *Journal of Mathematical Sociology* 4:103–20.

Mendelberg, Tali. 2001. *The Race Card: Campaign Strategy, Implicit Messages and the Norm of Equality*. Princeton: Princeton University Press.

Miller, Arthur H., and Michael MacKuen. 1979. "Learning about the Candidates: The 1976 Presidential Debates." *Public Opinion Quarterly* 3:326–46.

Miller, Joanne M., and Jon A. Krosnick. 1996. "News Media Impact on the Ingredients of

Presidential Evaluations: A Program of Research on the Priming Hypothesis." In *Political Persuasion and Attitude Change*, edited by Diana C. Mutz, Richard A. Brody, and Paul M. Sniderman. Ann Arbor: University of Michigan Press.

Mueller, John. 1970. "Presidential Popularity from Truman to Johnson." *American Political Science Review* 64:18–34.

Noelle-Neumann, Elisabeth. 1984. *The Spiral of Silence: A Theory of Public Opinion—Our Social Skin*. Chicago: University of Chicago Press.

Poole, Keith, and Howard Rosenthal. 2007. *Congress: A Political-Economic History of Roll Call Voting*. Oxford: Oxford University Press.

Popkin, Samuel L. 1991. *The Reasoning Voter: Communication and Persuasion in Presidential Campaigns*. Chicago: University of Chicago Press.

Rogoff, Kenneth, and Anne Sibert. 1988. "Elections and Macroeconomic Policy Cycles." *Review of Economic Studies* 55:1–16.

Rohde, Paul W., and Koleman S. Strumpf. 2004. "Historic Presidential Betting Markets." *Journal of Economic Perspectives* 18 (Spring): 127–42.

Rosenstone, Steven J. 1983. *Forecasting Presidential Elections*. New Haven: Yale University Press.

Shapiro, Robert Y., and Yaeli Bloch-Elkon. 2008. "Do the Facts Speak for Themselves? Partisan Disagreement as a Challenge to Democratic Competence." *Critical Review: A Journal of Politics and Society* 20:115–39.

Shaw, Daron R. 1999a. "The Effect of TV Ads and Candidate Appearances on Statewide Presidential Votes, 1988–1996." *American Political Science Review* 93:345–61.

———. 1999b. "A Study of Presidential Campaign Event Effects from 1952 to 1992." *Journal of Politics* 6:387–422.

———. 2006. *The Race to 270: The Electoral College and the Campaign Strategies of 2004 and 2004*. Chicago: University of Chicago Press.

Squire, Peverill. 1988. "Why the 1936 Literary Digest Poll Failed." *Public Opinion Quarterly* 52:125–33.

Stevenson, Randolph, and Lynn Vavreck. 2000. "Does Campaign Length Matter? Testing for Cross-National Effects." *British Journal of Political Science* 30: 217–35.

Stimson, James A. 1991, 1999. *Public Opinion in America: Moods, Cycles and Swings*. 1st and 2nd eds. Boulder, CO: Westview Press.

———. 2004. *Tides of Consent: How Public Opinion Shapes American Politics*. New York: Cambridge University Press.

Traugott, Michael. 2005. "The Accuracy of the National Preelection Polls in the 2004 Presidential Election." *Public Opinion Quarterly* 69:642–54.

Tufte, Edward. 1978. *Political Control of the Economy*. Princeton: Princeton University Press.

Vavreck, Lynn. 2009. *The Message Matters: The Economy and Presidential Campaigns*. Princeton: Princeton University Press.

Wlezien, Christopher. 2000. "An Essay on 'Combined' Time Series Processes." *Electoral Studies* 19:77–93.

Wlezien, Christopher, and Robert S. Erikson. 1996. "Temporal Horizons and Presidential Election Forecasts." *American Politics Quarterly* 24:492–505.

———. 2001. "Campaign Effects in Theory and Practice." *American Politics Research* 29:419–437.

———. 2002. "The Timeline of Presidential Election Campaigns." *Journal of Politics* 64: 969–93.

Wlezien, Christopher, Mark Franklin, and Daniel Twiggs. 1997. "Economic Perceptions and Vote Choice: Disentangling the Endogeneity." *Political Behavior* 19:7–17.

Wolfers, Justin, and Eric Zitzewitz. 2004. "Prediction Markets." *Journal of Economic Perspectives* 18 (Spring): 103–26.

———. 2008. "Prediction Markets in Theory and Practice." In *The New Palgrave Dictionary of Economics*, 2nd ed., edited by Larry Blume and Steve Durlauf. London: Palgrave Macmillan.

Zaller, John. 1992. *The Nature and Origins of Mass Opinion*. New York: Cambridge University Press.

———. 2002. "Assessing the Statistical Power of Election Studies to Detect Communication Effects in Political Campaigns." *Electoral Studies* 21:297–329.

———. 2004. "Floating Voters in U.S. Presidential Elections, 1948–2000. In *The Issue of Belief: Essays in the Intersection of Non-Attitudes and Attitude Change*, edited by Paul Sniderman and Willem Saris. Princeton: Princeton University Press.

advertising, 10, 12
African American voters, 142, 153, 154, 156, 192n9
age of voter, 153, 155, 156
Alvarez, R. Michael, 149
American National Election Studies (ANES): economy and, 192n10; pre- and post-election interviews, 139, 143–44, 145, 146, 154–57, 192n3; turnover in successive elections and, 140–42; variance compression and, 157, 160
April polls (ED-200), 2, 4, 61–63, 165
autoregressive (AR1) process, 46–49, 60, 63. *See also* random walk (integrated series); stationary time series

Bartels, Larry, 41
beginning of election year, 1, 4, 166
bounces, 44–46, 166; conventions and, 76–77, 107, 188n23; intensification effect and, 55; of stationary time series, 47, 49, 50, 52. *See also* late campaign effects; shocks
broadcast networks, 17, 166
Budge, Ian, 129, 167, 190n21
bumps, 44–46, 166; conventions and, 76–77, 107, 166; of stationary time series, 47, 50, 52. *See also* shocks
Business Retrospections, 112, 116, 117–18

campaign effects, 1–2; downward trend over the years, 144; events perspective on, 11–13 (*see also* convention season; debates); fundamentals and, 2, 5–7,

13, 15, 41–42, 57, 177–78; models of, 13–14, 41–42; overestimated by observers, 176–77; partisan predispositions and, 55–57, 148–49; predicting specific elections and, 169; seeming contradictions of, 165; time-series properties and, 49, 50, 51–52; voter decision-making and, 10–11; voters' relative utilities and, 53–55, 56. *See also* enlightenment (learning); fundamentals; late campaign effects; persuasion; priming; shocks
Campbell, James, 7
candidate attractiveness, partisan effects and, 57, 160. *See also* presidential approval; relative utility (relative liking)
candidate competence, 2; persuasion about, 10
candidate positions, 7. *See also* platform ideology
Catholic voters, 154, 156, 192n9
change in voter preferences, 15. *See also* campaign effects; volatility of voter preferences
Comparative Manifesto Project, 128
conservatism. *See* platform ideology; policy mood
convention season, 4, 12, 72–79, 102–7; bump associated with, 76–77, 107, 166; changes in scheduling of, 37, 60–61, 72; decline in poll variance over, 37–38; difference between Election Day vote and polls of, 90; economic factors independent of, 115; fundamentals and, 8, 167; learning in, 107, 131–32, 188n21; political model and, 130, 131–32; predicting

convention season (*continued*)
the Election Day vote and, 97, 99, 100,
101–7, 188n19; volatility of voter preferences in, 31, 32, 67, 72–75, 79, 166
cross-sectional analysis, 60–72; biweekly-
by-biweekly, 67; conventions and,
72–79; long-term equilibrium in,
69–72; mid-April vs. election eve,
61–63; of time series, 60–61; week-by-
week, 63–69
cross-sectional variance, 32–38. *See also*
variance compression, cross-sectional
crystallization of voter preferences, 2,
148–54, 155

daily analysis of vote division, 35–38; vs.
Election Day vote, 88–90; reliability in,
183n15
debates, 12, 79–81
decision-making by poll responders, 10–11
defections, partisan, 150–51
demographic variables, 140, 148; campaign
evolution and, 151–54; Election Day
vote and, 154–57
design effects on poll accuracy, 30
dropouts. *See* nonvoters
dynamics of vote intentions, 2, 3, 41–42;
conclusions of initial analysis, 57–58;
individual voter and, 42–44; models of,
46–52; shifting over time, 52–57; types
of shocks contributing to, 44–46. *See
also* random walk (integrated series);
shocks; stationary time series; time
series

early polls. *See* April polls (ED-200)
economic model, 109, 110–25; compared
to political model, 133–36; disparate
views of, 110; objective factors in,
110–11, 112–15, 117, 121–22, 123–25,
188n3; predicting Election Day vote
from, 110, 121–25; subjective factors in,
111–13, 115–19, 122, 123–25, 189n12;
summary of, 125
Economic News Heard, 189n13
Economic Perceptions, 117–18, 122, 123,
124, 125, 189n13; omitted from combined model, 134
economy, 2, 3, 5, 6, 7; as driver of vote
intentions, 167, 168; election of 2000
and, 8, 168; political variables and, 134;
predicting specific elections and, 169;

presidential approval and, 109, 119–24,
133, 190n15; priming about, 9, 115,
168; vote switchers and, 192n10. *See
also* fundamentals
ED-200 (April) polls, 2, 4, 61–63, 165
educational level of voter, 153, 155, 156
election markets, 176–77, 181n4,
193nn5–6
election of 2000: economy and, 8, 168;
intangibles in, 168
electoral (true) preferences, 27
enlightenment (learning), 8; in convention
season, 107, 131–32, 188n21; about
economy, 115, 119; fundamentals and,
6, 8, 41, 148, 168; individual-level relative utility and, 158; of least interested
voters, 11; moving equilibrium and, 14;
in primary season, 107; priming effect
on, 9
equilibrium: bounces or bumps and, 45;
campaign effects and, 13–14; of stationary time series, 47–48, 49, 52, 58
equilibrium, moving, 13–14, 50–51,
165–66; convention period and, 103;
fundamentals as driver of, 45–46, 167;
regression analysis of, 69–72, 87, 98,
100–102; year-specific, 69, 82
Erikson, Robert S. *See Macro Polity*
error. *See* sampling error; survey error
error correction model, 50
error variance, 27–28, 60. *See also* sampling
error
events. *See* shocks
external fundamentals, 6, 7; increasing
variance of, 159. *See also* economic
model; economy; fundamentals; political factors; political model; presidential
approval

final campaign weeks: graphs of polls by
year, 26; stability of vote division in,
66, 67–69, 166; two-stage least squares
analysis, 69–72; variance of polls
during, 26, 28–30, 31, 32. *See also* late
campaign effects
final week polls: convention effects and,
76–77; election outcome and, 83–88,
90; incumbent party vote and, 83–85;
shrinking lead and, 4, 69, 84, 87–88,
91; uncertainties of prediction and, 167
Finkel, Steven E., 148–49
first-time voters, 142

floating voters, 5. *See also* independent voters

forecasting. *See* predicting Election Day vote

fractionally integrated time series, 184n45

framing, 181n6

fundamentals, 167–68; campaign effects and, 2, 5–7, 13, 15, 41–42, 57, 177–78; defined, 5–6, 181n3; enlightenment and, 6, 8, 41, 148, 168; equilibrium representing, 45–46, 167; external vs. internal, 6–7; market predictions and, 177; poll-based predictions and, 177; post-convention slopes and, 103; predicting specific elections and, 169, 170–71, 193n1; in stock market, 181n4; in time-series model, 49, 50, 51; typical outcome and, 3, 11. *See also* economy; external fundamentals; internal fundamentals

Gallup polls, 17; demographics in, 152, 154; individual voters from, 139, 149; party identification in, 126, 150, 191n24; of presidential approval, 119; variance compression and, 157–58

Gallup Report, 19

gambling. *See* election markets

GDP growth, 110

Gelman, Andrew, 14, 148, 152

gender gap, 154

gender of voter, 154, 155, 156; priming based on, 9

group characteristics, 6. *See also* demographic variables

Hibbs, Douglas A., 111

Hispanic voters, 153, 154, 155

house effects on poll accuracy, 30, 183n10

ideological proximity of voters to parties, 2, 109, 126–27, 129, 134, 167, 191n23. *See also* platform ideology; policy mood

Income Growth, 111; political variables and, 134; predicting specific elections and, 170; presidential approval and, 121–22, 123–24; subjective measure correlated with, 117; vote and, 113–15

income growth, 110–11

income of voter, 152, 153, 154, 155, 156

incumbent party vote: over convention season, 75–77, 105–7; final week's polls and, 83–85

incumbent president. *See* presidential approval

independent voters, 5, 55, 56–57, 149. *See also* least politically involved voters

Index of Consumer Sentiment, 111, 116

index of leading economic indicators, 189n8

individual voter: factors influencing, 5; hypothetical time series of, 42–44; intensification effect and, 53–55; partisan effect and, 56; survey data sources, 139. *See also* internal fundamentals; relative utility (relative liking); vote shifts by individual voters

information: intensification effect and, 53; vote stability and, 10, 146–48, 192n7. *See also* enlightenment (learning)

in-person polls, 18

instrumental variable, 60, 69, 74, 87, 101

intangible forces, 5, 168

integrated time series. *See* random walk (integrated series)

intensification effect, 53–55

interactive voice response (IVR) polls, 18

intercepts: of daily equations, 187n11; of vote intention by lagged vote intention, 63

interests of voters, 6, 148–49. *See also* fundamentals

internal fundamentals, 6, 148–54, 162, 168. *See also* demographic variables; fundamentals; partisan predispositions; party identification

Internet as information source, 144

Internet polls, 18

interpolation: of daily economic measures, 112, 189nn5–6; of daily vote division, 35–36, 88–89, 183n15, 187nn6–7

Inter-University Consortium for Political and Social Research (ICPSR), 139. *See also* American National Election Studies (ANES)

Intrade commercial election markets, 176, 193n5

Iowa Electronic Market, 176, 193n5

iPOLL database, 19, 139

issues. *See* platform ideology; policy mood

Jewish voters, 154, 156

King, Gary, 14, 148, 152

late campaign effects, 6, 13–14, 15, 46, 166, 167, 178; in autoregressive model, 48, 49; as bounces, 44; regression coefficients and, 99–100; R-squared statistic and, 93. *See also* final campaign weeks
late-deciding walk-ins, 154, 160, 161, 162, 163, 167
late electoral shifting, 86–88
learning. *See* enlightenment (learning)
least politically involved voters, 10, 11, 56. *See also* independent voters
least squares. *See* OLS (ordinary least squares); TSLS (two-stage least squares)
Lenz, Gabriel, 181n7
liberal-conservative platform ideology. *See* platform ideology
liberal-conservative policy mood. *See* policy mood
likely voters, 19, 162, 167, 182nn5–6. *See also* late-deciding walk-ins; nonvoters
live-interviewer polls, 18, 19
long-term predispositions, 10–11, 182n8. *See also* internal fundamentals; partisan predispositions
lowess (locally weighted scatterplot smoothing), 192n4

MacKuen, Michael. *See Macro Polity*
macropartisanship, 109, 126, 127, 128, 190n16, 191n24; economy and, 134; Election Day vote and, 132–33, 134, 136, 191n25; major shifts in, 190n19; platform ideology and, 130. *See also* party identification
Macro Polity, 109, 126, 130, 191n24
marital status of voter, 156
markets, election prediction, 176–77, 181n4, 193nn5–6
memory-based processing, 11
"minimal effects" view of campaigns, 7, 13
minor-party candidates, 19, 142
missing data, 59–60, 61
mobilization efforts, 12
models of campaign timeline. *See* time series
models of campaign variables. *See* economic model; political model
mood. *See* policy mood
multistage random samples, 18, 182n3

national conventions. *See* convention season

near-integrated time series, 52, 184n3
newly eligible voters, 142
newspaper organizations, polls of, 17
nomination. *See* convention season; primary season
nonvoters, 88, 154, 160–61, 162–63, 167
normal vote, 57

OLS (ordinary least squares): conventions and, 74, 75, 77–79, 102–6; with lag-2 values, 185n6; late polls and, 87, 186n4; regression coefficients in, 98–100, 101–2; at various lag lengths, 71; of vote-by-last-poll relationship, 84; with weekly vote intentions, 63, 67–69
online processing, 10–11

partisan defections, 150–51
partisan predispositions: apparent rise in, 181n2; Bayesian models of, 184n9; campaign effects and, 55–57, 148–49; perceptions based on, 149; priming of, 9; pushing vote margin to the center, 55–57, 58, 159–60; stability of, 10, 11; state-level polls and, 192n12
party conventions. *See* convention season
party identification, 5, 6, 167; campaign evolution and, 149–52, 162; demographic variables and, 154; Election Day vote choice and, 155; policy mood and, 128; in political model, 109–10, 125–27; variance compression and, 159–60. *See also* macropartisanship
Personal Retrospections, 112, 189n11
persuasion, 1, 9–10
Pew polls, 148
platform ideology, 109, 126, 128–30, 132, 133, 134, 167, 190n21
policy mood, 109–10, 126, 127–28, 130, 132, 133, 167, 190n20, 191n24
policy preferences, 5, 6; long-term dispositions on, 182n8; persuasion about, 10
political factors, 2, 5, 7, 167. *See also* fundamentals
political knowledge, 146–48
political model, 109–10, 125–33; compared to economic model, 133–36; predicting Election Day vote, 110, 130, 132–33; testing over the campaign, 130–32; variables of, 109, 125–30
PoliticsNow website, 19
polling periods, 20, 21

PollingReport.com, 17, 19
poll of polls, 20–21
polls: decision-making by responders
    to, 10–11; historical development of,
    17–18; vs. market predictions, 177;
    "silence" of loser's supporters in, 88;
    wording of, 17, 19
polls included in analysis, 2, 3; of individ-
    ual vote decisions, 139–40; selection of,
    18–21; summarized graphically, 21–26
predictability of elections, 7–8, 175–77
"predictable campaign" perspective, 7, 8;
    priming and, 9
predicting Election Day vote: with
    combined model, 135–36, 191n27;
    conclusions about, 107–8; convention
    season and, 97, 99, 100, 101–7, 188n19;
    from economic variables, 110, 121–25;
    from final week polls, 83–88, 90; with
    political model, 110, 130, 132–33; from
    polls over campaign timeline, 88–90;
    presidential approval and, 119–22;
    regression coefficients and, 90, 97–102;
    R-squared statistic and, 90–97. See also
    economic model; political model
predicting specific elections, 168–77;
    compared to election markets, 175–77;
    graphical presentation of results,
    171–75; model for, 169–71
predicting vote intentions, 136–37; with
    economic model, 121–22, 134–35; with
    political model, 130–32, 134–35; with
    presidential approval, 121–22
predictive factors. See campaign effects;
    fundamentals
presidential approval, 7, 119–22, 167;
    the economy and, 109, 119–24, 133,
    190n15; with incumbent president run-
    ning for reelection, 190n14; as indicator
    of performance, 167; omitted from
    combined model, 134, 191n26; predict-
    ing from political model, 130–31; pre-
    dicting specific elections and, 170–75.
    See also candidate attractiveness
presidential performance, 3, 5, 6, 167. See
    also presidential approval
primary season, 4, 97
priming, 8–9, 41, 168, 181n7; about
    economy, 9, 115, 168; time-series mod-
    els and, 53
print media, 166
probit equations: demographics and,

152–53, 155, 156, 192n9; party iden-
    tification and, 149–50, 155; variance
    compression and, 158–59; Zaller infor-
    mation index and, 147
pseudo R-squared, 152–53, 155, 156
Public Opinion, 19
Public Perspective, 19

quota sampling, 18

race, 9, 148, 152, 154, 155, 156
random sampling, 18; departures from,
    183n11; multistage, 18, 182n3. See also
    sampling error
random walk (integrated series), 47, 48; for
    bounded variable, 184n4; of individual
    preferences, 53–54; problems with
    model using, 52; R-squared statistic
    and, 91, 93; with stationary component,
    50–51, 91; vs. stationary time series,
    49–50; two-stage least squares analysis
    and, 70. See also near-integrated time
    series
region of voter, 155, 156
registered voters, 19
regression. See OLS (ordinary least
    squares); TSLS (two-stage least squares)
regression coefficients, 90, 97–102; for
    convention period, 102–6
relative utility (relative liking), 43, 52; in-
    tensification effect on, 53–55; learning
    and, 158; partisan effect and, 55–57
reliability, statistical, 28, 30; in daily analy-
    sis, 35–36, 183n15; with lagged weekly
    vote intentions, 68–69
religion of voter, 152, 153, 154, 155, 156,
    192n9
rolling cross-sections, 34–38
Roper Center, 19, 139
R-squared statistic, 90–97; adjusted,
    definition of, 187n16; over campaign
    timeline, 94–97; conventions and, 76,
    102; in cross-sectional analysis, 64, 67,
    68, 71; debates and, 81; economy and,
    114; final week polls and, 86; theory of,
    90–94. See also pseudo R-squared

sampling error, 3, 4, 12, 165–66; daily
    analysis and, 35–36; dwarfed in the
    cross-section, 35, 60; estimation of,
    27–28; in fall campaign, 30; within-year
    variance adjusted for, 30–32

shocks, 44–46; content of, 109 (*see also* economic model; political model); individual voter and, 43; intensification effect and, 55; modeling effects of, 46–52; regression coefficients and, 98, 102, 103–5; R-squared statistic and, 93–94, 96, 97. *See also* bounces; bumps; campaign effects; late campaign effects

short-term influences, 6, 10–11, 15, 182n8. *See also* bounces; late campaign effects

shrinking leads: over campaign timeline, 99; final week polls and, 4, 69, 84, 87–88, 91

southern white voters, 153, 154, 156

speeches, 12

"spiral of silence" effect, 88

stability: of aggregate vote intentions, 140; of individual vote choice, 139–40, 144; of partisan predispositions, 10, 11; of vote division in final weeks, 66, 67–69, 166. *See also* volatility of voter preferences; vote shifts by individual voters

state-level polls, 192n12

stationary time series, 47–49; problems with model using, 51–52; vs. random walk, 49–50; random walk with component of, 50–51, 91; R-squared statistic and, 93

Stimson, James A., 126, 127–28, 167, 190n20, 191n24. See also *Macro Polity*

survey error, 12, 27, 30. *See also* sampling error

Survey of Consumers, University Of Michigan, 111, 115, 118

surveys. See polls

switching votes. *See* vote shifts by individual voters

telephone interviewing, transition to, 18

television, 17, 166

timeline, presidential campaign: crystallization of voter preferences over, 2, 148–54, 155; for fifteen specific elections, 171–75; four key points of, 139; most important periods of, 4, 166–67; pace of change over, 166–67; summary of, 165–68. *See also* campaign effects

time series: campaign effects and, 51–52, 93–94; difficulty of modeling poll data with, 34, 42, 59–61; of individual voter, 42–44; models of, 46–52; R-squared and, 90–94; vote intentions over the

campaign as, 165–66. *See also* random walk (integrated series); stationary time series

tracking polls, 17

trial-heat polls, 2–3, 4, 14, 17. *See also* polls

true preferences, 27

true variance, 27–30; in different periods of campaign, 30–32

TSLS (two-stage least squares), 69–72, 74, 185n11; conventions and, 77–79, 103–6; late polls and, 87, 186n4; regression coefficients in, 100–102; of vote-by-last-poll relationship, 84

undecided voters, 87–88, 148, 167, 186n5

underdog bias, 176, 193n7

union membership, 153, 156

University Of Michigan Survey of Consumers, 111, 115, 118

utility. *See* relative utility (relative liking)

variance: of autoregressive process, 47; cross-sectional, 32–38; induced by party identification, 149–50; of random walk (integrated series), 47, 50, 51; of stationary series, 47, 48–49; within-year, 22, 25–26, 30–32. See also R-squared statistic

variance compression, cross-sectional, 32–34, 36–38, 39, 157–63; over campaign timeline, 158–60; conclusions about, 58, 162–63; convention effect on, 37, 75; from fall campaign to final vote, 160–62; intensification effect and, 53–55; partisan activation and, 55–57, 159–60; random walk model and, 50, 51, 53; R-squared statistic and, 93; two-stage least squares analysis and, 71

variance compression, within-year, 26

Vavreck, Lynn, 9

volatility of voter preferences: in convention season, 31, 32, 67, 72–75, 79, 166; in debate periods, 81; over the election year, 30–32, 38–39, 183n13; across election years, 25, 29; in fall polls, 29; overestimated by election markets, 176–77. *See also* stability; vote shifts by individual voters

vote. *See* predicting Election Day vote

vote intentions, 1, 2; aggregate stability of, 140; slow evolution of, 177; as a time series, 165–66. *See also* dynamics of vote intentions; polls; predicting vote intentions

voter. *See* individual voter

vote shifts by individual voters, 140–48; across elections, 140–42, 146; information and, 146–48; from pre-election intention to Election Day choice, 143–44, 147, 154, 192n5; timeline of, 145–46. *See also* internal fundamentals; volatility of voter preferences

walk-ins, 154, 160, 161, 162, 163, 167

women voters, 153, 154, 156

Zaller, John, 146–47, 182n8

Chicago Studies in American Politics
A series edited by Benjamin I. Page, Susan Herbst,
Lawrence R. Jacobs, and James Druckman

Series titles, continued from front matter:

DEMOCRACY AT RISK: HOW TERRORIST
THREATS AFFECT THE PUBLIC *by Jennifer L.
Merolla and Elizabeth J. Zechmeister*

AGENDAS AND INSTABILITY IN AMERICAN
POLITICS, SECOND EDITION *by Frank R.
Baumgartner and Bryan D. Jones*

THE PRIVATE ABUSE OF THE PUBLIC INTEREST
by Lawrence D. Brown and Lawrence R. Jacobs

THE PARTY DECIDES: PRESIDENTIAL
NOMINATIONS BEFORE AND AFTER REFORM
*by Marty Cohen, David Karol, Hans Noel,
and John Zaller*

SAME SEX, DIFFERENT POLITICS: SUCCESS
AND FAILURE IN THE STRUGGLES OVER
GAY RIGHTS *by Gary Mucciaroni*